Pro Active Directory Certificate Services

Creating and Managing Digital Certificates for Use in Microsoft Networks

Lawrence E. Hughes

Apress®

Pro Active Directory Certificate Services: Creating and Managing Digital Certificates for Use in Microsoft Networks

Lawrence E. Hughes
Frisco, TX, USA

ISBN-13 (pbk): 978-1-4842-7488-0   ISBN-13 (electronic): 978-1-4842-7486-6
https://doi.org/10.1007/978-1-4842-7486-6

Managing Director, Apress Media LLC: Welmoed Spahr
Acquisitions Editor: Joan Murray
Development Editor: Laura Berendson
Coordinating Editor: Jill Balzano

Cover designed by eStudioCalamar

Cover image designed by Freepik (www.freepik.com)

Distributed to the book trade worldwide by Springer Science+Business Media New York, 1 New York Plaza, Suite 4600, New York, NY 10004-1562, USA. Phone 1-800-SPRINGER, fax (201) 348-4505, e-mail orders-ny@springer-sbm.com, or visit www.springeronline.com. Apress Media, LLC is a California LLC and the sole member (owner) is Springer Science + Business Media Finance Inc (SSBM Finance Inc). SSBM Finance Inc is a **Delaware** corporation.

For information on translations, please e-mail booktranslations@springernature.com; for reprint, paperback, or audio rights, please e-mail bookpermissions@springernature.com.

Apress titles may be purchased in bulk for academic, corporate, or promotional use. eBook versions and licenses are also available for most titles. For more information, reference our Print and eBook Bulk Sales web page at http://www.apress.com/bulk-sales.

Any source code or other supplementary material referenced by the author in this book is available to readers on GitHub via the book's product page, located at www.apress.com/978-1-4842-7488-0. For more detailed information, please visit http://www.apress.com/source-code.

Printed on acid-free paper

This book is dedicated to my daughter, Bronwen Ferry Hughes. I taught her C# and networking from an early age. We believe she may have been the youngest person to ever pass the IPv6 Forum's Certified Network Engineer for IPv6 test. Even though I was the instructor, she legitimately passed the exam at the age of 16. She created most of the diagrams used in the book, and they are beautifully done. She graduated from the Singapore Campus of Oxford Brookes University as Valedictorian and is now working in Texas in IT. My wife and I are both very proud of her.

Table of Contents

About the Author xi

About the Technical Reviewers xiii

Acknowledgments xv

Introduction xvii

Part I: Foundations in Cryptography, Digital Certificates, and PKI 1

Chapter 1: Basic Cryptography: Symmetric Key Encryption 3

Symmetric Key vs. Asymmetric Key Encryption 5

Key Management 7

Symmetric Key Encryption 7

Introducing Alice and Bob 8

Key Management with Symmetric Key Encryption 9

Common Symmetric Key Cryptographic Algorithms 10

Strength of Symmetric Key Algorithms Based on Key Length 11

Encryption Modes 12

Example of Symmetric Key Cryptography 13

Chapter 2: Basic Cryptography: Hash Function 19

Characteristics of a Good Message Digest Algorithm 20

Conceptual Representations 21

Primary Uses 21

Chapter 3: Basic Cryptography: Asymmetric Key Encryption 23

Comparing Asymmetric Key to Symmetric Key...28

Common Asymmetric Key Algorithms...29

Conceptual Model 30

Cryptographic Algorithm Performance..31

Crypto Challenge Demo 32

Chapter 4: Digital Signature and Digital Envelope...............................35

Digital Signature 35

Creating a Digital Signature..36

Validating a Digital Signature..37

Uses of Digital Signatures..39

Digital Envelope 40

Creating the Digital Envelope..40

Need for Recipient Certificates 41

Opening the Digital Envelope:..42

Chapter 5: X.509 Digital Certificate 45

Certificate Trustworthiness 48

Subject Distinguished Name...50

Sources of Digital Certificates..51

Sources of TLS Server (SSL) Certificates 51

Sources of TLS Client Certificates and S/MIME Certificates 54

The Windows Certificate Store..55

A Tour of a Digital Certificate's Contents...57

S/MIME Certificates for Microsoft Outlook...72

A Word on Let's Encrypt..73

Chapter 6: PKCS #10 Certificate-Signing Request (CSR) 75

Chapter 7: Certificate Revocation and Renewal 93

Certificate Renewal...95

Certificate Revocation...96

Certificate Revocation List (CRL)...97

OCSP (Online Certificate Status Protocol) 102

Supporting Certificate Revocation on Your Own CA....................104

Chapter 8: Key Management 105

Symmetric Key Management...105

Asymmetric Key Management 105

Public Key Management 106

Private Key Management..110

Key Backup and Recovery vs. Key Escrow 116

Chapter 9: Certificate Management Protocols......................119

CMP (Certificate Management Protocol).....................................120

CMC (Certificate Management over CMS)....................................121

SCEP (Simple Certificate Enrollment Protocol)............................122

EST (Enrollment over Secure Transport) 123

ACME (Automated Certificate Management Environment)...............125

IRP (Identity Registration Protocol) 125

Example of Certificate Request and Retrieval Using IRP...............128

CSRs (Create/Manage CSR) 132

CSRs (Reassociate Cert)...139

Chapter 10: Public Key Infrastructure (PKI) 147

Trust Chains 151

SixWallet Certificate Status..153

Chapter 11: SSL and TLS 155

Implicit TLS vs. Explicit TLS 158

TLS with Other Protocols (in Addition to HTTP) 161

Securing FTP with TLS 166

Strong Client Authentication with a TLS Client Certificate During the
TLS Handshake 167

TLS Cryptosuites 169

TLS Only Secures One Client/Server Network Link................................. 170

The Splintered IPv4 Internet (Public vs. Private Addresses) 171

IPv4 Address Exhaustion... 172

PeerTLS.. 173

Chapter 12: S/MIME Secure Email 177

MIME... 177

S/MIME – MIME with Security... 178

S/MIME Implementations 178

S/MIME Digital Certificates 181

Public vs. Private Certificate Hierarchies 183

Example: Signed Message 184

Example: Encrypted Message 186

Example: Signed and Encrypted Message 188

Installing an S/MIME Certificate in Microsoft Outlook 189

S/MIME with Applications Other Than Email... 211

Part II: Deploying and Using Active Directory
Certificate Services 213

Chapter 13: Deploy Microsoft Certificate Services 215

Two-Level Hierarchy 216

Three-Level Hierarchy... 218

Deploy Root CA..219

    Add Active Directory Certificate Services Role...221

Deploy Subordinate CA for Intermediate and End-Entity Certificates..............243

    Add Active Directory Certificate Services Role...245

PKIView..272

Chapter 14: Issue and Manage TLS Server Certificates...................275

Set Up Templates for Root CA 277

Prepare for Issuing TLS Server Certs..284

Request and Issue a TLS Server Certificate Using mmc.exe 287

Install Server Cert in Internet Information Server 299

Manage Subordinate CA 305

Check CA Health in PKIView...307

Force Publication of a New CRL..313

Install OCSP Responder 316

Chapter 15: Issue and Manage TLS Client Certificates....................327

Create TLS Client Certificate 330

Set Up Template for TLS Client Certificate 331

Prepare for Issuing TLS Client Certificates..339

Request and Obtain a TLS Client Certificate Using mmc.exe 342

Test TLS Client Certificate for SCA with PKIEduRootCA...................................349

PeerTLS..358

Chapter 16: Issue and Manage S/MIME Secure Email Certificates....359

Issuing S/MIME Digital Certificates with Microsoft AD CS 361

Create Template for S/MIME Certificate..364

Prepare for Issuing S/MIME Certificates 372

Request and Obtain an S/MIME Certificate Using mmc.exe 375

Test Your New S/MIME Certificate...386

Create a Digitally Signed Email..390

Send a Digitally Enveloped Message 396

Chapter 17: Issue and Manage Windows Logon Certificates...........405

Configure Active Directory Certificate Services to Issue Windows
Logon Certificates 406

Create Template for Windows Logon Certificate 407

Prepare for Issuing Windows Logon Certificates 413

Request and Obtain a Windows Logon Certificate Using mmc.exe.................416

Logging into Windows with a Windows Logon Certificate 424

Appendix: Relevant Standards..437

PKCS – Public Key Cryptography Standards 437

    PKCS #1 – RSA Cryptography Standard 438

    PKCS #2 – RSA Encryption of Message Digests (Withdrawn) 438

    PKCS #3 – Diffie-Hellman Key Agreement.................................439

    PKCS #4 – RSA Key Syntax (Withdrawn) 439

    PKCS #5 – Password-Based Encryption Standard 440

    PKCS #6 – Extended-Certificate Syntax Standard
    (Obsoleted by X.509 v3)..441

    PKCS #7 Cryptographic Message Syntax Standard....................441

    PKCS #8 – Private-Key Information Syntax Standard.................443

    PKCS #9 – Selected Attribute Types 443

    PKCS #10: Certification Request Standard 443

    PKCS #11 – Cryptographic Token Interface (Cryptoki) 445

    PKCS #12 – Personal Information Exchange Syntax Standard...................446

Internet Request for Comments (RFCs)..446

Federal Information Processing Standards (FIPS)............................448

Index...451

About the Author

Lawrence E. Hughes is an internationally renowned expert in cryptography and PKI. He learned PKI from the top people in the field while working at VeriSign. He created and taught the courseware at VeriSign and presented it internationally to affiliates and large customers. He is a security author and was heavily involved in the deployment of several national certification authorities in the UK, Netherlands, and Australia. He later co founded and was the first CTO at CipherTrust (who created a secure email proxy appliance). In 2014, he co-founded Sixscape Communications Pte Ltd in Singapore where he was responsible for creating much of their technology.

About the Technical Reviewers

Hans Van de Looy is probably best known as ethical hacker, and allround IT security guy with over 35 years of experience. Mid 2017 he sold his shares in Madison Gurkha, the company he started in 2000, together with two friends. This company delivered high quality penetration testing services and security consultancy to the top-1000 organisations (enterprises, (research) institutions and government) in The Netherlands. During this time the organisation was regarded one of the top-3 penetration test specialists in The Netherlands. Before building this company Hans was involved as a senior security consultant with the RISC team at PinkRoccade. Hans started his professional carreer as a software engineer at the R&D department of Positronika Data Systems, after which he has different roles in various companies including Vicorp, and Sequent Computer Systems. In the past Hans has delivered presentations and workshops at (international (hacker)) conferences, including (but not limited to): SANE, HOPE, Black Hat and HAL, and he still shares information and knowledge in presentations and workshops at company meetings, at universities and other educational institutions. Today Hans helps his customers to ensure the privacy of PII and protect their IP and other data from his new company UNICORN Security. He is always looking for new exciting projects in both The Netherlands and abroad.

 **Merike Kaeo** is currently the CISO at Uniphore where she is responsible for the overall security strategy and its execution. Prior to joining Uniphore, Merike held positions as CTO of Farsight Security, CISO for Internet Identity (IID), and founder of Doubleshot Security. Merike has over 25 years of experience in pioneering core Internet technology deployments and leading strategic digital security transformations. She instigated and led the first security initiative for Cisco Systems in the mid 1990s and authored the first Cisco book on security, Designing Network Security, which was translated into multiple languages and leveraged for prominent security accreditation programs such as CISSP.

Merike is a senior member of the IEEE, a pioneer member of ISOC and has been an active contributor in the IETF since 1992. She was named an IPv6 Forum Fellow in 2007 for her continued efforts to raise awareness of IPv6 related security paradigms. Merike was appointed to the ARIN Board of Trustees in 2016 to serve a one year term from Jan 1, 2017 to Dec 31, 2017. Since 2010 she has been an active member on ICANN's Security and Stability Advisory Council (SSAC) and from 2018 thru 2021 served as the SSAC Liaison to the ICANN Board.

Merike earned a MSEE from George Washington University and a BSEE from Rutgers University.

Acknowledgments

I would like to acknowledge the many people from whom I have learned cryptography and PKI over the years, especially the technical wizards at VeriSign.

Some 30 years ago, a friend of mine, Winn Schwartau, who has run many Information Warfare conferences over the years, approached me with an opportunity to make the communication software I had created for CP/M and MSDOS encrypt files and chat for the US IRS. We actually delivered a working product (which used a hardware DES board), and they accepted it. Unfortunately, congress never authorized funding for this, so it was never deployed, and the IRS continued sending sensitive financial information in plaintext over phone lines via modems for some time. Hopefully, they fixed this somewhere along the way! However, this got me started in the fascinating field of cryptography (using DES at the time).

I also learned a lot about cryptography from a great book on the subject, *Applied Cryptography*, by Bruce Schneier (one of my favorite authors on computer security). Thanks for the insight and knowledge, Bruce!

In 1998, I was working for a computer security company called SecureIT, founded by Jay Chaudhry (now CEO of Zscaler). We did white hat hacking plus firewall consulting and training. One of our customers was VeriSign. We made it further into their layers of security than anyone else, and they apparently decided we were safer on the inside than on the outside, so they bought us. They thought since we made great training for CheckPoint Firewall-1, we would be able to make equally great training for cryptography and PKI. Unfortunately, the two areas are quite different and the attempts by our firewall trainers did not go well. I was not a trainer, but I offered to try, since my degree was in math and I had learned at least some cryptography in the IRS project some years before. VeriSign loved what I came up with, and I spent the next two years traveling all over the world, teaching PKI to large customers and affiliates.

Since I was creating the training, I was allowed to ask anyone at HQ any question, and they were required to answer. I was "drinking from a firehose," learning from literally the top people in the field. I also did very well there with Incentive Stock Options. Those helped me to co-found CipherTrust in 2000 (again with Jay Chaudhry), where I applied much of the technology I had learned at VeriSign.

I would also like to acknowledge the contributions of my two technical reviewers who have made this book better, more technically correct, and easier to understand.

The first half was reviewed by Merike Kaeo. I have known her for some 20 years and consider her one of the top people in the computer security field. She is also a senior advisor at my venture in Singapore, Sixscape Communications Pte Ltd. I am very honored that she was willing to spend some of her valuable time reviewing the first half.

The second half was reviewed by one of my students from my VeriSign days, Hans van de Looy. He is based in the Netherlands and was working for a networking company called Pink Roccade when I met him in my VeriSign training classes there. He is also an elite (white hat) hacker and is well known at DefCon and Black Hat Briefings.

Introduction

This book contains two very different parts.

The first part covers the concepts, algorithms, and protocols used in modern cryptography and Public Key Infrastructure (PKI). It covers essentially the same information I taught in the VeriSign training classes (except for the VeriSign-specific content). We charged roughly $1000 a day for a four-day course, so you are getting quite a deal considering the very reasonable cost of this book.

Cryptography is an arcane area of technology that has grown vastly more powerful with the advent of digital computers. One area of it involves scrambling information using algorithms and cryptographic keys to provide privacy, authentication, and detection of tampering. This is used in many kinds of digital communications today. We could not have the modern Internet today without it. TLS (formerly called SSL) is widely used to secure not only web traffic but also email and other protocols. S/MIME can provide true end-to-end encryption and sender-to-recipient authentication in email, although I have also pioneered using it in file transfer.

PKI is a technology developed to do secure cryptography key management, in technologies such as TLS. Public keys must be wrapped in a digital certificate, where the identifying information has been validated. The certificate is digitally signed by a trusted third party (Certification Authority), such as VeriSign. VeriSign is no longer around, but there are other companies doing the same thing today, such as Entrust, DigiCert, and Sectigo. Digital certificates provide *trust* in cryptographic systems.

The second part of the book explains in detail how to deploy Microsoft's Active Directory Certificate Services, which is a PKI you can deploy and run in-house, on Microsoft servers. It requires considerable knowledge of cryptography and PKI to run it correctly, hence the first part of this book.

It not only covers deployment of MS AD Certificate Services but also shows how to issue various kinds of digital certificates (TLS Server Certs, TLS Client Certs, S/MIME Certs, and Windows Logon Certs). It also covers examples of using these certs in Microsoft networks.

PART I

Foundations in Cryptography, Digital Certificates, and PKI

CHAPTER 1

Basic Cryptography: Symmetric Key Encryption

Cryptography is a deep mystery to many people (even techies). Many people assume you must be an accomplished mathematician to understand it. There are two basic kinds of encryption: symmetric key, where the same key is used to encrypt and decrypt, and asymmetric key, where there are two interrelated keys, a public key and a private key. While there are some deep math issues in asymmetric key algorithms, symmetric key algorithms involve very little math, and you can make very good use of even asymmetric key algorithms without a deep understanding of the math involved. Just assume that the cryptographers that created the algorithms knew what they were doing, and everything will work just fine.

Cryptography has been around for literally thousands of years. A very simple algorithm is actually called the Caesar Cipher and is attributed to Julius Caesar. For much of its lifetime, it has been involved with scrambling one or a few letters at a time. All this changed when computers arrived – previously complex algorithms (like the German Enigma) can now be cracked in seconds. But we can also scramble information in far more

© Lawrence E. Hughes 2022
L. E. Hughes, *Pro Active Directory Certificate Services*,
https://doi.org/10.1007/978-1-4842-7486-6_1

complex ways in a short time. We can even scramble binary data (e.g., an audio track or an image file) as easily as we can ASCII text. We can slice and dice the binary data at the bit level now and do thousands of simple ciphers in milliseconds.

The process of scrambling information is called *encryption* from *plaintext* (the unscrambled form) into *ciphertext* (the scrambled form). The reverse process of recovering the plaintext from the ciphertext is called *decryption*.

While it would be possible to create a symmetric key algorithm with no key, you would have to keep the details of the encryption algorithm *secret*, or anyone could decrypt an encrypted message. Modern algorithms use a *key* (an ordered sequence of bits, which can be thought of as an integer or a sequence of characters). The symmetric key has a role similar to that of a camshaft in a car engine. A camshaft is a device that controls the sequence of operations in a complex machine such as a car engine. If you use a different camshaft, the same engine will behave in a very different way. If you use a different encryption key, the same algorithm encrypts in a very different way, resulting in different ciphertext from the same plaintext. You can only recover the plaintext by using the *same* key that you used to encrypt it. This moves the need for secrecy from the *algorithm* to the *key*. You can publish all the details of your encryption algorithm (to standardize it and for peer review), but nobody will be able to decrypt a message encrypted with it without having a copy of the specific key used to encrypt it. You can think of this as a pair of mathematical functions:

```
ciphertext = encrypt(plaintext, K1)
plaintext = decrypt(ciphertext, K1)
```

If you encrypted some plaintext with a given algorithm (AES128) and a given key (K1), you can only recover the plaintext by using the same algorithm (AES128) and the same key (K1). If you use a different key (K2), you get gibberish, not the plaintext. With a good algorithm, like AES (Advanced Encryption Standard), if even a single bit of the key is wrong, you get total gibberish.

```
gibberish = decrypt(ciphertext, K2)
```

Even with detailed knowledge of the algorithm with a good one, it is extremely difficult to recover the plaintext from ciphertext without the appropriate decryption key. Not impossible, just *extremely* difficult, expensive, and/or time-consuming. One approach (brute force) involves trying every possible key until the plaintext is discovered. Since the number of keys is equal to 2 to the number of bits in the key, for sufficiently long keys (e.g., 128 bits or longer), this is a very, very large number of keys, making it difficult, time-consuming, and/or expensive to try them all.

So what does a 128-bit key look like? In decimal (base 10), it would be a 39-digit number between 0 and 340,282,366,920,938,463,463,374,607,431,768,211,455. A 256-bit key would be a 78-digit number between 0 and 115,792,089,237,316,195,423,570,985,008,687,907,853,269,984,665,640,564,039,457,584,007,913,129,639,935. These are very large numbers indeed.

Ciphertext can be safely transmitted via insecure channels (email, chat, file transfer, network protocol) or stored in insecure storage systems (hard disk, optical disk, thumb drive). Even if someone is able to intercept the ciphertext, the plaintext within it remains safe from discovery by anyone without the decryption key. If a hacker modifies the ciphertext, it will usually result in the decryption failing.

Symmetric Key vs. Asymmetric Key Encryption

All encryption algorithms fall into two general classes: **symmetric key** and **asymmetric key**. Everything up until the last few decades has been symmetric key based. Asymmetric key algorithms are possible only with the use of computers and involve some fairly obscure math (to create the algorithms, not to use them). The difference is quite simple.

Symmetric key algorithms use the *same* key to encrypt and decrypt. This is easy to conceptualize as it is similar to house keys. I use the same key to lock and unlock my house.

Asymmetric key algorithms have a matched pair of keys (one public, one private). You can encrypt with either key of the pair but can only decrypt with the *other* key of the matched pair. You cannot decrypt something encrypted with the public key with the public key, only with the corresponding private key. And you can only decrypt something encrypted with the private key with the corresponding public key. This is difficult to conceptualize. The locks and keys we use in real life don't work this way. For privacy, you encrypt a message with the recipient's public key, as only they have the corresponding private key to decrypt it (to read the message). To create a digital signature, you encrypt something with your own private key, and anyone can use your public key to decrypt it (to verify the signature).

Even with detailed knowledge of the algorithm with a good one, it is extremely difficult to recover the plaintext from ciphertext without the appropriate decryption key. Not impossible, just *extremely* difficult, expensive, and/or time-consuming. One approach (brute force) involves trying every possible key until the plaintext is discovered. Since the number of keys is equal to 2 to the number of bits in the key, for sufficiently long keys (e.g., 128 bits or longer), this is a very, very large number of keys, making it difficult, time-consuming, and/or expensive to try them all.

Ciphertext can be safely transmitted via insecure channels (email, chat, file transfer, network protocol) or stored in insecure storage systems (hard disk, optical disk, thumb drive). Even if someone is able to intercept the ciphertext, the plaintext within it remains safe from discovery by anyone without the decryption key. If a hacker modifies the ciphertext, it will usually result in the decryption failing. If it does happen to work, the result is gibberish.

Key Management

Key management involves communicating the decryption key to the recipient in a secure manner. This can be done in person, via a different channel, or protected via other kinds of cryptography (e.g., asymmetric key).

The ciphertext *contains* the entire plaintext (just in scrambled form), hence is at least as large as the plaintext and often just a bit larger. In some cases (e.g., asymmetric key cryptography), the ciphertext may be *significantly* larger than the plaintext. It is possible to reduce the size of the plaintext (and hence ciphertext) via compression *before* encryption and decompression of the recovered plaintext *after* decryption. While in ciphertext form, it is generally not possible to compress the information much at all, since compression depends on finding repeating patterns in the data, which are destroyed by the encryption process.

Symmetric Key Encryption

Symmetric key cryptographic algorithms are simple to understand and have been around far longer than asymmetric key algorithms. They are conceptually similar to physical keys. You use the same key to lock your house when you leave it and unlock it when you return. In terms of the mathematical representation of encryption and decryption discussed later, AES is the encryption algorithm, AES^{-1} (read "AES inverse") is the decryption algorithm, and K1 is the symmetric key. The same key is used to encrypt and decrypt. Actually when you decrypt, you run the encryption algorithm in the reverse direction (which undoes all the slicing and dicing you did to encrypt the plaintext).

```
ciphertext = AES(plaintext, K1)
plaintext = AES⁻¹(ciphertext, K1)
```

These diagrams are another way to envision this, as shown in Figure 1-1. Note that I use AES^{-1} to represent running the AES algorithm in the reverse direction.

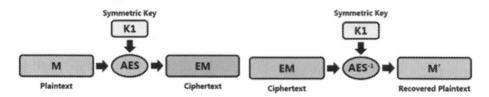

Figure 1-1. *Symmetric key encryption diagram*

Introducing Alice and Bob

Allow me to introduce you to the two parties involved in a simple secured message transmission, Alice and Bob. *Alice* encrypts some plaintext message (M) using a symmetric key algorithm (AES) and key (K1) and sends the resulting ciphertext (EM) to Bob. *Bob* receives the ciphertext (EM) from Alice and decrypts it using the same algorithm in decrypt mode (AES^{-1}) and key (K1) to recover the plaintext message (M'). Sometimes the messages may go from Bob to Alice.

To describe some scenarios, we also will use Alice and Bob's other friends, **Charlie** and **Donna**. There is a passive adversary named **Eve** who tries to passively eavesdrop on their messaging. Eve is easily foiled by the use of even simple encryption. In some scenarios, there is a very evil adversary named **Mallet** who launches active attacks. He is harder to foil.

Key Management with Symmetric Key Encryption

With symmetric key algorithms, Alice must somehow securely provide the key she used to Bob, without anyone else (e.g., *Eve*) discovering the key and hence the secret message. In general, with only symmetric key algorithms, this is a very difficult thing to do. One solution is an ANSI X9.17 *Key Management Facility* (KMF), where Alice and Bob each have a keying relationship with the KMF. Alice can send the key for communicating with Bob to the KMF using the key she shares with the KMF, and Bob can retrieve it from the KMF using the key he shares with the KMF. While an exchanged key is on the KMF, it is not protected. This means the KMF must be very well secured and operated by trusted personnel, as anyone who has access to the KMF can obtain any key used.

Without a KMF, there is a *combinatorial explosion* in terms of the number of keys needed, since Alice and Bob need one key, while Alice and Charlie need another key and Bob and Charlie yet another. With 50 people, 2,450 keys are needed (in general, $n \times (n-1)$ keys for n people).

Prior to the development of asymmetric key algorithms, key management was handled by something like ANSI X9.17, a Key Management Facility. This involves establishing a symmetric key protected channel between each user and a central KMF (e.g., Alice<->KMF, Bob<->KMF, etc.). Alice would create a key and send it to the KMF over her channel to the KMF, which would relay it to Bob over his secured channel to the KMF. This prevents the combinatorial explosion in symmetric keys without a KMF. The weakness of this system is if someone can compromise the KMF, the entire system is compromised.

Common Symmetric Key Cryptographic Algorithms

There are many well-known symmetric key cryptographic algorithms, some of which are now *deprecated* (considered weak and should not be used).

DES – Data Encryption Standard (1975), used by the US government for many years. DES encrypts or decrypts a 64-bit block at a time. Key length was 64 bits, but every 8th bit was a checksum bit, resulting in an effective key length of 56 bits, for 72 quadrillion (7.2 E+16) possible keys. While this sounds like a lot, the Deep Crack DES cracker (Figure 1-2) could try every possible DES key in about 9 days, at 90 billion keys a second.

Figure 1-2. *Paul Kocker, principal designer of Deep Crack (at the EFF)*

IDEA (International Data Encryption Algorithm, 1991) – used a 128-bit key and encrypts or decrypts a 64-bit block at a time. This was mostly used in Europe.

Blowfish (1991) – 32- to 442-bit keys, 64-bit block size.

CAST-128 (1996) – 40- to 128-bit keys, 64-bit block size.

CAST-256 (1998) – 128-, 160-, 192-, 224-, or 256-bit keys, 128-bit block size.

3DES (Triple DES, 1998) – Kludge to improve the strength of DES by applying it three times in a row (with the same key or with three different keys). Still used in PKCS12 key containers.

Serpent (1998) – 128-, 192-, or 256-bit keys, 128-bit block size.

Twofish (updated Blowfish, 1998) – 128-, 192-, or 256-bit keys, 128-bit block size.

Camellia (Japan, 2000) – Block size of 128 bits, key size of 128, 192, or 256 bits. Comparable to AES.

AES – Advanced Encryption Standard (2001), original name Rijndael, which replaced DES in 2001 as the official US symmetric cipher, after an international competition (128-, 192-, or 256-bit keys, 128-bit block size). AES is the most common symmetric cipher in use today.

Strength of Symmetric Key Algorithms Based on Key Length

The typical speed of a dedicated symmetric key cracking machine (Deep Crack discussed earlier) is about 90 billion keys per second, as shown in Figure 1-3. At that speed, various key lengths will require the following amount of time to try all possible keys.

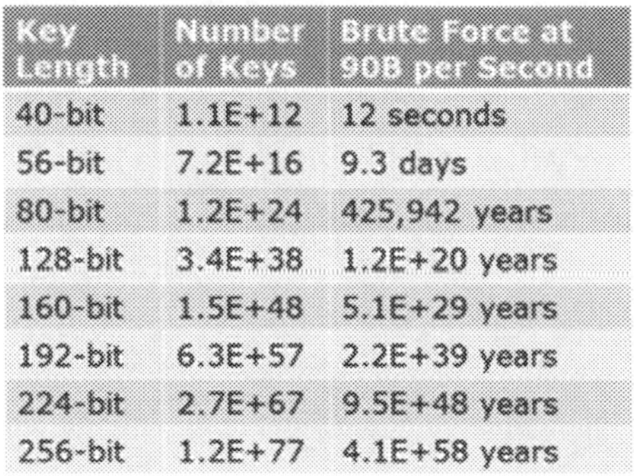

Key Length	Number of Keys	Brute Force at 90B per Second
40-bit	1.1E+12	12 seconds
56-bit	7.2E+16	9.3 days
80-bit	1.2E+24	425,942 years
128-bit	3.4E+38	1.2E+20 years
160-bit	1.5E+48	5.1E+29 years
192-bit	6.3E+57	2.2E+39 years
224-bit	2.7E+67	9.5E+48 years
256-bit	1.2E+77	4.1E+58 years

Figure 1-3. *Number of possible keys*

The number of possible keys and time to try all of them at 90 billion keys per second, for various key lengths. The larger numbers are in scientific notation, for example, 1.2E+20 = 1.2 times 10 to the 20th. For comparison, the universe is about 13.8 billion or 1.38E+10 years old.

In general, symmetric key ciphers are very fast (they can process millions of bytes of plaintext per second), hence are good for bulk encryption. They are very poor at key management and not very effective for creating digital signatures. There is little risk of even 128-bit ciphers (let alone 256 bits) being rendered useless by increasingly fast computers. Even quantum computers will only cut the effective key length roughly in half (a good reason to use 256-bit keys).

Encryption Modes

If you process each block (e.g., 128 bits) independently, that is called ECB (Electronic Code Book). The main problem with this is that many files have repeating or well-known patterns at the start. If you can use that to crack one block, the same key can decrypt all other blocks. There are various schemes for adding feedback across blocks – to work information from a previous block into the current one. This breaks up any repeating patterns. This feedback adds very little additional processing time but makes it far more difficult to crack a given encryption.

The common modes are

ECB – Electronic Code Book – each block is independent of every other block (no feedback).

CBC – Cipher Block Chaining – each block XORed with the previous ciphertext block before encryption.

CFB – Cipher Feedback – encrypts the previous block of ciphertext and XOR with the current block of plaintext

CTR – Counter-XOR with an incrementing counter – very effective for removing repeating patterns and will not "get back into sync" after a few blocks (the other schemes have a problem with this).

When you specify a symmetric cipher, you should include the algorithm name, key length, and mode, for example, *AES-256 with CTR*.

Example of Symmetric Key Cryptography

I created a demo program (Figure 1-4) in C# and .NET that allows you to play with various algorithms, key lengths, and encryption modes for symmetric key cryptography.

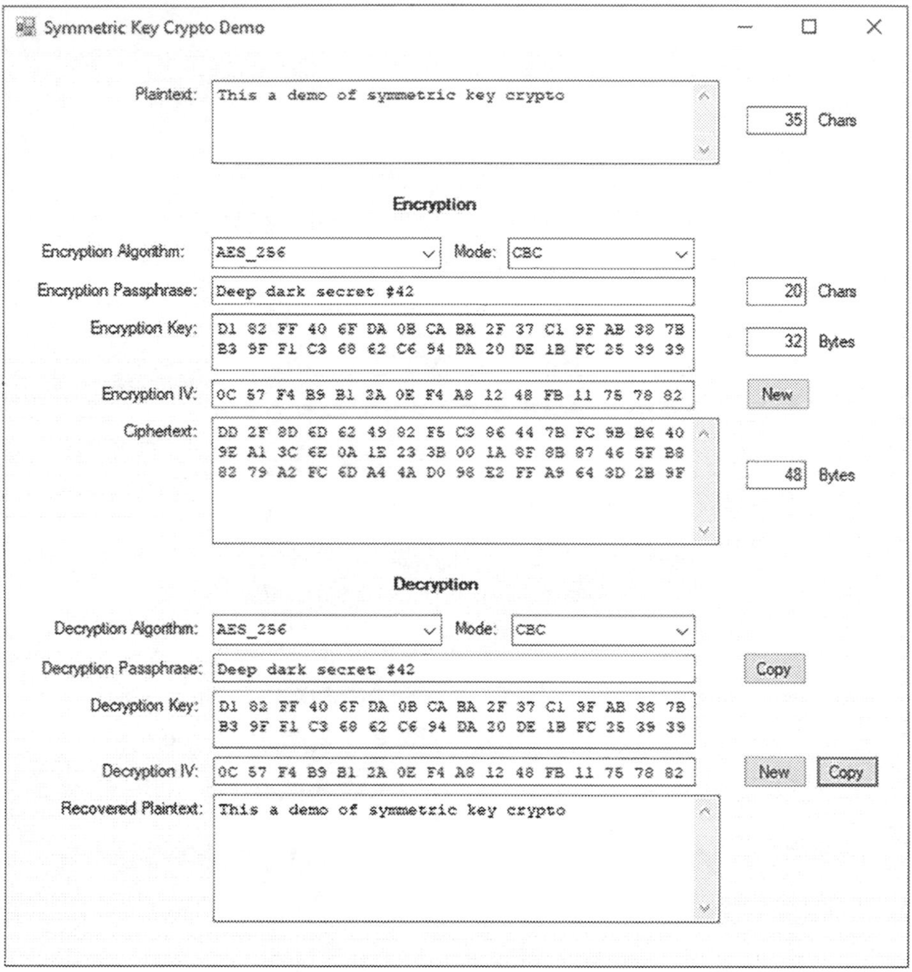

Figure 1-4. *Symmetric Key Crypto Demo*

In this figure, the plaintext is "This is a demo of symmetric key crypto." I selected the AES_256 algorithm (AES with 256-bit keys), using CBC (Cipher Block Chaining) mode. The app supports various algorithms, including AES_128, AES_256, IDEA, Blowfish, Twofish, and even DES and Triple DES. It supports ECB, CBC, CFB, and CTR encryption modes.

The *passphrase* "Deep dark secret #42" produced the earlier binary encryption key (using PKCS #5/RFC 2898). Regardless of the length of the passphrase, the key length is always 256 bits (32 bytes) (for AES_256). The key is actually binary but is displayed in hexadecimal in the app. CBC uses an initialization vector (IV).

These choices produce the displayed ciphertext (actually binary, displayed in hexadecimal in the app).

When the same decryption algorithm, mode, and passphrase (hence key) and initialization vector are used, the plaintext is recovered.

If you change the decryption passphrase, you get gibberish. If you use the wrong algorithm or mode, you get gibberish. If you use the wrong initialization vector, you get gibberish.

For example, changing the decryption passphrase to "Deep dark secret #43" changes the decryption key to a completely different value, which results in gibberish, even though everything else is correct (Figure 1-5).

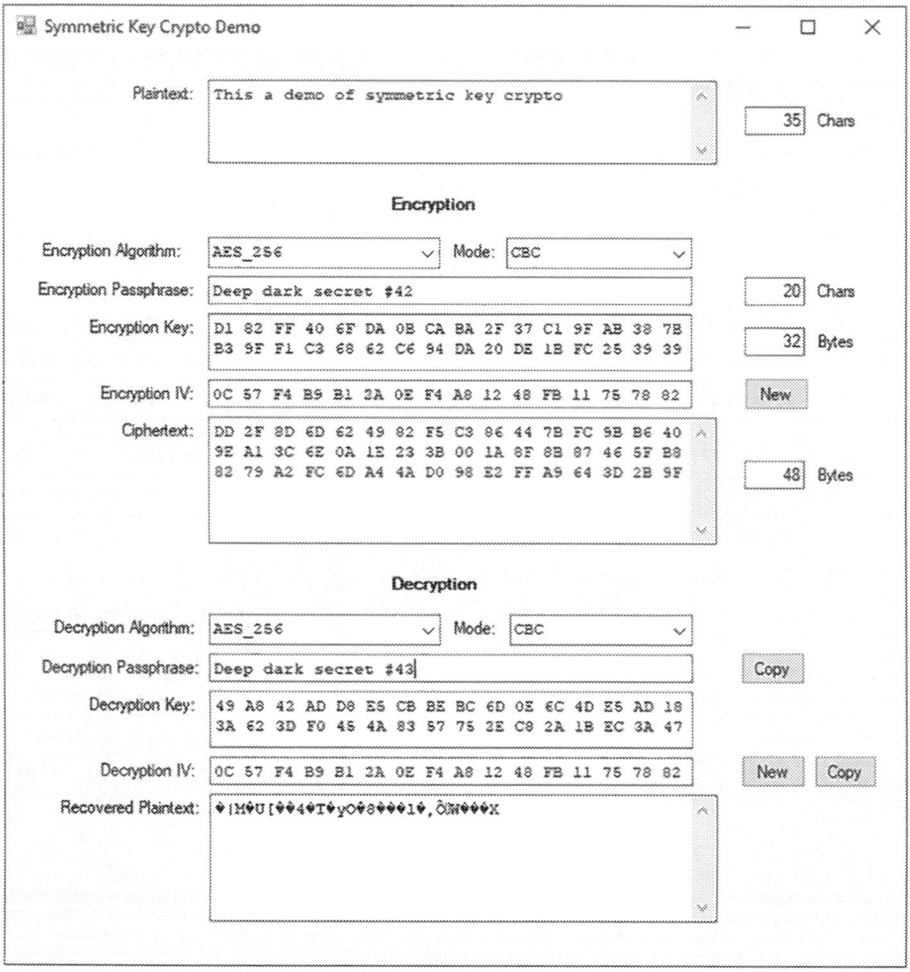

Figure 1-5. *Symmetric Key Crypto Demo*

You can even modify the decryption key itself by one bit (first byte changed from D1 to C1) and still get total gibberish, as seen in Figure 1-6.

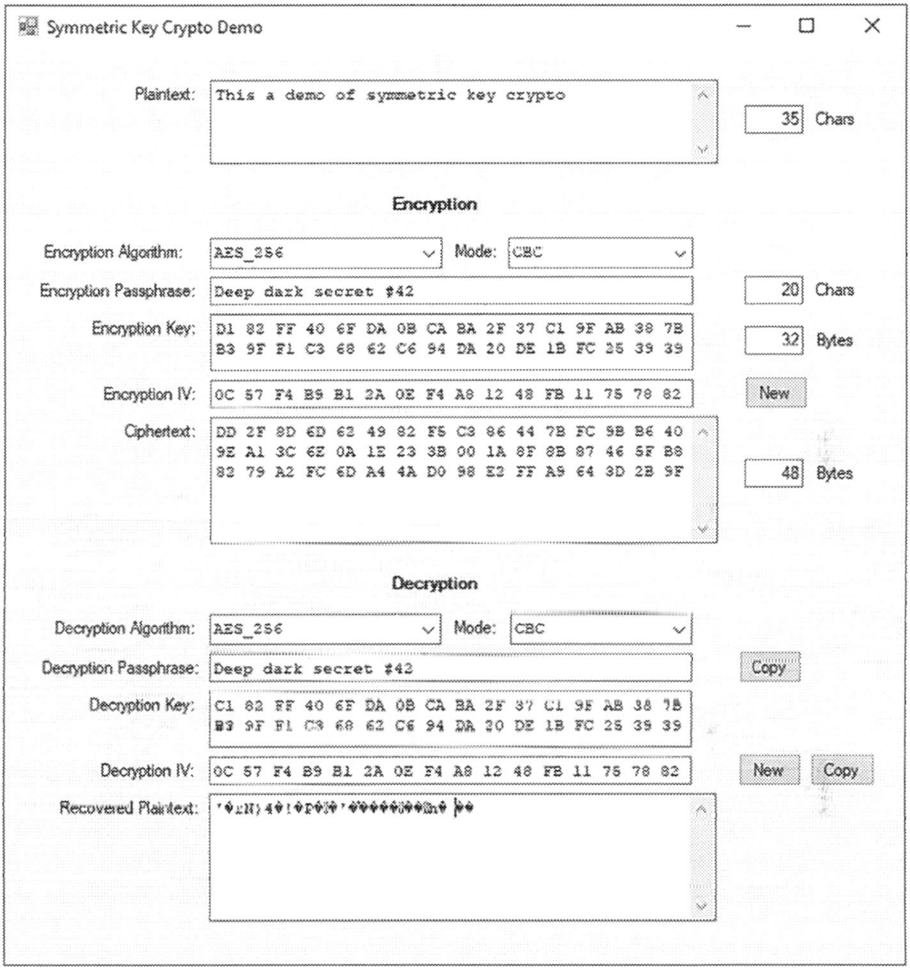

Figure 1-6. *Symmetric Key Crypto Demo*

If you type in additional plaintext in ECB, you will see the ciphertext grow in multiples of 128 bits or 16 bytes (the *block size* of AES). If you change the plaintext, the passphrase, or even the keys, the results update in real time as you type.

In conclusion, this is a fun tool that is useful for getting an intuitive feel for how symmetric key cryptography works.

CHAPTER 2

Basic Cryptography: Hash Function

There is another type of cryptographic algorithm similar to encryption, but with several very important differences. The technical term for this is *hash function*. It is sometimes also called a message digest algorithm. Technically though, the algorithm is a hash function, and the output of that function is a message digest.

Here, the object is not to *hide* information by scrambling it in a reversible manner, but to *characterize* a digital document (of any length) with a single large number (e.g., 224 to 512 bits in length). Since the result is always a fixed length for a given hash algorithm, it can't contain the entire source file as encryption does. One of the goals is to make it extremely difficult to recover *any* of the source document from the message digest (unlike encryption which *must* be reversible given the key, a message digest *must not* be reversible).

Unlike encryption, there is no *key*. A given hash function algorithm (e.g., SHA2-256) will always produce exactly the same digest from a given source document, no matter who does it or when it is done. On the other hand, it is *very* sensitive to changes in the source document. Even a single bit change in a ten-megabyte source document will result in a completely different message digest.

There were early attempts at creating good hash algorithms like MD2, MD4, MD5 (128 bits), and more recently SHA-1 (160 bits). SHA stands

© Lawrence E. Hughes 2022
L. E. Hughes, *Pro Active Directory Certificate Services*,
https://doi.org/10.1007/978-1-4842-7486-6_2

for *Secure Hash Algorithm*. Those have all been *deprecated* (found to be weak and no longer recommended for use). Currently, there are two sets of message digest algorithms that are approved for use, called SHA-2 and SHA-3. Both have versions with 224-, 256-, 384-, and 512-bit digests. The longer the digest, the better characteristics it has (of course, longer digests also take more computing power for a given source document than shorter digests). SHA-2/256 bits is the most commonly used message digest today. It is sometimes referred to as SHA256. SHA-3 is kind of a backup algorithm in the event that SHA-2 is broken.

Characteristics of a Good Message Digest Algorithm

- Good cryptographic dispersion, so that tiny changes are amplified – ideally, every bit of the message affects the final digest.

- It is created using many *one-way* transformations (compare to encryption where every transformation *must* be one to one onto or reversible). There is no way to recover any part of the message given in the digest.

- It should be extremely difficult or impossible for someone to make changes to a file and then make offsetting changes and still produce the same digest (this can easily be done with simpler schemes like a checksum or even CRC-32).

While there are a very large number of 160-bit digests (2 to the 160th), there are far more *possible* messages (most of which are total gibberish). While it is possible that two different emails or books could produce the same digest, it is *very, very* difficult to cause that to happen on purpose. That is called a collision, and finding a way to cause collisions with a message digest algorithm is one way to "break" it.

The total number of books ever published, or even the total number of email messages sent, is a vanishingly tiny number compared to the number of possible 160-bit (let alone 256-, 384-, or 512-bit) digests. It is unlikely that any two books or emails ever published or sent would produce the same message digest, but it is not impossible, just *very, very* unlikely. These are called collisions, and a message digest can be broken by being able to produce a collision on purpose.

One approach to breaking hash algorithms is to precompute a ton of hashes in rainbow tables.

Conceptual Representations

You can think of message digest as a mathematical function or transform:

$$MD = SHA(message)$$

Or for those more visually oriented, refer to Figure 2-1.

Figure 2-1. *Visual of a message digest as a mathematical function or transform*

Primary Uses

The main use today for message digests is in digital signatures.

To digitally sign a message, you produce a message digest of it and then encrypt that digest with an asymmetric algorithm and your own private key.

To verify a signature, you decrypt the signature with the signer's public key (from their digital certificate) to recover the original digest and then produce a new digest of the message. If those match, the signature is valid. This lets you know two things:

- **Message integrity** – the message has not changed in any way since it was signed.

- **Signer authentication** – only the owner of the private key corresponding to the certificate used to validate the signature could have created such a signature.

If the signature fails, then one or both of the following are true (there is no way to know which is true, but in either event, you should not trust the message):

- Something has changed in the file since it was signed (could be malicious or from a transmission or storage error).

- It was signed by some other person than the one whose certificate you are using to validate the signature.

CHAPTER 3

Basic Cryptography: Asymmetric Key Encryption

There is another type of encryption that is very different from symmetric key encryption. It is based on some recent technology and algorithms. The technical term for it is *asymmetric key encryption*, but it also sometimes is called *public-private key encryption.*

The first paper on asymmetric key cryptography was by Whitfield Diffie and Martin Hellman in 1975. In 1976, they released their first asymmetric key algorithm, Diffie-Hellman Key Exchange. In 1977, RSA released a scheme for general asymmetric key encryption and decryption now known as the RSA algorithm. It was patented by RSA, so widespread use didn't happen until the patent expired in 2000.

Although it was not made public until long after this, Clifford Cocks and Malcolm Williams at GCHQ in the UK were actually the first to invent the Diffie-Hellmann algorithm in 1974.

In comparison, the "Caesar Cipher," which is a form of symmetric key cryptography, literally dates from Roman times (2000 years ago).

Symmetric key encryption uses the same key for both encrypting and decrypting. If Alice encrypts something with a particular symmetric key, then Bob needs a copy of that same key to decrypt it.

© Lawrence E. Hughes 2022
L. E. Hughes, *Pro Active Directory Certificate Services*,
https://doi.org/10.1007/978-1-4842-7486-6_3

Asymmetric key encryption uses a matched pair of keys, usually called *public* and *private* keys, as the key owner should *publish* the public key (e.g., in Active Directory), but keep the private key secret (never reveal it or share it with anyone). Anyone can encrypt something with Alice's public key, but only she can decrypt the resulting ciphertext, using her private key. This is ideal for authentication and key management (securely sharing a symmetric session key with someone else).

This is used in TLS (Transport Layer Security) (formerly known as SSL – Secure Sockets Layer) for authentication using a crypto challenge, both for server-to-client authentication and (less commonly) for client-to-server authentication. For server authentication, the steps involved are as follows:

- The server sends its server certificate (including its public key) to the client.

- The client verifies the server certificate as valid, trusted, unexpired, and unrevoked.

- The client extracts the server's public key.

- The client creates a random string of characters and encrypts it with the server's public key.

- The client sends the resulting ciphertext to the server as a crypto challenge.

- The server decrypts the challenge using its private key and returns the recovered plaintext as the challenge response.

- The client compares the returned challenge response to the original string – if they match, that proves the server possesses the private key corresponding to its server certificate (without revealing it), which provides strong authentication.

Client-to-server authentication (aka Strong Client Authentication) does the same thing using an X.509 client certificate (which identifies a person, not a node), with the roles reversed. This is not widely used due to the cost and complexity of providing every user with a unique, trusted client certificate.

It can also be used in TLS to securely exchange a symmetric session key. This assumes the server has already provided its server certificate to the client (mentioned earlier). The steps involved in this are

- The client securely creates a symmetric session key (unique to this connection).

- The client encrypts the symmetric session key with the server's public key (from its server certificate).

- The client sends the resulting ciphertext to the server.

- The server decrypts the encrypted session key with its private key, recovering the original symmetric session key created by the client.

- The server and client have now securely exchanged a symmetric session key.

Note that today, this key exchange is often done using Diffie Hellman Key Exchange instead of the preceding.

Public keys are always provided in the context of a signed X.509 digital certificate, ideally from a trusted third party (Certificate Authority) to prevent the "public key substitution threat." Without a certificate, a hacker could trick you into using a public key they created, thereby assuming the victim's identity. The certificate is protected by a digital signature to prevent tampering with any of the items as well as authentication of the issuer. It "binds" the certificate subject's identity to the public key. A great deal of the security provided by PKI depends on this mechanism. There is more detail on X.509 certificates and PKI provided in later chapters.

Note that there is no such thing as a "private key digital certificate," since you never publish private keys nor need to determine if one belongs to the purported owner.

We showed examples of some of the very large numbers used in symmetric key cryptography in an earlier chapter. Those are tiny compared to the numbers used in asymmetric cryptography. For example, a 1024-bit number takes 309 digits to represent it in decimal, while a 2048-bit number takes 617 digits. When creating a key pair for 2018-bit keys, you multiply together two 2048-bit prime numbers resulting in a mind-boggling 1,234-digit number.

Likewise, Alice can encrypt something with her private key, and anyone can decrypt the resulting ciphertext with her public key. This is ideal for digital signatures. Only Alice can digitally sign something with her private key, but anyone can verify her digital signature. Note that symmetric key encryption does not do either of these things well. Hence, asymmetric key encryption is *complementary* to symmetric key encryption. It is not a competitor to it. Most modern cryptographic tools use both symmetric key and asymmetric key cryptography often including hash algorithms as well.

The math behind asymmetric key cryptography is complex, but you don't need to understand that in order to *use* it.

In practice, each pair of users exchanging things securely using symmetric key encryption needs a unique symmetric key. This can get complicated in a hurry with a large number of users. In comparison, with asymmetric key encryption, each user has exactly *two* keys, one public and one private. And only the private one needs to be secured. The public key can be shared with everyone. The two keys are related mathematically, but it is extremely difficult, time-consuming, and/or expensive to derive one from the other. At the current state of the art, a 2048-bit RSA key would require thousands of years of computer time to derive the private key from the public one.

Unfortunately, when practical quantum computers arrive, many current existing asymmetric algorithms will be crackable in a very short time (minutes or hours). Many groups are now creating quantum safe asymmetric key algorithms for applications that may be used for a long time.

Typical key lengths with symmetric key encryption today range from 128 bits to 256 bits. Asymmetric keys are usually much longer. With RSA keys, the minimum recommended length today is 2,048 bits, and high-security (e.g., DoD Top Secret) users may use RSA keys over 15,000 bits long! There is a more recent set of asymmetric key algorithms based on *Elliptic Curve Cryptography* (ECC). The key lengths for equivalent cryptographic strength for these algorithms are much shorter (e.g., 384-bit ECC is as strong as 8,192-bit RSA).

The math behind ECC is similar to that for RSA, but the two primes must be a coordinate pair that lies on one of a list of possible elliptic curves. For reasons we won't go into here, the strength of the encryption goes up far more rapidly with increasing key length than with RSA. Due to the shorter key lengths in ECC, it is an ideal solution for low-end devices (as in IoT) that have limited CPU power.

Asymmetric key encryption is also *much* slower than symmetric key encryption. You typically only encrypt or decrypt short things, like a 128- to 256-bit symmetric key or a 256- to 512-bit message digest. You would never encrypt an entire one-megabyte file with asymmetric key cryptography.

To send an encrypted message, you would create a random symmetric session key, encrypt the message with that session key, and then encrypt the symmetric session key with the recipient's public key. The recipient would decrypt the encrypted session key with their own private key and then decrypt the message using the recovered symmetric session key. Most real-world systems use *both* symmetric key and asymmetric key algorithms: symmetric key for bulk encryption and asymmetric key for secure session key exchange.

For a digital signature, you would create a message digest of the message (e.g., using SHA-256, producing a 256-bit digest) and then encrypt that using the signer's private key. The recipient would recover that digest by decrypting it with the sender's public key and then generate a new message digest of the received message. If the recovered digest and the regenerated digest match, that is a valid signature. That provides message integrity (you know the message has not been tampered with since it was signed) and sender authentication (you know for certain who signed the message). Here, asymmetric key and message digest algorithms are used together.

Comparing Asymmetric Key to Symmetric Key

Symmetric key cryptography is based on "slice and dice" operations (substitution and transposition ciphers), while asymmetric key cryptography is based on complex mathematical operations ("trap door functions") that require *far* more time to reverse than to create. For example, RSA keys are created by multiplying together two giant (300-digit) prime numbers. Deriving the private key from the public key requires factoring that product into the two original primes (a known difficult problem in math). This can take tens of thousands of times longer than multiplying two primes together.

If I encrypt something with someone's public key, only *that person's* private key can decrypt it. The public key it was encrypted with cannot decrypt it. If I encrypt a message digest with my private key (to create a digital signature), only *my* public key can decrypt it to validate my signature.

Common Asymmetric Key Algorithms

Diffie-Hellman Key Exchange (1976) – A scheme for remote symmetric key agreement, based on the discrete logarithm problem.

RSA (1978) – Specified in PKCS #1. Note that "PKCS" was a set of standards (Public Key Cryptography Standards) published by RSA. These have since been incorporated in IETF RFCs, but most people still refer to them by their RSA names. For example, PKCS #1 is now specified in RFC 8017. General asymmetric encryption and decryption are based on the "factoring the product of two large primes" problem. It was patented, but that expired in 2000. Key lengths currently range from 2048 bits to over 15,000 bits. We are now reaching the point of diminishing returns for increasing key length. RSA was patented for a long time, but that expired, and anyone can implement or use it with no royalties today.

El-Gamal (1985) – General asymmetric encryption/decryption based on Diffie-Hellman Key Exchange and the discrete logarithm problem.

DSA – Digital Signature Algorithm (adopted as FIPS 186 in 1993) – derived from the El Gamal algorithm. Only used for digital signatures, not encryption. Available worldwide royalty-free.

ECC – Elliptic Curve Cryptography (first introduced in 2004–2005) – similar to RSA, but the two primes must be coordinate pairs that fall on one of a number of "elliptic curve" functions. With ECC, good curves are patented, and you must pay royalties to use them. ECC is now starting to replace RSA. For example, 256-bit ECC is roughly as strong as 2048-bit RSA, and the strength goes up much faster with increasing key length than with RSA. It is also much faster for a given cryptographic strength than RSA, so is being used heavily on low-end devices, as are often found in IoT products.

Conceptual Model

As before, encryption and decryption with asymmetric key algorithms can be represented as mathematical functions or transforms:

```
ciphertext = RSA(plaintext, alice's public key)
plaintext = RSA⁻¹(ciphertext, alice's private key)
```

Or if you are more visually oriented, see Figure 3-1.

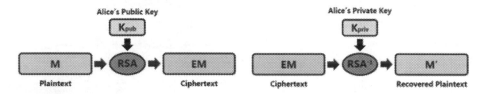

Figure 3-1. *Visual representation of mathematical functions or transforms*

This would be the way to use it to encrypt something. You must obtain the client certificate of the recipient in order to send them an encrypted object. The recipient would use their own private key to decrypt it.

You can reverse this (encrypt with a private key and decrypt with the corresponding public key) to create a digital signature. In this case, the signer uses their own private key, and the signature validator needs the signer's public key (in a digital certificate). It is actually typical to include the signer's digital certificate as a part of the message, since it doesn't matter how you get that certificate (it can be verified no matter how you got it).

```
ciphertext = RSA(plaintext, Alice's private key)
plaintext = RSA⁻¹(ciphertext, Alice's public key)
```

Or for the visually oriented, see Figure 3-2.

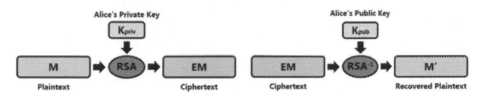

Figure 3-2. *Visual of encrypting with a private key and decrypting with the corresponding public key*

Asymmetric keys tend to be rather larger (thousands of bits) than symmetric keys (128 to 256 bits). Asymmetric key algorithms are *very, very* slow compared to symmetric key algorithms. Typically, only relatively small things (a symmetric key, a message digest, or a short random string of characters) are ever encrypted or decrypted using asymmetric key algorithms. They are ideal for key management or creating digital signatures. They are not suitable for bulk encryption or decryption (like an entire message or file). Most real-world systems use both symmetric key and asymmetric key algorithms.

Cryptographic Algorithm Performance

The following is a comparison of speed of various cryptographic algorithms on a typical desktop PC (Figure 3-3).

Cipher	Performance
SHA-1	253 MB/sec
SHA-256	111 MB/sec
SHA-512	99 MB/sec
RIPEMD-160	106 MB/sec
AES128-CBC	103 MB/sec
AES192-CBC	92 MB/sec
AES256-CBC	80 MB/sec
RSA 1024 Encryption	.08 msec/operation
RSA 1024 Decryption	1.46 msec/operation
RSA 2048 Encryption	.16 msec/operation
RSA 2048 Decryption	6.08 msec/operation

Figure 3-3. Comparison of speed of various cryptographic algorithms on a typical desktop PC

Crypto Challenge Demo

This screenshot from a demo app I wrote can give you a better idea of how this all works. I load the public key (from a certificate) and the corresponding private key. I then generate the plaintext (the *random string*) and encrypt it with the RSA and the loaded public key (producing the ciphertext or *challenge string*). I finally decrypt the ciphertext with the private key, recovering the original plaintext (the *challenge response*). Normally, one computer would create the challenge and send it to another computer. The other computer would respond to the challenge by decrypting it and returning the result to the first computer which would compare that result to the original random string.

Note how much larger the ciphertext is than the plaintext. The ciphertext is actually a binary object, but it is represented here encoded with base64. This *crypto challenge* is used in various places, like TLS authentication, as shown in Figure 3-4.

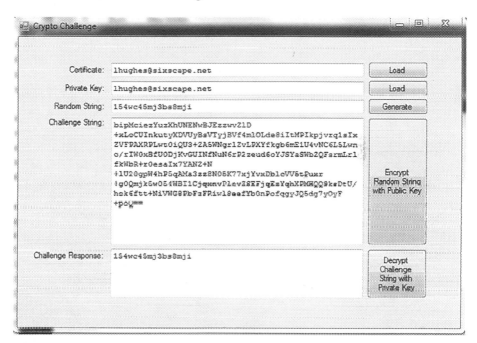

Figure 3-4. *Ciphertext is a binary object, but is represented here encoded with base64*

To use this app, you load the certificate and corresponding private key, then enter or generate a random string (e.g., by clicking *Generate*), and then produce the challenge string by clicking *Encrypt Random String with Public Key*. Finally, you recover the random string by clicking *Decrypt Challenge String with Private Key*. If an attacker makes any change at all to the challenge string, the decryption will fail.

CHAPTER 4

Digital Signature and Digital Envelope

Now that you understand the basic mechanisms of cryptography, we can move on to some applications of cryptography, which are used in actual real-world systems, such as TLS and S/MIME (Secure MIME). The first of these is the *digital signature*.

Digital Signature

A digital signature is *not* your handwritten signature scanned into a jpeg. That is not bound to you in any way, and a malicious actor can scan anyone's handwritten signature and embed that into a document.

A real digital signature is a binary object that *is* bound to you, which only you can affix to a document (since you are the only person that has your private key), and anyone can verify that it is *your* digital signature (through the use of your digital certificate, which contains your public key that is needed to verify the signature). Furthermore, a digital signature provides *message integrity*, so any change at all to the document since you signed it can be easily detected by anyone.

You create a message digest of the document (using a hash function, such as SHA256) that you want to digitally sign and then encrypt that digest (using an asymmetric key algorithm such as RSA) and your private

© Lawrence E. Hughes 2022
L. E. Hughes, *Pro Active Directory Certificate Services*,
https://doi.org/10.1007/978-1-4842-7486-6_4

key. The encrypted message digest (EMD) *is* your digital signature. Anyone can validate your signature by decrypting the signature using your public key (after validating your certificate that contains your public key). This yields the recovered message digest. The recipient then produces a *new* message digest of the received document using the same hash function used by the sender. If those two digests match, it's a valid signature. This provides the recipient with three things:

Signer authentication – Nobody but you could have produced a digital signature that validates with your digital certificate (since only you have the necessary private key to do this).

Message integrity – Had there been any changes whatsoever to the message after you signed it, the signature would fail when you validate it. A digital signature cannot *prevent* changes to the message, but it can definitely detect them – even a single bit in a digital copy of *War and Peace*.

Non-repudiation – Since you are the only one who could have signed it, you cannot repudiate it having come from you. Don't digitally sign any message that might incriminate you!

Note that a digital signature does not provide any *privacy*. That requires a digital envelope. Digital envelopes are discussed later and involve encryption. The message (M) is still in plaintext, and anyone can read it. It cannot detect whether anyone has read your message along the way.

Creating a Digital Signature

In the following example (Figure 4-1), Alice (the sender) produces a digest (MD) from the message (M) using a hash function, such as SHA256.

Creating a Digital Signature

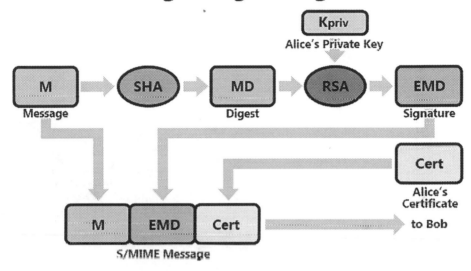

Figure 4-1. *Creating a digital signature*

The MD is encrypted using an asymmetric key algorithm such as RSA and Alice's private key, producing the signature (EMD for encrypted message digest).

The message (M), the signature (EMD), and Alice's certificate (Cert) are then sent to Bob.

Validating a Digital Signature

From there, Bob receives the message (M), the signature (EMD), and Alice's certificate (Cert) from Alice (Figure 4-2).

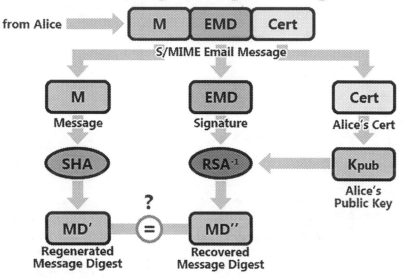

Figure 4-2. Validating a digital signature

He generates a new message digest (MD') using the same hash function used by the sender, from the received message (M).

He extracts Alice's public key (Kpub) from her certificate (after validating the certificate).

He then decrypts the signature (EMD) using RSA⁻¹ (the same asymmetric key algorithm used by the sender, but running in the decrypt direction) and Alice's public key (Kpub), which yields the recovered message digest (MD").

Finally, he compares MD' and MD". If they match, it's a good signature.

Note that I use the notation RSA-1 (to be read "RSA inverse") to indicate running an encryption algorithm in decrypt direction.

Uses of Digital Signatures

Digital signatures are used in S/MIME Secure Email to authenticate the sender to the recipient. It also will detect any changes to the message while it is in transit. If the sender wants for the recipient to acknowledge receipt of the message and authenticate themselves to the sender, the recipient must return a *signed receipt* (most S/MIME-compliant email clients have the ability to do that).

Digital signatures are used in digital certificates to ensure that nothing in the certificate can be changed without detection and to let everyone know for certain that the certificate was issued by the Certification Authority (CA) shown in the Issuer Distinguished Name.

A Certification Authority is the organization that issues digital certificates to applicants. It will be described in great detail in the chapter on PKI. The Issuer Distinguished Name is a list of name/value pairs that identifies the CA who issued this certificate. A typical IssuerDN is "CN=Sectigo RSA Domain Validation Secure Server CA, O=Sectigo Limited, L=Salford, S=Greater Manchester, C=GB."

You can affix a digital signature to *any* digital document to detect changes (message integrity) and to establish who signed it (signer authentication). This includes PDF files, drawings, MS Office documents, etc. You can even digitally sign binary files, like images or digitized music. Not all applications support adding or verifying a digital signature, but you can create a signed document that includes any of these, for example, an S/MIME email with attachments. MS Office allows affixing and validating digital signatures in any Office document. Adobe supports adding digital signatures to a PDF document and validating them.

Digital Envelope

A digital envelope is built using both symmetric key and asymmetric key cryptography. The encryption of the message is done with *symmetric key cryptography*, and the symmetric session key is sent to the recipient securely using *asymmetric key cryptography*.

It only provides privacy, but it also *prevents* tampering (not just detects it) since the content cannot be seen or modified without the symmetric session key. It doesn't guarantee delivery – a hacker could still delete or reroute a message (the message headers are not encrypted or signed). But only the intended recipient can open the message body or attachments.

Digital signature and digital envelope are independent. A given message can use either, neither, or both. If you use both, you digitally sign the entire message first, and then all message components are encrypted in a single digital envelope.

Creating the Digital Envelope

Next, Alice (the sender) first generates a symmetric session key (SSK) using a cryptographic random number generator (Figure 4-3).

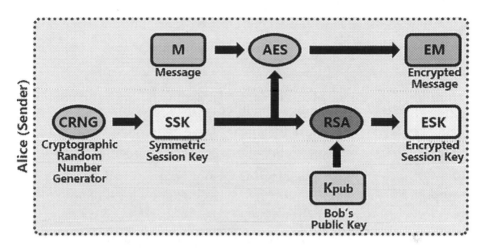

Figure 4-3. *Creating a digital envelope*

She then encrypts the message (M) with the symmetric key algorithm (e.g., AES) and the SSK, producing the Encrypted Message (EM).

Then she encrypts the SSK with RSA and Bob's public key (Kpub), producing the Encrypted Session Key (ESK).

The Encrypted Message (EM) and Encrypted Session Key (ESK) are sent to Bob.

Need for Recipient Certificates

To *send* a digitally enveloped message to someone, you need *their* S/MIME Certificate which contains their public key, at the time you send the message. This can be done with a local "personal address book" or a "shared address book" (e.g., with Active Directory). To *open* a digitally enveloped message to you, you need only your own private key.

One common way to get someone's digital certificate is to ask them to send you a digitally signed message, as their certificate is usually included with it. Microsoft Outlook has a way to store the S/MIME Certificate on a signed message in your personal address book. It is much better if the network administrator can create a shared address book for use by all users.

If there are multiple recipients, you need the S/MIME Certificate for each recipient. When sending to multiple recipients, a single symmetric session key is generated, and then the message is encrypted with it. Then that symmetric session key is encrypted with each recipient's public key (from their respective certificates). So, the message contains a single encrypted message plus one encrypted session key for each recipient. When each recipient gets this message, they use their private key to decrypt the session key encrypted with their public key and then decrypt the message using that recovered session key.

Opening the Digital Envelope:

Next, Bob receives the Encrypted Message (EM) and Encrypted Session Key (ESK) from Alice (Figure 4-4).

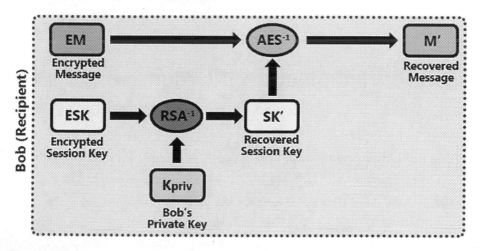

Figure 4-4. *Opening a digital envelope*

He first decrypts the ESK using his own private key (KPriv) and RSA in decryption mode, producing the Recovered Session Key (SK').

Then the Encrypted Message (EM) is decrypted using the selected symmetric key algorithm in decrypt mode (AES^{-1}) and the Recovered Session Key (SK'), producing the Recovered Message (M').

CHAPTER 5

X.509 Digital Certificate

An X.509 certificate is a digital document (file) that uniquely identifies something connected to a network. It contains several things, depending on the type of certificate. X.509 is a standard that was part of the OSI X.500 Directory Service (the "authentication framework"). A digital certificate has the following items in it:

- A **Subject Distinguished Name** that uniquely identifies a person, device, or computer (node), for example, *CN=www.pkiedu.com, O=PKIEdu Inc., L=Frisco, ST=Texas, C=US*

- An **Issuer Distinguished Name** that uniquely identifies the Certification Authority that issued the cert, for example, CN=Sectigo RSA Domain Validation Secure Server CA, O=Sectigo Limited, L=Salfor, S=Greater Manchester, C=GB

- A 128-bit **serial number**, for example, 00bb06fab4d512a3dea09b19e54361050a

- A start (**ValidFrom**) date and time, for example, Friday, May 8, 2020, 7:00:00 PM

L. E. Hughes, *Pro Active Directory Certificate Services*, https://doi.org/10.1007/978-1-4842-7486-6_5

- An end (**ValidTo**) date and time, for example, Sunday, May 9, 2021, 6:59:59 PM

- A **public key** (e.g., 2048-bit RSA key)

- **Key Usage Flags**, for example, *digital signature* and *key encipherment*

- **Enhanced Key Usage Flags**, for example, *Server Authentication*, *Client Authentication*, and *Email Security*

- The URL where the **Certificate Revocation List** (CRL) for this cert can be found

- The URL where the **OCSP** (Online Certificate Status Protocol) server for this cert can be found (if any)

- A **digital signature** created by the Certification Authority at time of issue using their signing private key, covering all of the earlier information

To understand Public Key Infrastructure (PKI), you must first understand digital certificates, as those are what a PKI issues and manages. If you are going to secure a website with TLS, you must understand TLS Server Certificates and optionally TLS Client Certificates, as those make TLS possible. Note that TLS (Transport Layer Security) used to be known as SSL (Secure Sockets Layer), although some people incorrectly continue using the old name. It has been officially known as TLS since January 1999 when Netscape handed SSL off to the IETF. If you are going to deploy S/MIME Secure Email, you must understand S/MIME Digital Certificates, as every user must obtain one of these.

A **TLS Server Certificate** identifies a particular server computer connected to a network (or the Internet). It enables TLS on a server, for example, HTTPS for a web server. It also is used to authenticate the server to a client (server-to-client authentication). One TLS Server Certificate is sufficient for any number of clients using a given TLS-secured server.

A **TLS Client Certificate** identifies a particular person or device. The primary difference from a server certificate is the Subject Distinguished Name, which might be something like *CN=Lawrence Hughes, E=lhughes@ pkiedu.com, L=Frisco, S=Texas, C=US*. It also has slightly different usage flags, and if it is an S/MIME Cert, it will contain a *Subject Alternative Name* such as *RFC822Name=lhughes@pkiedu.com*.

An **S/MIME Certificate** identifies a particular person and is used in secure email. It allows adding a *digital signature* to a message to provide message integrity and sender-to-recipient authentication. It can also enclose an email message in a *digital envelope* to provide privacy.

There are various other things in some certificates, but the earlier mentioned are the basic items. The specification for digital certificates is in ISO X.509. This specification has been adopted into the IETF RFC repository as RFC 5280, "Internet X.509 Public Key Infrastructure Certificate and Certificate Revocation List (CRL) Profile," May 2008.

Without digital certificates, it would be easy to trick someone into using a bogus public key. This is called the public key substitution threat. With the public key embedded in a digital certificate, anyone can be assured that

- It is the *correct* public key for the person, node, or device named in the Subject Distinguished Name and that it is the public key corresponding to that person's private key.

- That the certificate is currently valid and has not expired.

- The certificate was issued by a specific trusted Certification Authority (named in the certificate), including a pointer to that authority's *Certification Practices Statement*.

- The items in the SubjectDN have been validated to be correct and current by a Registration Authority (RA) at the issuing Certification Authority.

- None of the information in the cert has been modified in any way since it was issued by the CA.

- The certificate has not been revoked by the issuing authority (this requires checking of the Certificate Revocation List or the OCSP server for this certificate).

All of the preceding provides *trust*.

All of the equipment, legal agreements, and trusted operations needed to securely issue and manage certificates are called a **Public Key Infrastructure** or PKI.

There are a number of commercial Certification Authorities that have met all requirements for issuing trusted certificates, but you can also deploy your own in-house Certification Authority and issue certificates for use within your own organization. Microsoft Certificate Services is one tool for doing that.

Note that the Subject Distinguished Name in a digital certificate is a list of name-value pairs that uniquely identifies some person or device as the owner (subject) of the certificate. A typical SubjectDN looks like: E=lhughes@megacorp.com, O=Megacorp, OU=IT, L=Frisco, ST=Texas, C=US. These will be covered in more detail later.

Certificate Trustworthiness

A digital certificate contains everything required to check its trustworthiness. Every application or service that uses digital certificates must check several things before accepting it as valid and using it:

- **Validity** – The certificate must be within its validity period, after the *ValidFrom* date and before the *ValidTo* date. If the current date and time is *before* the *ValidFrom* date, you cannot yet use the certificate ("Not yet Valid"). If the current date and time is *after* the *ValidTo* date, you cannot use the corticate ("Expired"). The purpose of this is to force the certificate owner to periodically have the contents verified as accurate and current. Names change. Organizations change. People change jobs. Periodic verification helps keep certificate contents from being out of date.

- **Trust** – The digital signature on the certificate needs to be validated, using the public key of the parent cert (also known as the *issuing certificate* of the Certification Authority that issued the certificate). If the parent cert is a Trusted Root Certificate, the check is done. If not, then you must validate the parent cert as well. This continues up the *trust chain* until you reach a Trusted Root Certificate.

- **Revocation status** – Whether the certificate has been revoked by the Certification Authority that issued it. This requires access to a current *Certificate Revocation List* or OCSP server for the certificate hierarchy that includes this certificate. Those things are maintained by the issuing Certification Authority, and the URLs for these things are included in any valid certificate.

This validation is one of the most powerful aspects of PKI. No other security scheme has this kind of mechanism.

Subject Distinguished Name

One of the fields in an X.509 cert (the *Subject Distinguished Name*) uniquely specifies one person, device, or Internet node that the certificate (and hence the embedded public key) belongs to. It can have various fields, each of which is a name/value pair, for example, *CN=Lawrence Hughes*. Some of the fields are

- CN or CommonName, e.g., CN=Lawrence Hughes

- E or Email, e.g., E=lhughes@pkiedu.com

- OU or OrganizationalUnit, e.g., OU=IT

- O or Organization, e.g., O=PKIEdu Inc.

- L or Locality (city), e.g., L=Frisco

- ST or State (or province), e.g., ST=Texas

- C or Country, e.g., C=US

The applicant creates a public/private key pair and supplies the preceding SubjectDN information to the Registration Authority at a Certification Authority in a PKCS #10 *Certificate-Signing Request* (CSR), along with their public key. The private key never leaves their possession. The Registration Authority (RA) verifies (validates) all the submitted information (e.g., by reviewing passports, billing statements, birth certificates, etc.). The Certification Authority then creates an X.509 certificate from the CSR, adding in new items like start and end dates, Issuer Distinguished Name, URLs for obtaining the appropriate CRL or OCSP service, and usage flags, and finally digitally signs it. The CA may remove fields from the submitted SubjectDN that they either didn't or couldn't validate. The issued certificate is returned to the applicant who links it back together with the private key.

Sources of Digital Certificates

There are many places from which you can obtain a *TLS Server Digital Certificate* (aka *SSL Certificate*). These can be used to enable TLS on various servers, including Web (HTTPS), email (SMTPS, IMAPS), LDAP (LDAPs), FTP (FTPS), etc. In general, users do not require a client certificate in order to get privacy and server-to-client authentication (if the site uses username/password authentication [UPA] for the client).

With most TLS secured servers, it is possible to configure it to support *Strong Client Authentication* (SCA) with a TLS Client Certificate. In this case, each user will require a unique client certificate specific to them (which is trusted by the server). You can enable "Require Client Cert" (*only* SCA is allowed) or "Allow Client Cert" (if a user doesn't have a client cert, the server will fall back to username/password authentication).

Unfortunately, many mobile-based browsers do not support TLS Client Certificates, and even browsers that do support TLS Client Certificates have odd behavior – for example, once they accept one client cert, there is no way to change to a different cert without killing every instance of that browser. Sixscape provides a mobile device-based alternative for doing SCA with any online service that combines crypto challenge with push notification. This also automates getting the client cert on your mobile device via IRP. Basically, your phone becomes your authentication token.

Sources of TLS Server (SSL) Certificates

The leading vendors of TLS Server Certificates are

- GlobalSign

- Entrust

- DigiCert

- Sectigo (formerly Comodo)

There are a number of resellers of certificates from various CAs, where you can get better prices (especially from Sectigo), including

- GoGetSSL

- SSLs

- Namecheap

Note that these companies do not operate their own Certification Authorities or issue certificates. They are just resellers for real CAs. Some of them resell certificates for several real CAs.

Many website hosting companies will be glad to sell you an SSL cert as part of their package, such as DreamHost. I got the $15 a year DV cert from Sectigo, which was installed automatically (SSL Certificates on shared hosting can be a bit tricky to do yourself). DreamHost also will provide a free IPv6 address even for shared hosting (most hosting companies do not support IPv6, or if they do, it is only on their high-priced VPS offerings).

If you need more than a few TLS Server Certificates, all CAs have "Managed PKI" offerings, where you can verify your company and domain once and then manage the issuance of any number of certificates yourself. You will still have to pay for each cert as issued. You can issue TLS Server Certificates and Client Certificates (which TLS Server Certificates and Client Certificates (which also are SMIME) certificate with these offerings).

- DigiCert Enterprise PKI Manager

- GlobalSign Managed PKI Platform

There are different levels of TLS Server Certificates for various needs. The basic level is "DV" or *Domain Validation*. The SubjectDN will have only *CN=yourdomain.com*. Here, you only need to prove that you have control over your domain through one of the following methods:

- Access to key email addresses such as postmaster@ yourdomain.com

- Ability to upload a file into yourdomain.com website

- Ability to publish a CNAME record in DNS for yourdomain.com

For higher assurance, you can also validate ownership of your company name. There are various ways the CA can verify you have rights to use that corporate identity (e.g., DUNS, business registration documents, etc.). For these certificates, the SubjectDN will contain *CN=www.yourdomain.com, O=yourcompany.*

For very high assurance (and an even higher price), you can get EV (extended validation) TLS Server Certificates. You will have to provide numerous documents to the CA to validate more fields of the Subject DN. Some browsers will indicate an EV cert, for example, by showing the site owner in green, as seen in Figure 5-1.

Figure 5-1. *Example of a browser indicating an EV cert*

The TLS Server Certificate on `www.sixscape.com` is an EV cert. If you check the SubjectDN on our certificate, it includes the following fields (all of which we had to validate to the CA):

```
CN = www.sixscape.com
OU = COMODO EV SSL
O = Sixscape Communications Pte Ltd
STREET = 33 Ubi Ave 3 #08-26
L = Singapore
```

```
ST = Singapore
PostalCode = 408868
C = SG
2.5.4.15 = Private Organization
1.3.6.1.4.1.311.60.2.1.3 = SG
SERIALNUMBER = 201414391K
```

Sources of TLS Client Certificates and S/MIME Certificates

Many of the earlier TLS Server Certificate vendors also can provide TLS Client Certificates and S/MIME Certificates (actually they usually combine these functions into one multipurpose certificate that can do both Client Authentication and Email Security). If you are issuing TLS Client Certificates to your employees or customers, a Managed PKI solution may be the best bet. This is a scheme where you validate your organization identity once and then can issue any number of certificates (being charged per certificate issued). You control only the Common Name (CN), Organizational Unit (OU), and Email Address (E) in each issued certificate. All other fields are the same for all issued certificates.

Sixscape has a Managed PKI plan from one of the leading Certification Authorities. As the administrator, I can issue certificates with many fields in the SubjectDN (the domain name, O, L, and C fields are specific to our Managed PKI plan). This cert works for both TLS Client Authentication and S/MIME Secure Email. The SubjectDN from my cert is

```
E = lhughes@sixscape.com
CN = Lawrence Hughes
OU = Administration
O = Sixscape Communications, Pte. Ltd.
L = Singapore
C = SG
```

You can obtain an individual S/MIME Cert at Sectigo for about $12.95 per year (three-year plan). These are only email validated (they verify your identity by sending you an email which you must reply to). The SubjectDN includes only *E=<your email>* (no CN=<your name> or other fields). I consider this weak identity validation, as it is possible to intercept other people's email and obtain a certificate fraudulently. I prefer client certificates that include at least the applicant's validated name (*CN=<your name>*) in addition to the email address (*E=<your email>*). This requires proving your identity to the CA, for example, by submitting your passport.

As an individual, I have had good luck getting S/MIME Certificates from SSL.com. They have email-validated client certificates for $20 a year (three-year plan) and "Pro" client certificates with *CN=<your name>* and *E=<your email>* for $30 a year (three-year plan). They also have "Business" client certificates that can also be used for Adobe PDF signing for $299 a year (one-year plan). Most of the additional cost is related to the PDF signing.

I got a "Class 3" client cert from SSL.com. I had to verify all of the included fields in the SubjectDN, which is very complete:

```
E = lhughes@sixscape.com
CN = Lawrence Hughes
OU = IT
O = Sixscape Communications, Pte Ltd
L = Singapore
S = Singapore
C = SG
```

The Windows Certificate Store

Here, "store" means a place where certificates are *stored*, not a place to *buy* certificates. This store is part of Microsoft Windows, not any browser. This store has several "folders" in it, including

- **Personal** – Certificates that belong to you and usually include a private key.

- **Other People** – Certificates that belong to other people (no private key), to use when sending encrypted messages.

- **Intermediate Certificate Authorities** – Parent certificates to the End-Entity Certificates discussed earlier. These are normally obtained and installed automatically when you use an End-Entity Certificate, although there are a number provided by the operating system vendor (e.g., Microsoft) along with the Trusted Root Certificates. You can manually add additional Intermediate Certificates.

- **Trusted Root Certificate Authorities** – Parent certificates to the earlier mentioned Intermediate Certificates, usually provided by Microsoft (all CAs approved by WebTrust). Trusted Root Certificates are self-signed (signed by the corresponding private key, rather than a higher-level private key). You can add more (with a strong warning when you install since you will now trust *all* certificates in that certificate hierarchy). Be careful installing new Trusted Root Certificates!

IE included a tool to view and do limited management of the Certificate Store (Internet Options/Content/Certificates), as seen in Figure 5-2.

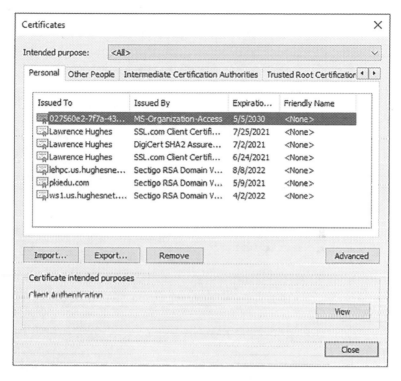

Figure 5-2. *Tool to view and do limited management of the Certificate Store*

A Tour of a Digital Certificate's Contents

If you double-click any certificate in any of these folders, you can see information on that certificate (Figure 5-3).

Figure 5-3. *Double-click any certificate in a folder to see information*

This dialog displays some basic information about the certificate, including who it was issued to, who it was issued by, the validity period, and whether you also have the private key corresponding to this certificate in your Certificate Store (private keys are never included in a digital certificate, and there is no such thing as a private key certificate). You can also install the certificate in the Microsoft Certificate Store with the *Install Certificate...* button.

If you click the *Details* tab, you can see additional information within this certificate. For example, if you select *Subject*, you can see the Subject Distinguished Name (see Figure 5-4).

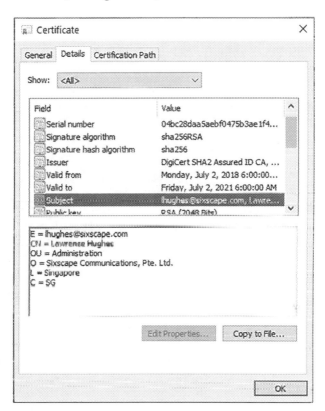

Figure 5-4. *Select Subject so you can see the Subject Distinguished Name*

If you click *Issuer*, you can see the Issuer Distinguished Name, as shown in Figure 5-5.

Figure 5-5. *Click Issuer so you can see the Issuer Distinguished Name*

By clicking *Public key*, you can see the actual Public Key (there is nothing secret about this; it is a public key), including the key type (RSA) and length (2048 bits), as shown in Figure 5-6.

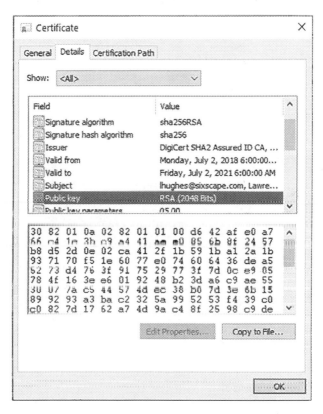

Figure 5-6. *Click Public key to see the actual Public Key*

If you click *Enhanced Key Usage*, you can see what things you can use this particular certificate for. In this case, it can be used for *TLS Client Authentication* and *S/MIME Secure Email.* A TLS Server Certificate would include *Server Authentication.* (See Figure 5-7.)

Figure 5-7. *Click Enhanced Key Usage to see what you can use the certificate for*

If you click *Certificate Policies*, you can find a link to the Certification Practices Statement for the Issuing Certification Authority. If I surf to the URL in this certificate, it has a list of many legal documents including the CPS, as shown in Figure 5-8.

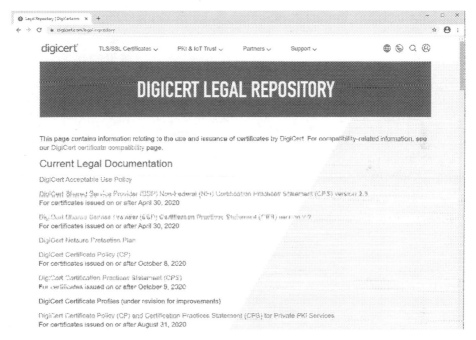

Figure 5-8. *Click Certificate Policies to find a link to the Certification Practices Statement*

If I click the Certification Practices Statement link, there is an 82-page document that details exactly how DigiCert operates its Certification Authority (see Figure 5-9).

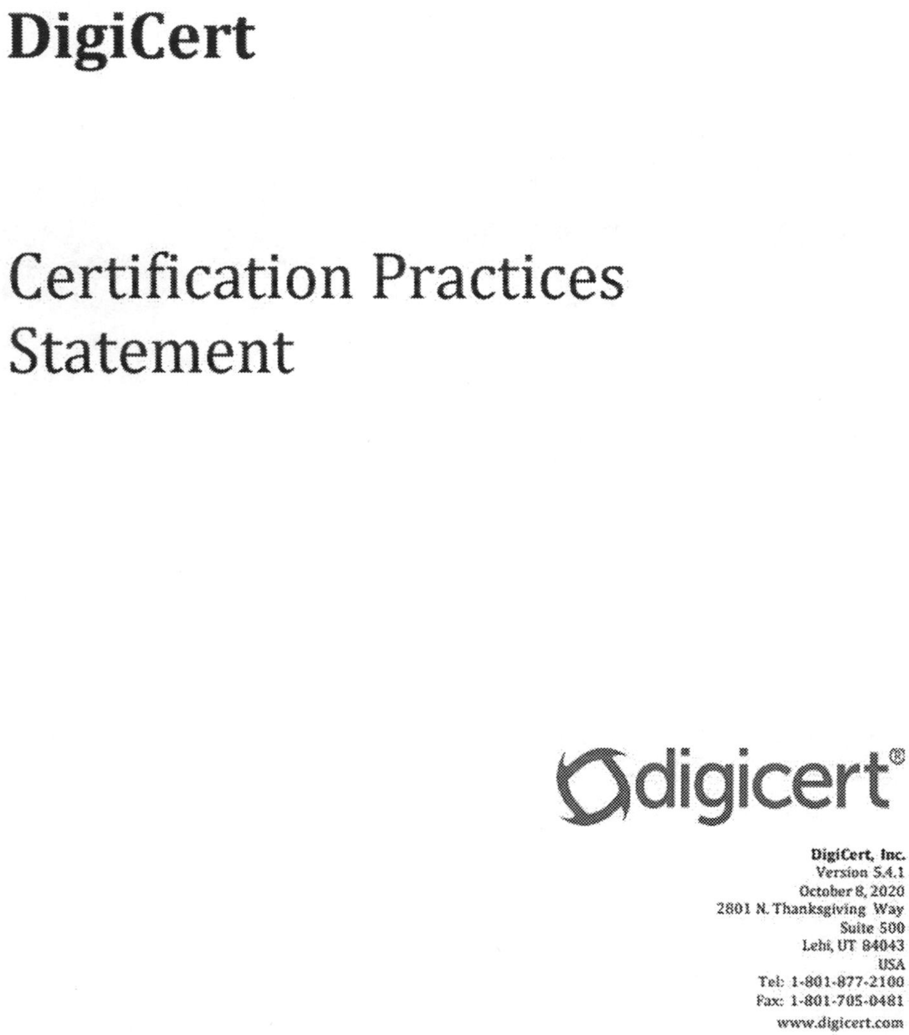

DigiCert

Certification Practices Statement

DigiCert, Inc.
Version 5.4.1
October 8, 2020
2801 N. Thanksgiving Way
Suite 500
Lehi, UT 84043
USA
Tel: 1-801-877-2100
Fax: 1-801-705-0481
www.digicert.com

Figure 5-9. *Cover of document that details how DigiCert operates its Certification Authority*

This is a complex legal document that any Cortication Authority should create and maintain and provide a link to it in all certificates issued by that CA.

If I click *CRL Distribution Points*, I get the URLs where I can retrieve current CRLs for the certificate hierarchy this certificate is a member of:

```
[1]CRL Distribution Point
    Distribution Point Name:
        Full Name:
            URL=http://crl3.digicert.com/
            DigiCertSHA2AssuredIDCA-g2.crl
[2]CRL Distribution Point
    Distribution Point Name:
        Full Name:
            URL=http://crl4.digicert.com/
            DigiCertSHA2AssuredIDCA-g2.crl
```

If I surf to one of these URLs, it allows me to download the current CRL as a file. If I open that file with the Microsoft *Crypto Shell Extensions*, I can see details on the CRL (see Figure 5-10).

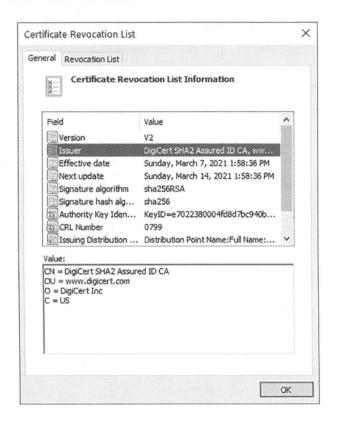

Figure 5-10. *View of the details on the CRL*

If I click the *Revocation List* tab, I can see a list of revoked certificates from this hierarchy, including the serial number and date the certificate was revoked (see Figure 5-11).

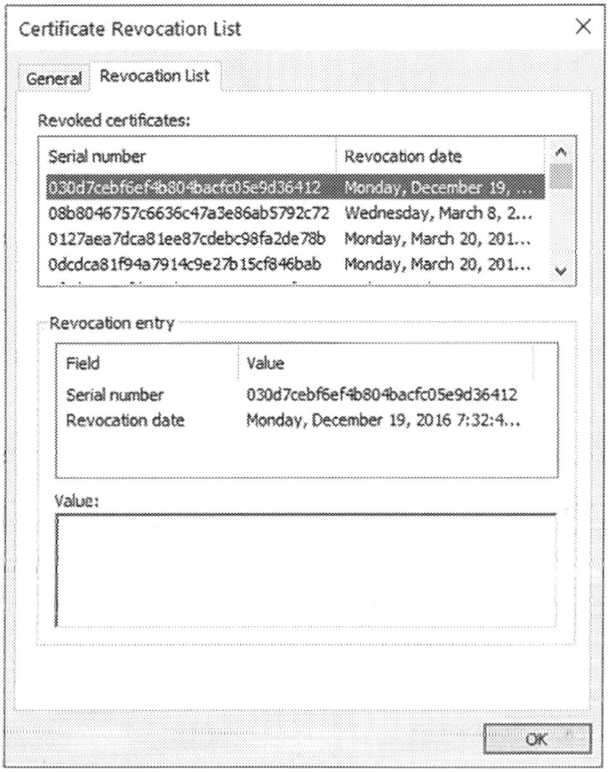

Figure 5-11. *View of a list of revoked certificates from this hierarchy*

There is more information on CRLs in a later chapter.

If I click *Authority Information Access* (AIA), I find URLs where I can find the OCSP server for determining revocation status for any certificate in this hierarchy (this server is run by the Certification Authority). I can also find a copy of the *issuing certificate* that was used to sign this certificate.

```
[1]Authority Info Access
    Access Method=On-line Certificate Status Protocol
    (1.3.6.1.5.5.7.48.1)
    Alternative Name:
        URL=http://ocsp.digicert.com
```

```
[2]Authority Info Access
     Access Method=Certification Authority Issuer
     (1.3.6.1.5.5.7.48.2)
     Alternative Name:
         URL=http://cacerts.digicert.com/
         DigiCertSHA2AssuredIDCA.crt
```

I created my own version of the Microsoft Certificate Store Viewer (IDWallet), which shows you a lot of information on the current status of any certificate (see Figure 5-12).

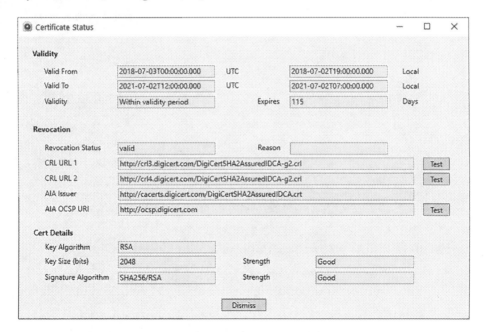

Figure 5-12. *Information on the current status of a certificate*

If you click the *Test* button after a CRL URL, it will retrieve information about this certificate on the CRL (see Figure 5-13).

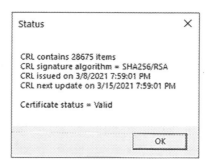

Figure 5-13. *Click Test to retrieve information about this certificate*

If you click the *Test* button after the AIA OCSP URI, it will retrieve information from that OCSP server for this certificate (see Figure 5-14).

Figure 5-14. *Click Test to retrieve information from that OCSP server*

Finally, if I click the *Certification Path* tab in the viewer, I can see the trust chain from this certificate up to its Trusted Root Certificate (see Figure 5-15).

Figure 5-15. *Image of the trust chain from this certificate*

You can view details about the parent certs by clicking them in this list. For example, if I click the Intermediate Certificate (parent of the original certificate), I can see information on that certificate. Note that the IssuerDN of this certificate is the same as the SubjectDN of the End-Entity Certificate (the original one we viewed), as seen in Figure 5-16.

Figure 5-16. *Intermediate Certificate (parent of the original certificate)*

This same Certificate Store Viewer dialog is available in the current Microsoft Chromium-based Edge browser, but it is buried even more deeply than in IE. To start it, right-click the three dots, and select *Settings*. Under *Settings*, select *Privacy, Search and Services*. On that page, look for *Security*. Under *Security*, click *Manage Certificates*. The same GUI will appear, with the same functionality.

If you have installed *Visual Studio*, there is yet another way to run this dialog. Bring up a *Visual Studio Command Prompt*, and type the command *certmgr.exe*.

Note that Mozilla software (Firefox and Thunderbird) does have a simple Certificate Store Viewer, but that is not for the Microsoft Certificate Store; it is for a proprietary Mozilla-specific Certificate Store, which is not used by most Windows applications (primarily Firefox and Thunderbird). The contents of the Microsoft and Mozilla Certificate Stores are completely disjoint. Loading a certificate into either does not load it into the other. Applications such as Outlook, Edge Chrome, and Opera use the Microsoft Certificate Store. The Firefox browser and Thunderbird Email client use only the Mozilla Certificate Store. You *can* export a certificate from either store in PKCS12 format and then import it into the other store, but that is the only way to move certificates between the two stores or install a certificate into both.

S/MIME Certificates for Microsoft Outlook

Microsoft made it really difficult to install an S/MIME Certificate for an account in Outlook – it is actually too difficult for most people to manage. My company Sixscape Communications (based in Singapore) created an add-in for Microsoft Outlook called SixMail, which vastly simplifies the process. Once the add-in is installed, the next time you send an email, it will say "You don't currently have an S/MIME Certificate, don't worry I WILL GET ONE FOR YOU." And about ten seconds later, you will have a public hierarchy S/MIME Certificate installed in your Outlook ready to use. It can get this certificate from any Certification Authority that supports our Identity Registration Protocol (IRP). That is currently Entrust and GlobalSign. It will automatically add the certificate into AD (as well as your key material in PKCS12 form). It can optionally also escrow your key material for compliance issues. This allows the organization to recover encrypted emails even if the user's private key is lost or destroyed.

This requires setting up some infrastructure, so it is best suited to deployment in an organization. This will be set up by our deployment team as part of the contract.

We also support private hierarchy S/MIME using certificates from your own EJBCA or PKI-In-A-Box. Contact Sixscape for other options (we can add IRP to almost any CA).

SixMail makes secure email (with just signing or signing and encrypting) easy and safe enough for any organization to use.

The chapter on S/MIME includes the details of how to install an S/MIME Certificate in Outlook.

A Word on Let's Encrypt

I am not a fan of Let's Encrypt. This is a "free" source of TLS Server Certificates. The certificates are free but have to be renewed every 90 days. Many content management systems for web servers (e.g., WordPress) can automate getting these TLS Server Certificates (e.g., "Really Simple SSL" plug-in). A while back, they had to reissue millions of certificates because they had used noncompliant serial numbers. There is no source of revenue to cover the costs of running a full PKI (e.g., good revocation support).

I don't have much confidence in the security of sites that use Let's Encrypt certificates. On my websites, I opted to get a real Sectigo TLS Server Certificate instead of the free Let's Encrypt certificate. I validated my control of domain pkiedu.com by adding a CNAME resource record into DNS (which I manage for my domains). The SubjectDN does only show CN=pkiedu.com, but at least it's not from Let's Encrypt.

Basically, a Let's Encrypt protected site does provide *privacy* (via encryption), but the *authentication* normally provided by a real certificate is very weak or nonexistent. Any user of your site that understands security may not have much confidence in the security of your site if you use *Let's Encrypt*.

If you feel comfortable with using a Let's Encrypt certificate, they do work for now. There are millions of people using these.

CHAPTER 6

PKCS #10 Certificate-Signing Request (CSR)

Now that you know what a digital certificate is, how do you request one from a Certification Authority?

First, the requester must create a public/private *key pair* (a public key and a corresponding private key). The private key is kept secret by the requester and is never submitted to the CA. The requester also creates a *Subject Distinguished Name* for the certificate owner.

Whether is it exposed or not, the requester creates a complex digital document called a *Certificate-Signing Request.* This syntax of this file is specified in PKCS #10 (from the RSA Public Key Cryptography Standards) and is now included in IETF RFC 2986, "PKCS #10: Certification Request Syntax Specification Version 1.7," November 2000. For more details on the PKCS series, see the Relevant Standards appendix.

A number of other items can be specified in a CSR and can be accepted or ignored by the Certification Authority. Only the fields of the SubjectDN that are validated by the Registration Authority are included in the resulting certificate.

© Lawrence E. Hughes 2022
L. E. Hughes, *Pro Active Directory Certificate Services,*
https://doi.org/10.1007/978-1-4842-7486-6_6

Typically, the completed CSR is submitted to the Certification Authority, and the resulting Certificate is returned to the requester (e.g., via email). This certificate is then reassociated with the private key created when the CSR was created. The resulting key material is typically stored in the Microsoft Certificate Store. It can be exported in PCKS #12 format and securely backed up, if the original key material is lost or needs to be installed on another computer (e.g., your home computer).

There are various tools for creating CSRs – many CAs provide online web pages that allow you to provide a public key and fields from the SubjectDN, then create the CSR, and submit it for you. You can also create a CSR using command-line tools, such as the one found in OpenSSL.

I created a tool (IDWallet) that can simplify the creation of CSRs. For example, I can right-click the CSR page and select *Create New CSR*. I would see the following form shown in Figure 6-1.

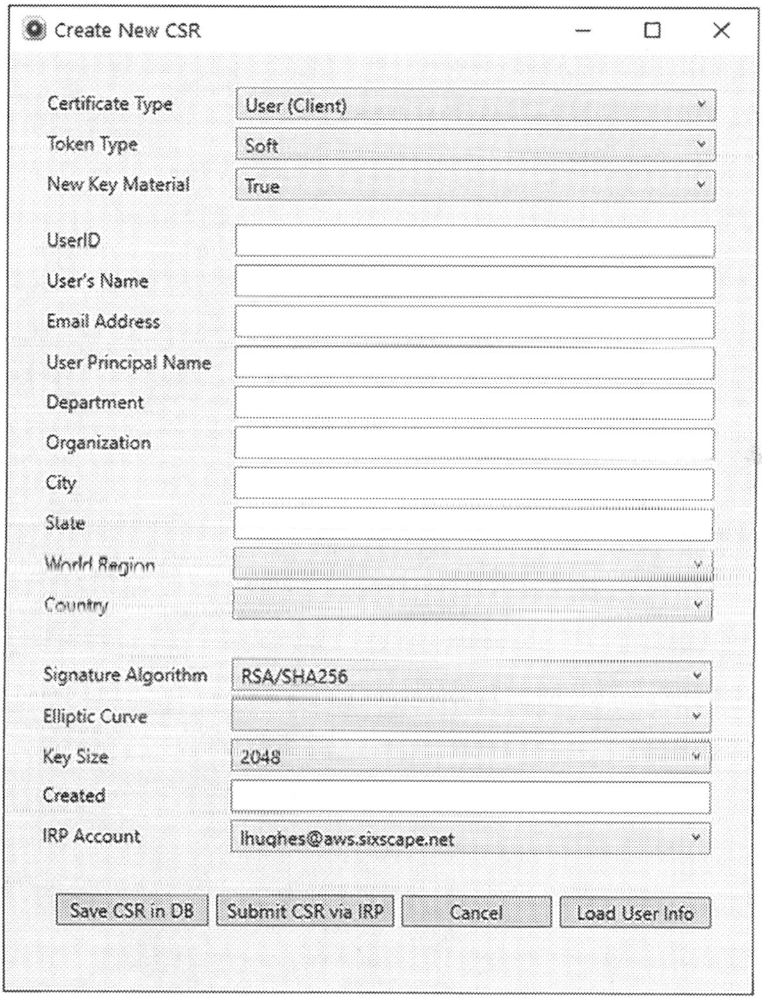

Figure 6-1. *Right-click the CSR page and select Create New CSR*

I can manually fill in the fields that comprise the Subject DN and click *Save CSR in DB*. That will generate a public/private key pair using best practices to ensure randomness and strong keys, then build the SubjectDN from the fields in Figure 6-1, build a PKCS #10 CSR from the public key and SubjectDN, and then save the result in the local database, along with the private key in encrypted form (Figure 6-2).

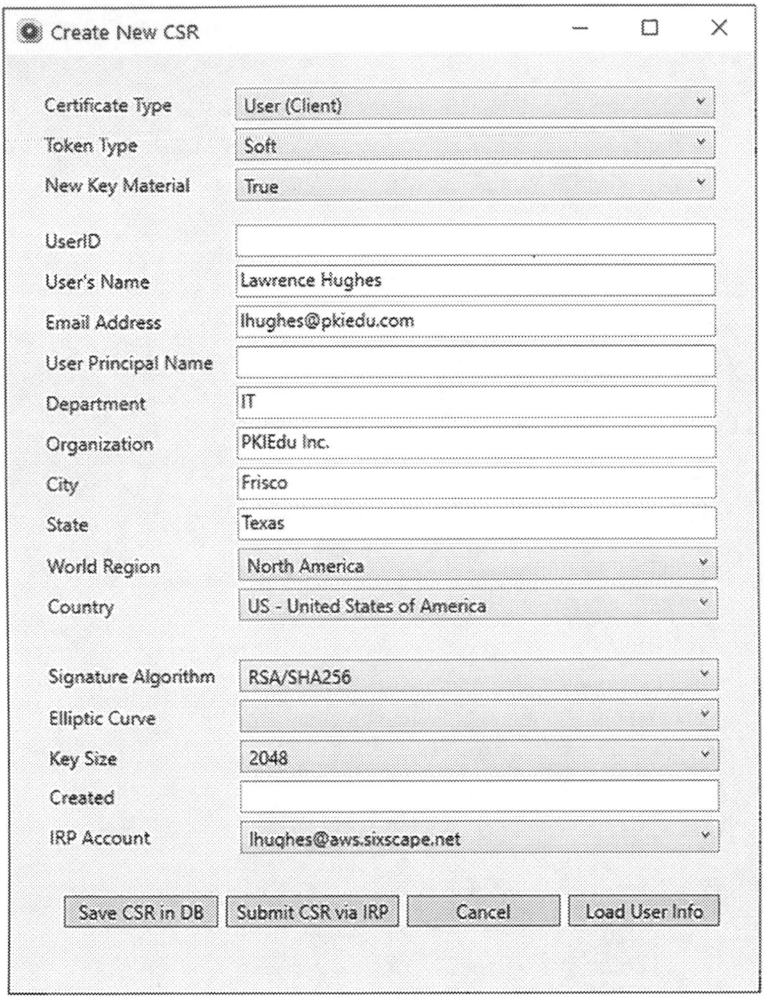

Figure 6-2. *Save the result in the local database, along with the private key in encrypted form*

When I click *Save CSR in DB*, it asks for a passphrase from which to create a symmetric key to protect the private key, shown in Figure 6-3.

Figure 6-3. Create a symmetric key to protect the private key

When I click *OK* here, it will save the CSR and encrypted private key in the local database (Figure 6-4).

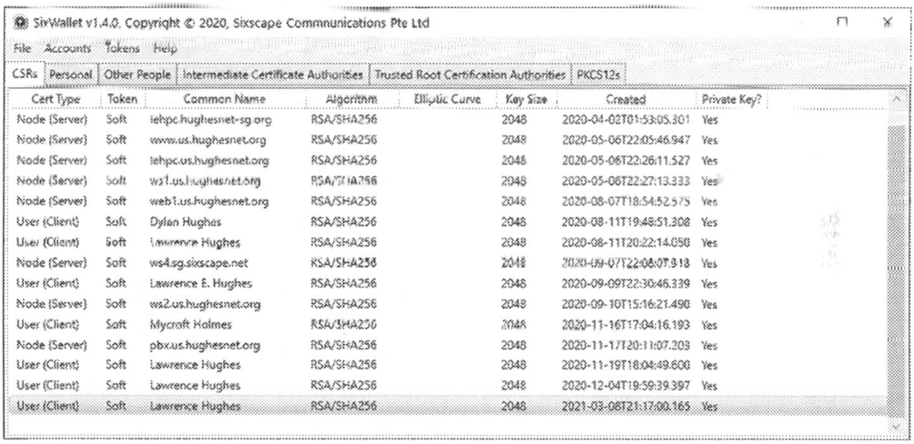

Figure 6-4. Save the CSR and encrypted private key in the local database

If I want to submit this CSR to a CA, I can view it in PEM (Privacy-Enhanced Mail) format (Figure 6-5).

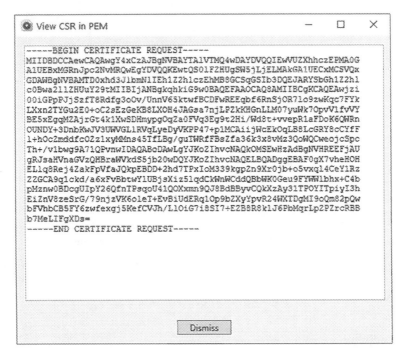

Figure 6-5. *View CSR in PEM format*

Note   PEM refers to an older standard called Privacy Enhanced Mail. This was specified in RFC 1421 in February 1993. PEM was replaced by S/MIME later. We still use some of the file formats created for Privacy Enhanced Mail. This is one of them. PEM format files are ASCII text files that start with a header (e.g., "-----BEGIN CERTIFICATE REQUEST -----" and end with a trailer (e.g., "----- END CERTIFICATE REQUEST -----"). The lines in between are a binary object encoded into base64 notation.

The Open Source OpenSSL cryptographic library makes extensive use of PEM format files.

Some CAs allow you to submit a CSR in PEM format.

To verify this, I can go to various CSR viewers, for example, `http://digicert.com/ssltools/view-csr/`. I can paste this CSR in PEM format there (Figure 6-6).

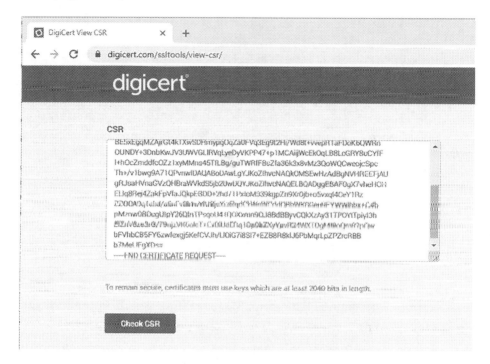

Figure 6-6. *Example of a CSR viewer*

When I click *Check CSR*, I see the following (Figure 6-7).

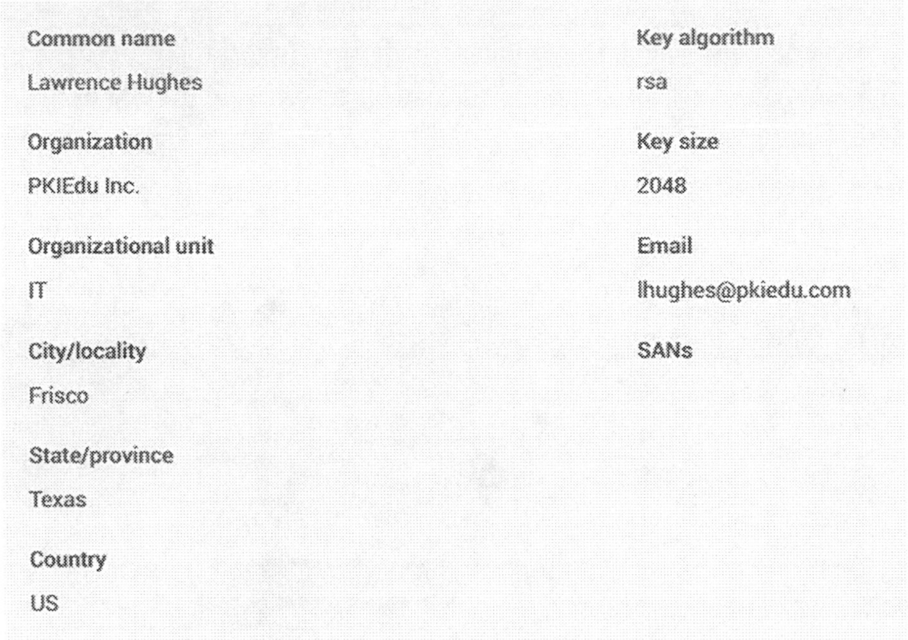

Common name	Key algorithm
Lawrence Hughes	rsa
Organization	Key size
PKIEdu Inc.	2048
Organizational unit	Email
IT	lhughes@pkiedu.com
City/locality	SANs
Frisco	
State/province	
Texas	
Country	
US	

Figure 6-7. *View of Check CSR*

Many CAs have a page that allows you to submit a CSR in this format. After you submit the request, you can retrieve the issued certificate and link it back together with the saved private key (which requires the passphrase you protected the private key with).

If you have a CA that supports Sixscape's Identity Registration Protocol, you can actually submit the CSR over that, retrieve the issued certificate (also over IRP), and save the result into your Certificate Store.

Sixscape Communications created their own Certification Authority (called IDCentral) that supports IRP. I am running a copy of that in AWS. As an example, I have created a CSR for this (loading the fields for my SubjectDN from the IRP server) as in Figure 6-8.

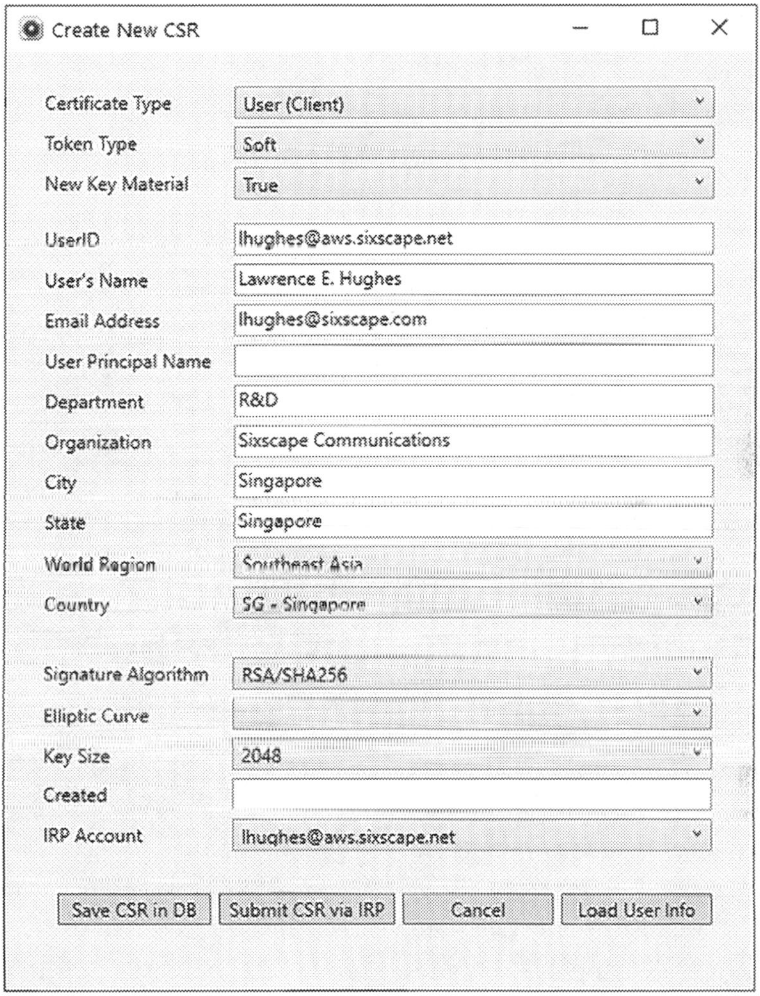

Figure 6-8. *Create a CSR*

When I click *Submit CSR via IRP*, it asks for a passphrase to protect the private key.

It then submits the CSR over IRP to request a certificate from IDCentral, with the response (see Figure 6-9).

Figure 6-9. *Response when you request a certificate from IDCentral*

The new CSR appears in the CSR tab (Figure 6-10).

Cert Type	Token	Common Name	Algorithm	Elliptic Curve	Key Size	Created	Private Key?
Node (Server)	Soft	www.us.hughesnet.org	RSA/SHA256		2048	2020-05-06T22:05:46.947	Yes
Node (Server)	Soft	lehpc.us.hughesnet.org	RSA/SHA256		2048	2020-05-06T22:26:11.527	Yes
Node (Server)	Soft	ws1.us.hughesnet.org	RSA/SHA256		2048	2020-05-06T22:27:13.333	Yes
Node (Server)	Soft	web1.us.hughesnet.org	RSA/SHA256		2048	2020-08-07T18:54:52.575	Yes
User (Client)	Soft	Dylan Hughes	RSA/SHA256		2048	2020-08-11T19:48:51.308	Yes
User (Client)	Soft	Lawrence Hughes	RSA/SHA256		2048	2020-08-11T20:22:14.050	Yes
Node (Server)	Soft	ws4.sg.sixscape.net	RSA/SHA256		2048	2020-09-07T22:08:07.918	Yes
User (Client)	Soft	Lawrence E. Hughes	RSA/SHA256		2048	2020-09-09T22:30:46.339	Yes
Node (Server)	Soft	ws2.us.hughesnet.org	RSA/SHA256		2048	2020-09-10T15:16:21.490	Yes
User (Client)	Soft	Mycroft Holmes	RSA/SHA256		2048	2020-11-16T17:04:16.193	Yes
Node (Server)	Soft	pbx.us.hughesnet.org	RSA/SHA256		2048	2020-11-17T20:11:07.203	Yes
User (Client)	Soft	Lawrence Hughes	RSA/SHA256		2048	2020-11-19T18:04:49.600	Yes
User (Client)	Soft	Lawrence Hughes	RSA/SHA256		2048	2020-12-04T19:59:39.397	Yes
User (Client)	Soft	Lawrence Hughes	RSA/SHA256		2048	2021-03-08T21:17:00.165	Yes
User (Client)	Soft	Lawrence E. Hughes	RSA/SHA256		2048	2021-03-08T21:28:25.443	Yes

Figure 6-10. *Visual of new CSR*

I can then retrieve the generated certificate and save it in my Certificate Store by right-clicking the CSR and selecting *Reassociate Certificate*.

This first shows the fields from the existing CSR (note this is all read-only), as shown in Figure 6-11.

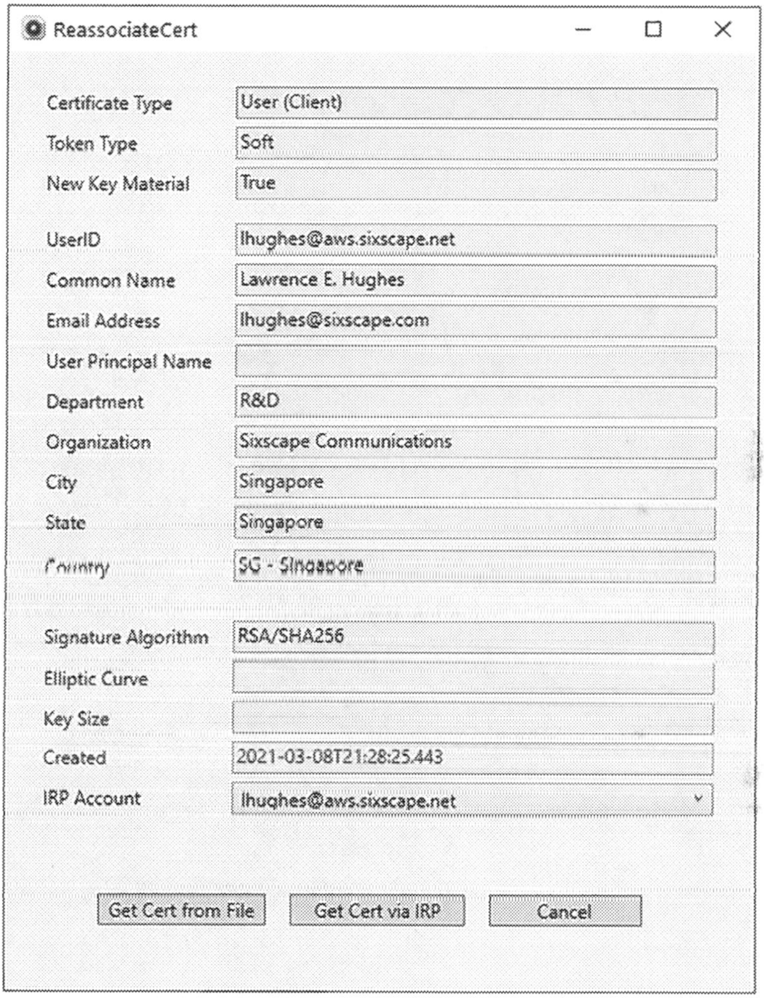

ReassociateCert	— ☐ ✕
Certificate Type	User (Client)
Token Type	Soft
New Key Material	True
UserID	lhughes@aws.sixscape.net
Common Name	Lawrence E. Hughes
Email Address	lhughes@sixscape.com
User Principal Name	
Department	R&D
Organization	Sixscape Communications
City	Singapore
State	Singapore
Country	SG - Singapore
Signature Algorithm	RSA/SHA256
Elliptic Curve	
Key Size	
Created	2021-03-08T21:28:25.443
IRP Account	lhughes@aws.sixscape.net ∨

Get Cert from File   Get Cert via IRP   Cancel

Figure 6-11. *Fields from the existing CSR*

I can then click *Get Cert via IRP* to retrieve the generated certificate.

It asks for the passphrase I used to protect the private key (see Figure 6-12).

Figure 6-12. *Enter passphrase*

When I click *OK*, it gets the cert from IDCentral via IRP, reassociates it with the private key, and saves the result in my Certificate Store. It allows me to select the level of protection for the private key, as shown in Figure 6-13.

Figure 6-13. *Select the level of protection for the private key*

The status is then displayed (Figure 6-14).

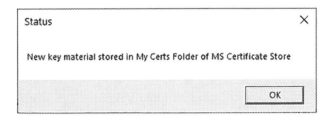

Figure 6-14. *View of the status*

It allows me to specify a passphrase to also store the key material in PKCS12 format (Figure 6-15).

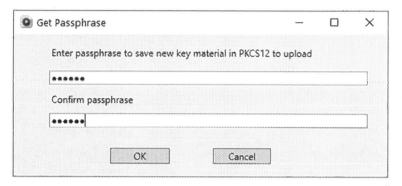

Figure 6-15. *Specify a passphrase to store key material in PKCS12 format*

When I click *OK*, the status shows success (Figure 6-16).

Figure 6-16. *Status success*

And it also uploads the PCKS12 file to the IRP server (Figure 6-17).

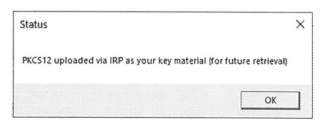

Figure 6-17. *Upload of PCKS12 file to the IRP server*

Now when I look in my Personal folder, I see the new certificate, as shown in Figure 6-18.

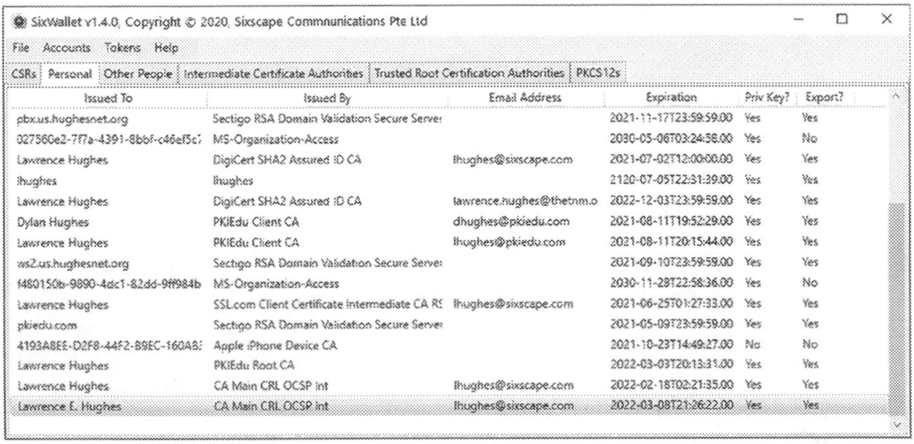

Figure 6-18. *View of new certificate*

If I double-click that certificate, I see (Figure 6-19).

Figure 6-19. *Certificate information*

And the private key is in the Certificate Store.

If I check the SubjectDN, I see the fields from the CSR (Figure 6-20).

Figure 6-20. *View the fields from the CSR*

Finally, if I check the PCKS12 page, I see the new PKCS12 stored locally (Figure 6-21).

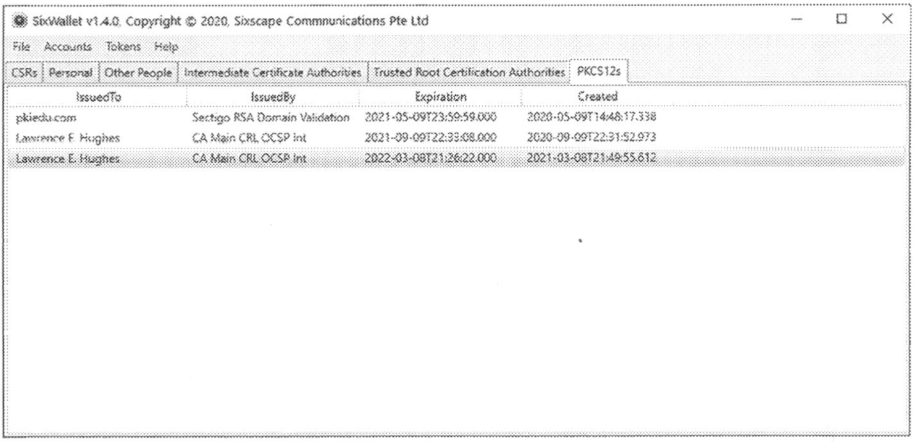

SixWallet v1.4.0, Copyright © 2020, Sixscape Communications Pte Ltd
File Accounts Tokens Help
CSRs Personal Other People Intermediate Certificate Authorities Trusted Root Certification Authorities PKCS12s
IssuedTo IssuedBy Expiration Created
pkiedu.com Sectigo RSA Domain Validation 2021-05-09T23:59:59.000 2020-05-09T14:48:17.338
Lawrence E. Hughes CA Main CRL OCSP Int 2021-09-09T22:33:08.000 2020-09-09T22:31:52.973
Lawrence E. Hughes CA Main CRL OCSP Int 2022-03-08T21:26:22.000 2021-03-08T21:49:55.612

Figure 6-21. *View the new PKCS12 stored locally*

This shows the complete process of requesting a certificate, retrieving it, and backing it up securely.

Note that PKCS12 (or "PKCS #12") is a secure container (file) that can hold one or more digital certificates and one or more private keys. Most hold one of each. The contents are usually encrypted with 3DES symmetric key cryptography, using a symmetric key derived from a passphrase using PKCS #5.

The PKCS (Public Key Cryptography Standards) series were issued by RSA long ago. The useful ones have been adopted into IETF RFCs, but most people still refer to them by the PKCS numbers. For example, PKCS #12 is now specified in RFC 7292, "PKCS #12: Personal Information Exchange Syntax v1.1," July 2014. I have personally never heard anyone refer to an "RFC 7292 container." For more details on the PKCS series, see the "Relevant Standards" appendix.

CHAPTER 7

Certificate Revocation and Renewal

A digital certificate has a limited validity period, but sometimes you want to "expire" a certificate before its expiration date. There is no way to know even how many copies of a given certificate there are, let alone where they are located. So, there is no way to reach out and delete them or change their expiration date (which would make the digital signature fail anyway).

The same problem happens with credit cards. Sometimes people don't pay their bill, so you want to stop people from using them. Originally, credit card companies published booklets of revoked credit card numbers (sorted by card number to make it easier to look up). Clerks would check the booklet before accepting a card, which took time. If the number of the card they were checking was not listed, they would accept the card (the booklet is what is known as a "blacklist" – a "whitelist" would be a list of all the *valid* credit cards, which would be enormous).

Later, credit card companies provided little machines that could dial in to their computers, check for a revoked credit card number, and even verify if the current transaction was covered by available credit. This was much faster and did not require little booklets to be published frequently. That is still in use today, only many of the machines actually connect over the Internet.

© Lawrence E. Hughes 2022
L. E. Hughes, *Pro Active Directory Certificate Services*,
https://doi.org/10.1007/978-1-4842-7486-6_7

With certificates, the first approach corresponds to using Certificate Revocation Lists (CRLs). The second approach corresponds to the Online Certificate Status Protocol (OCSP).

It is the responsibility of every relying application to check either CRL or OCSP for the current revocation status of a certificate before it is used.

Like credit cards, digital certificates have expiration (*ValidTo*) dates. They also have start (*ValidFrom*) dates, which most credit cards don't have. Normally, the start date is the issue date, but it doesn't have to be. You could start the validity period a week or a month after the issue date. The end date is normally one year (or however long you paid for) after the start date. The certificate is only valid between the start and end dates. It is up to the software that uses the certs to not use it outside of the validity period. There are times you have to use an expired cert (or the corresponding private key), for example, to open old encrypted messages in your email message store. One solution is when you renew your certificate to go through the message store and decrypt any encrypted messages with your old private key and then encrypt them again with your new public key. Once that is done, you can toss your old cert and private key (or at least archive them).

Certs can be issued for any validity period. It is common to issue them for one year, two years, or even three years. The longer the cert life, the less frequently you have to renew them, but the more likely it is that the information in the cert will no longer be current or accurate. Recently, some vendors (like Apple) have said that they will not accept certs longer than 13 months after their start date. Now this is standard industry practice.

You can ask a CA to renew your cert any time (usually for free if it is not yet expired). The end date will normally not change unless you paid for a cert lifetime longer than the original validity period. You don't get additional certificate lifetime unless you paid for it. In some cases, you can even change the SubjectDN information when you renew (say if you changed your name or email address). Of course, the new information must be validated the same as for the initial issue.

Some people believe that CAs put expiration dates on certs just so they can charge you again for a new cert once a year. The real reason is to force the issuing CA to review the identifying information in the cert's SubjectDN and update anything that is no longer valid or current. There is nothing that says the CA has to charge a full certificate price when they renew a cert or charge anything at all. Some CAs still sell two- and three-year certs and will renew them for free (for 13 months each time) until you have used up the lifetime you paid for.

Another reason for an expiration date is to keep the revocation list from growing without bound. Once a cert reaches its expiration date (actually a bit after that), it can be purged from the appropriate CRL (or OCSP database). Without expiration, CRLs could grow without bound.

Certificate Renewal

Once a cert has expired, if you want to continue using it, it must be renewed. Most cryptographic tools will reject expired certificates, just like most stores won't accept an expired credit card. This is very similar to doing the initial certificate request. You can create a new CSR and new private key with the same info as the existing cert and submit it to the CA for signing as usual. If you happened to save the old CSR and private key, you can just resubmit it (which would be *renewal with rollover*).

There are two ways you can renew a cert:

Renewal with rollover – You keep the old public and private keys but create a new certificate with a later expiration date. I call this "old wine in new bottles." In this case, you can still open all your old encrypted emails. You still need to update your cert in shared address books, since the old cert will now be rejected as "expired." The downside is that the longer you use a given key pair, the more likely it is to have been compromised. At some point, you really should do renewal with replacement.

Renewal with replacement – You create a new key pair and use that to create the renewal CSR. I call this "new wine in new bottles." In this case, you will need the old private key to open old emails (unless you bulk re-encrypt all old messages with the new public key). You also need to publish your new cert in any directories the old one was published in (and hopefully notify people using your cert to refresh their copy from the shared address book). The longer you use a given key pair, the more likely it is to be compromised. So, *renewal with replacement* limits the time you use a given key pair.

It is possible to construct a valid CSR from any existing cert (even ones from other issuers), and then the new CSR can be submitted for signing as usual. You can even make changes to the SubjectDN information before submitting it if needed. It can do it with key pair replacement or rollover. The CA will happily sign the certs either way. They don't keep track of your old key material to compare your public key with.

Certificate Revocation

If you don't pay your credit card bill, the credit card company will revoke your charging privileges. In some cases, if you present your card to a store after it is revoked, they may confiscate your card or cut it in half. If you only use your card online, there is no way anyone could seize or destroy your card.

Years ago, credit card companies published little booklets with a list of all revoked credit card numbers (sorted by card number). Before they would accept your card, stores would check if your card number was in that booklet, and if it wasn't, they would accept your card (it was a *blacklist*, not a *whitelist*). Sorting the card numbers made it quicker to check for a given card.

A user could still charge things until a new booklet came out, which the card company might have to take a loss on. If a store didn't check and the card number was already in the booklet, the store might be liable for bogus charges.

Certificate Revocation List (CRL)

Certificates have a similar scheme called **Certificate Revocation List** (CRL). A CRL is a list of all certificate serial numbers that have been revoked, but not yet expired. Once expired, the certs should not be accepted regardless, and the serial number can be removed from the CRL.

The CRL is specified in RFC 5280, "Internet X.509 Public Key Infrastructure Certificate and Certificate Revocation List (CRL) Profile," May 2008.

Each certificate hierarchy (e.g., DigiCert SHA2 Assured ID CA) has a separate CRL. Each certificate in that hierarchy will contain a CRL Distribution Point for CRLs for that hierarchy. You may have quite a few cached CRLs for different hierarchies on your computer at any given time, each with its own *Next Update* date and time. A public CA may have quite a few certificate hierarchies.

A certificate hierarchy consists of a Root Cert, one or more Intermediate Certs, and any number of End-Entity Certs. An End-Entity Cert chains up to an Intermediate Cert. It is possible to have multiple Intermediate Certs in a hierarchy, each chaining up to the next one. The top of the chain is the Root Cert, which the top Intermediate Cert chains up to. See Figure 7-1.

Figure 7-1. *A certificate hierarchy*

In this certificate, the End-Entity Cert (tz270.us.hughesnet.org) is a
TLS server cert. It chains up to the Sectigo RSA Domain Validation Secure
Server CA Intermediate Cert. That in turn chains up to the USERTrust RSA
Certification Authority Intermediate Cert. Finally, that one chains up to
the root of this hierarchy, the Sectigo AAA Root Cert. The entire hierarchy
consists of the Root Cert, the two Intermediate Certs, and possibly
thousands of End-Entity Certs.

The CRL is a complex structure, just like CSRs and certificates.
Microsoft has a viewer for them if you double-click a CRL file (Figure 7-2).

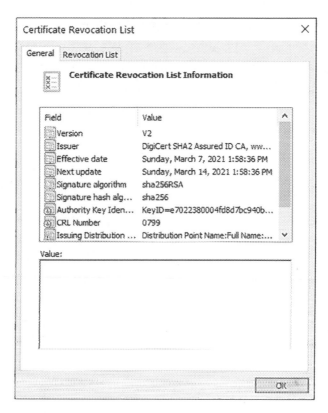

Figure 7-2. *Microsoft viewer for the CRL*

If I click *Issuer*, it shows who issued this CRL (the same CA that issued the certificate you are checking):

```
CN = DigiCert SHA2 Assured ID CA
OU = www.digicert.com
O = DigiCert Inc
C = US
```

If I click *Effective Date*, it will show when this CRL becomes effective (when your application should start using it), for example:

```
Sunday, March 7, 2021 1:58:36 PM
```

If I click *Next Update*, that is when the CA will issue a new CRL for this certificate hierarchy. Anytime after that date, if your application is presented with a certificate, you should first obtain the new CRL before checking. Usually, that CRL is cached, so you can use it for checking additional certificates until yet another CRL is issued. For example:

```
Sunday, March 14, 2021 1:58:36 PM
```

From this, you can see that DigiCert issues a new CRL every week. Basically, if there are no CRLs cached on a given system for this certificate's hierarchy, the next time you need to check a certificate from this hierarchy, you need to download the current CRL from the CRL Distribution Point in the certificate. You can use that CRL for this hierarchy until a new CRL is issued (which is in the CRL as *Next Update*). At that time, you need to obtain the new CRL and cache it.

If I select the *Revocation List* tab, you can see the entire list of certificates that have been revoked (but not yet expired) for this certificate hierarchy (Figure 7-3).

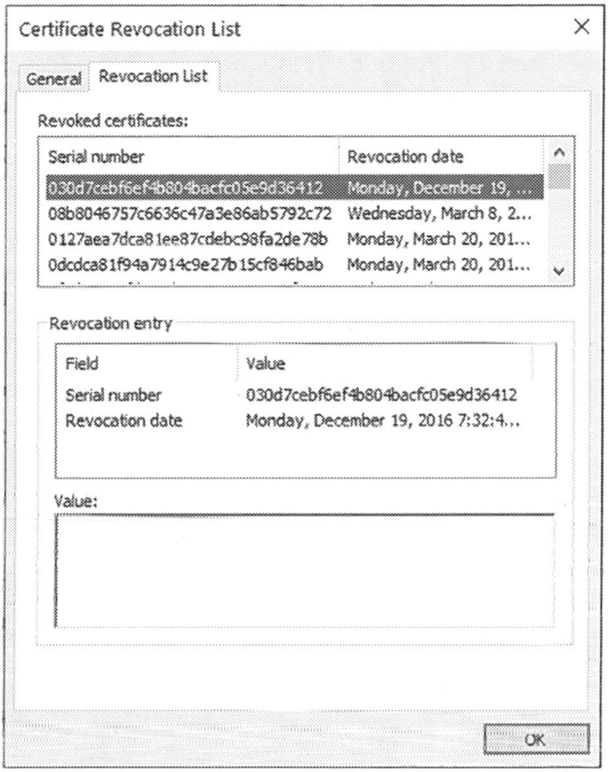

Figure 7-3. *The entire list of certificates that have been revoked*

Each entry in this list has a 128-bit serial number of a specific certificate and the date and time it was revoked. Even though it is not shown here, it also includes a reason why the certificate was revoked.

The list is digitally signed by the CA when it is issued, so each client can know that it is the authentic CRL for this certificate hierarchy and has not been tampered with in any way since it was issued. Every time a client node uses a CRL, it checks that signature before trusting the information in the list.

Each computer has a separate CRL cache, so when my desktop downloads a new CRL, that new CRL isn't available to my notebook computer, which must also download the new CRL the next time *it* has to check a certificate from that hierarchy.

As with credit cards, with CRLs, there is a delay between the time the CA revokes the certificate and the relying parties become aware of that revocation. The more frequently CRLs are issued, the shorter that delay is, but the more often CRLs have to be downloaded. It is common for CRLs to be reissued every 24 hours, but some CAs have premium service to reissue them every hour. Because of the "next issue time" and caching, CRLs don't use that much bandwidth.

OCSP (Online Certificate Status Protocol)

To minimize the gap between revoking a credit card and stores becoming aware of it and to speed up the process of checking for invalid credit cards, credit card companies abandoned the revocation booklets and introduced little machines that could check the revocation status of cards online. The store would swipe the customer's card and enter the amount of the transaction. The machine (Figure 7-4) would dial in and check the revocation status of the card (and the available balance as well). It would reject or approve the transaction and give the store an approval code if accepted. Once the store got that approval code, the card company was responsible for any loss.

Figure 7-4. *Checking the revocation status of a card*

CAs came up with a similar scheme, based on a new protocol called **Open Certificate Status Protocol** (OCSP). A new company called ValiCert split off from VeriSign and opened just down the street. They specialized in OCSP deployments. OCSP is currently specified in RFC 6960, "X.509 Internet Public Key Infrastructure Online Certificate Status Protocol – OCSP," June 2014.

Anytime a relying party is presented with a cert, it can send just that serial number to the CA (based on information in the cert) via OCSP and get back a go/no-go status reflecting the current revocation status of that cert. Once it gets back a "revoked" status on a given cert, it can cache that, because once a CA revokes a cert, it will never "unrevoke" it.

In theory, this could reduce the delay from revocation to end users becoming aware of it to near zero, but many OCSP servers just provided another way to access the CRL information, so there was still a delay, but it was easier to determine revocation status.

OCSP queries can be the majority of the network traffic at a CA. Most people don't request or renew certs all that often (typically once a year for a given cert), but OCSP could be used every time a cert is presented. It is possible to have a local cache that is queried instead of going all the way to the CA on every request. In practice, an OCSP response also includes a "next issue" timestamp, and each client can cache the OCSP response until the next issue time arrives. This holds down the traffic related to revocation checking significantly.

OCSP is simpler to implement than CRLs but can involve a lot more network traffic. If you want to minimize total network traffic, it is better to use CRLs.

Supporting Certificate Revocation on Your Own CA

If you deploy your own CA, for example, with Microsoft Certificate Services, you must generate CRLs and/or deploy an OCSP server to allow relying applications to check the current revocation status. Microsoft Active Directory Certificate Services takes care of all this for you, storing the information in your Active Directory and providing URLs to that information. It also periodically updates the CRLs in Active Directory. Every relying application needs to have access to the http or ldap servers that publish the CRLs or provide OCSP service.

CHAPTER 8

Key Management

Symmetric Key Management

Symmetric keys are very good for bulk encryption but are difficult to manage and exchange if only symmetric key cryptography is available. In real-world systems, symmetric keys are typically "use once and throw away." You create a new random symmetric key for each S/MIME email message or for each connection with TLS. Once you are finished with a particular symmetric session key, you destroy it. In fact, with TLS, a new session key is generated and exchanged periodically since the longer you use a symmetric key (or the more data you process with it), the easier it is to crack that key. You typically use asymmetric key cryptography to exchange a symmetric session key between the communicating parties.

You can protect symmetric keys in an HSM, hardware cryptographic token, or PKCS12 container, but for most uses, treat them as "use once, throw away."

Asymmetric Key Management

There are two kinds of asymmetric keys that require management: public and private. There are two places that key management must be implemented: locally on each user's client and centrally on the PKI.

There are two very different goals when managing public and private keys.

© Lawrence E. Hughes 2022
L. E. Hughes, *Pro Active Directory Certificate Services*,
https://doi.org/10.1007/978-1-4842-7486-6_8

Public Key Management

With public keys, you should never use or exchange a "naked" public key – use them only protected within an X.509 digital certificate. A digital certificate provides

- Detection of tampering with items in the certificate, including the public key (via digital signature)

- Binding of the public key to the certificate owner's identity (via SubjectDN and digital signature)

- Knowing who issued the certificate (IssuerDN)

- Validity period (ValidFrom and ValidTo fields)

- Trust chain from End-Entity Certificate to Trusted Root Authority Certificate

- A way to determine current revocation status (CRL and/or OCSP distribution points)

Otherwise, the public key is a *public* object. It is not only OK for other people to see it; you want to make it as easy as possible for other people to get a copy of it. However, you want them to be certain that the key they are getting is the *actual* key for you.

All email clients provide a local address book (usually called the *personal address book* or PAB) on each user's computer. It is possible to save contact information in this, including name, email address, and S/MIME Certificate, and even PKCS #12 container. When you receive a digitally signed message, there is usually some way to capture the sender's email address and certificate in the PAB. It is also usually possible to make a copy of any contact's information from a shared address book into the PAB for future use. However, this requires every user keeping track of this information on all users they correspond with. It is much easier to have a shared address book, for example, in LDAP or Active Directory.

This only has to be built once for everyone sharing it, and updates with new information can be available to everyone at the same time. Most email clients allow you to select recipients from either a PAB or a shared address book.

One good approach to publishing user's digital certificates is in a *directory* (e.g., LDAP or Active Directory). Client software can then access the directory any time it needs another user's digital certificate. Such a directory can be created and maintained by a network engineer. An ideal way to do this is to automate certificate creation, so that anytime you create a certificate for a user, you add their certificate into their directory entry. This requires some kind of *Certificate Management Protocol* (CMP), like *Identity Registration Protocol* (from Sixscape), SCEP (Simple Certificate Enrollment Protocol), or EST, specified in RFC 7030, "Enrollment over Secure Transport," October 2013. If you have competent users, they can get their certificate from anywhere (e.g., online) and publish their own certificate in your directory using various tools, for example, using SixWallet (Figure 8-1).

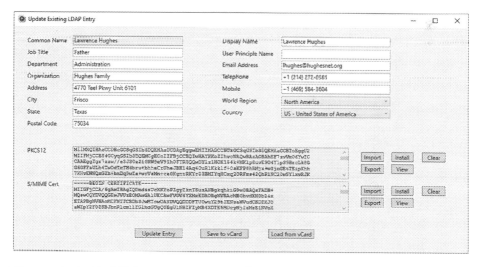

Figure 8-1. *Publish your own certificate in your directory*

This allows you to connect to an LDAP/AD server, list the entries on it, then bring up any entry, and view the relevant attributes, including S/MIME Certificate and PKCS12 file. If it is your own entry, or you have an admin account, you can update those for this entry. If it is someone else's entry, you can view and download their certificate. It would not be any use to export their PKCS12 without the passphrase used to encrypt it.

Any general-purpose LDAP management tool can do similar things with any LDAP attribute. LDAPSoft has management tools for this.

A good email client should include tools for managing certificates and PKCS12 containers for the current user. It should also be able to automatically obtain recipient certificates from LDAP when you send a message.

Microsoft provides access to AD entries to network admins, who can manually view, export, and post certificates for any user (not PKCS12 containers). This is done via *Active Directory Users and Computers*, as shown in Figure 8-2.

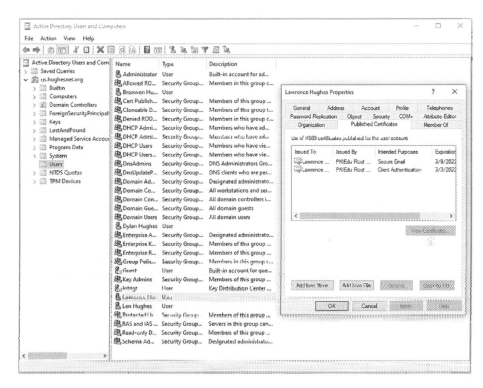

Figure 8-2. *View of Active Directory Users and Computers*

If your organization has deployed MS Certificate Services, you can use mmc.exe or certmgr.msc to view and post your certificates in your AD entry (but not your PKCS12). See Figure 8-3.

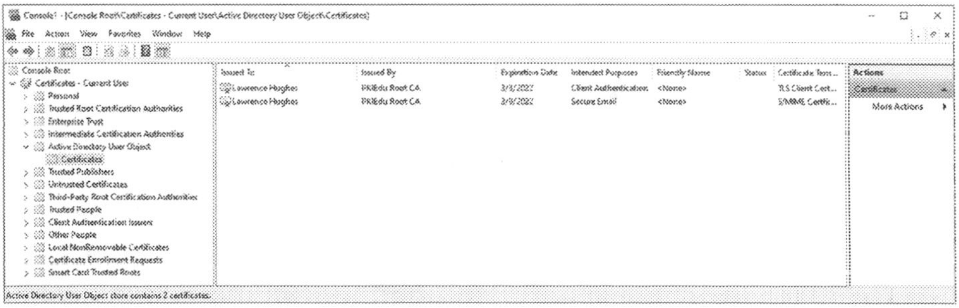

Figure 8-3. *Post certificates in your AD entry*

There are automated systems for organizations that can combine the following functions:

- An "add-in" for MS Outlook that can obtain public hierarchy certificates from various CAs via a Certificate Management Protocol and automatically install them in Outlook for use by S/MIME. This can also automate retrieval of recipient certificates when sending encrypted messages.

- Building a shared address book in Active Directory for all users, including S/MIME Certificate and PKCS12 container, with automated posting of certificates and PKCS12 containers as they are requested.

- Optional key escrow to allow the organization to obtain any user's private key if they lose theirs or they leave the organization without surrendering their private key. Without this, all of their encrypted messages can be irretrievably lost.

Sixscape Communications Pte Ltd has such a system, called the *Email Security Suite*. This is distributed globally by Entrust and GlobalSign. I was heavily involved in the creation of this product. For details, see `https://sixscape.com/products/emailsecuritysuite/`.

Private Key Management

When you store key material into your Certificate Store, if there is a private key, it asks you how you want to protect the private key. One question is whether you want to allow the private key to be exported (which is pretty obvious). The other asks whether you want it protected and, if so, what level of protection. See Figure 8-4.

Figure 8-4. *Private key management*

If I select *Protected,* it lets me choose which *level* of protection I want (Figure 8-5).

Figure 8-5. *Select level of protection*

The default is *Medium* level. If I click *Set Security Level,* I can select the security level (Figure 8-6).

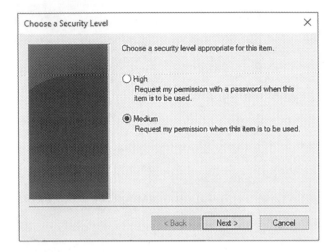

Figure 8-6. *Default is set at Medium*

Medium means anytime I try to use the key, it will warn me that it is being used and ask if that is OK. This prevents malware in the background from using the key without your knowledge. If you are not using a key and you see a warning that it is about to be used, the answer is *NO*.

High will request a passphrase which you must enter every time you use the private key. This is enforced by the operating system; the application merely allows you to select the level, if any. See Figure 8-7.

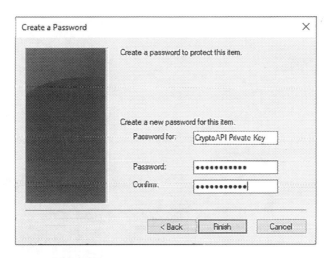

Figure 8-7. *Selecting "High" will request a passphrase which you must enter every time*

If you don't select *any* protection, the private key can be used without any password or warning that it is being used, so long as I am logged into the computer.

There is no protective certificate for *private keys* like the ones for *public keys*. This is because you do not normally share your private key with anyone else (unless your organization does key escrow). You normally keep your private keys on your own computer or in a cryptographic hardware token (USB or smart card). Ideally, only *you* have access to your private key.

When you request a digital certificate, normally, this is done *from* your client computer. You generate the public/private key locally on your computer, create a PKCS10 CSR (Certificate-Signing Request) including the private key, and then submit the CSR to the CA (e.g., via cut and paste on a web page or via some protocol). The CA does not *want* your private key. When the certificate is issued, they return it to you (either over a protocol or by email). You link it back together with your private key to create your full *key material* and put it in your Certificate Store personal folder or possibly in a hardware security token. All vendors of security tokens provide simple apps to let you manage the contents of a token.

For example, Feitian provides the following app for their ePass2003 USB hardware tokens (Figure 8-8).

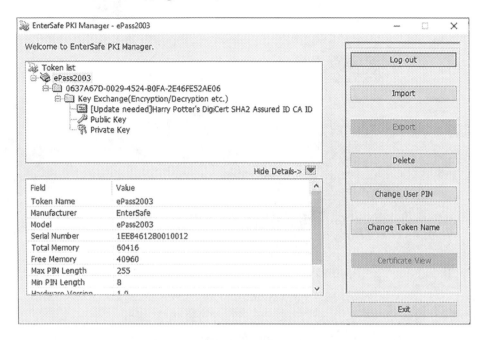

Figure 8-8. *An app for USB hardware tokens*

When you insert a USB token containing key material (certificate and private key) and log in (enter the PIN for the token), the Certificate Store will connect to it over PKCS11 (the standard for interacting with hardware cryptographic tokens) and make the certificate and private key *appear* to be in the Certificate Store. In reality, the private key never leaves the token (it can't – that is the whole purpose of the token). When you encrypt or decrypt something using the private key, that object (e.g., message digest, symmetric session key, etc.) is transmitted into the token, the encryption or decryption happens *within* the token, and the result is sent back to your computer, all via PKCS11. The token actually has a small CPU and firmware to do various cryptographic algorithms. This is *far* more secure than doing cryptographic functions in your own computer.

There are other applications that allow you to manage hardware tokens, such as my own SixWallet, shown in Figure 8-9.

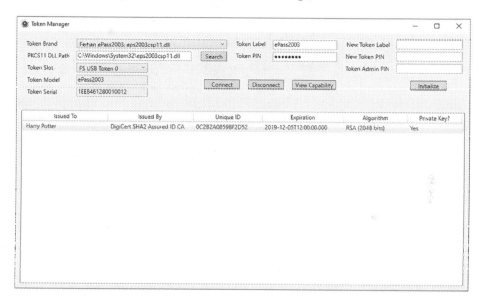

Figure 8-9. *Example of other applications that allow you to manage hardware tokens*

When you enter the PIN, it will show a list of all key material in the token. You can view any of the certificates listed by double-clicking one, or right-click and import, export, or delete certificates.

Notice that Harry Potter's key material *appears* to be in the Certificate Store *Personal* folder when the token is inserted in my computer (and I have logged into it with the PIN) and can be used just as if it were in my Certificate Store. When I remove the hardware token, his certificate disappears from the Certificate Store. Note that the private key is marked as *unexportable*. You can still export the certificate, but not the private key. You *can* move the hardware token to another computer (in which you have installed the token driver) and use the key material from *that* computer. This in effect makes the key material *portable*. See Figure 8-10.

Figure 8-10. *Making the key material portable*

Key Backup and Recovery vs. Key Escrow

Part of good key management is to keep your key material backed up in case you lose it or want to install it on another computer. This is especially important if you are encrypting things with your private key.

There are two approaches to this:

Key backup and recovery involves you exporting your key material into a PKCS12 container (file). PKCS12 is specified in RFC 7292, "PKCS #12: Personal Information Exchange Syntax v1.1," July 2014. The file type is usually .pfx. When you save key material in a PKCS12 container, you are asked for a *passphrase*. That phrase is used to generate a 3DES or AES key with PKCS5, which is used to encrypt the key material inside the container. PKCS #5 is a scheme for creating a symmetric key from an ASCII phrase in a repeatable manner. It is specified in RFC 8018, "PKCS #5: Password-Based Cryptography Specification v2.1," January 2017. You cannot recover the key material in the container without that passphrase. It is therefore safe to back up the PKCS12 container even in an unsecured file system or database. You can even back it to a thumb drive, optical disk, etc. Just don't forget the passphrase! This requires your knowledge and cooperation to back up or restore key material. As long as you keep your passphrase confidential, you are the only one that can recover key material backed up this way. It is safe to upload your PKCS12 to the CA for safe keeping.

Key escrow is another matter entirely. The goal here is to be able to recover a user's key material without the key owner's cooperation or even knowledge. If law enforcement is investigating you, or if you have left your organization without handing over your private key, it may be necessary to do this (they would not want you tipped off that they are investigating you). One way is to store your PKCS12 container and the passphrase that protects it, encrypted with a special escrow certificate. The corresponding private key is kept very securely (i.e., in a safe), and any access to it requires approval by a court order, a company officer, etc. Also, any access to an escrowed key must be very securely audited, including who accessed it, why they accessed it, and when they accessed it. This is necessary in case any legal issues arise in the future. It is particularly dangerous to escrow a *signing* key, and there is no reason to do that. Escrow is for *encrypting* keys.

Because of this, if key escrow is used, you can issue *dual key pairs*. This involves creating not just *one* key pair and certificate, but *two*: one certificate for signing and one certificate for encrypting. This can be enforced with Key Usage Flags. The Signing Certificate can have the *digital signature* flag set, and the *Encrypting* Certificate can have only the *key encipherment* flag set. Then it is not possible to use either certificate for the wrong purpose. Normally, both of those flags are set in a single certificate. Note that Outlook supports dual key pairs for S/MIME Certificates.

Whether you issue dual key pairs or not, many organizations will not deploy S/MIME secure email without some form of key escrow. They could lose company critical information otherwise.

CHAPTER 9

Certificate Management Protocols

Years ago, the primary way to obtain a certificate from a Certification Authority was via a web browser. It involved the following steps:

- You surfed to a special web page at the CA, filled in information for your SubjectDN (name, email, organization, city, state, and country), and clicked submit.

- Your browser then created an asymmetric key pair the public key and built a PKCS #10 Certificate-Signing Request from the public key and SubjectDN and then submitted it to the CA (along with payment information).

- The CA then approved or rejected the request. If it was rejected, nothing further was done.

- When the certificate was issued by the CA, a "please pick up your certificate" message was sent to the user, along with a URL.

© Lawrence E. Hughes 2022
L. E. Hughes, *Pro Active Directory Certificate Services*,
https://doi.org/10.1007/978-1-4842-7486-6_9

- When you clicked the URL, your browser downloaded your certificate and linked it back with the private key (which was stored in the browser) and created your full key material (certificate and private key) in your Certificate Store.

This scheme used a *KeyGen* mechanism in the browser that has since been deprecated. No modern browser supports this mechanism. Internet Explorer 11 has it, but that is being phased out by Microsoft.

There are alternative ways to request a certificate from a CA today, using any of a number of Certificate Management Protocols. These include some older protocols including CMP, CMC, and SCEP and some newer ones including EST, ACME, and Sixscape's IRP.

SCEP and EST are mostly concerned with enrollment and issuance of certificates, while CMP and CMC are more concerned with certificate management, including revocation, current status, and certificate request. IRP is concerned with simplifying creation of a PKCS #10 CSR, submitting a CSR to a CA, and retrieving the issued certificate.

CMP (Certificate Management Protocol)

CMP (Certificate Management Protocol) is specified in IETF RFC 4210, "Internet X.509 Public Key Infrastructure Certificate Management Protocol (CMP)," September 2005. It uses CRMF, which is specified in IETF RFC 4211, "Internet X.509 Public Key Infrastructure Certificate Request Message Format (CRMF)," September 2005.

CMP uses messages in ASN.1 (Abstract Syntax Notation One). This is a very complex format for objects and is used in X.509 digital certificates, PKCS #10 Certificate-Signing Requests, and other cryptographic objects. It is very difficult to implement CMP because of this, and most implementations are only partially compliant. This leads to issues of interoperability between products using CMP.

CMP messages can be embedded in HTTP, layered over TCP, sent as a file over FTP or SCP, or sent via MIME-compliant email. Implementations exist in OpenSSL, Bouncy Castle, EJBCA, and other libraries.

CMP does not support user authentication, with username/password or Strong Client Authentication. It cannot manage per user information for forming a SubjectDN in a request. It does support submission of a CSR and retrieval of the generated certificate, among other functions.

CMC (Certificate Management over CMS)

CMC – Certificate Management over CMS. It is specified in IETF RFC 5272, "Certificate Management over CMS (CMC)," June 2008. It is based on PKCS #10 and CRMF (Certificate Request Message Format), specified in RFC 4211, "Internet X.509 Public Key Infrastructure Certificate Request Message Format (CRMF)," September 2005.

CMS is Cryptographic Message Syntax, which is specified in IETF RFC 5652, "Cryptographic Message Syntax (CMS)," September 2009. It is based on PCKS #7, which was based on the older Privacy-Enhanced Mail (PEM) standard. CMS is similar to S/MIME digital envelopes.

CMC messages can be sent over MIME-compliant email or as files via FTP, SCP, etc. It includes a *Proof of Possession* mechanism to ensure that the requester possesses the private key corresponding to the submitted public key. This is basically the crypto challenge described elsewhere in this book.

The more recent EST (Enrollment over Secure Transport) is a *profile* of CMC.

SCEP (Simple Certificate Enrollment Protocol)

SCEP (Simple Certificate Enrollment Protocol) was originally created and maintained by Cisco. Its original purpose was to allow a network administrator to automate enrollment of digital certificates by various Cisco network devices from a central SCEP server. No user management or authentication was required as all nodes including the server were managed by one person (or group).

There was a long attempt to standardize SCEP in an RFC which kept failing. Finally in September 2020, SCEP was finally specified in RFC 8894, "Simple Certificate Enrollment Protocol," September 2020. More recently, SCEP has been replaced by EST.

There are many commercial and open source implementations of SCEP, some of which will not interoperate due to the long-delayed standardization effort.

SCEP is based on CMS and PKCS #10. It is a simple client/server protocol. There is no user database or per user authentication (either username/password or Strong Client Authentication). This makes it of limited use in many situations. There is a way for each SCEP client to be issued a special certificate that can be used in SCEP Secure Messages to identify the requester, but this is not done during the connection (as is the case with many network protocols). See Section 3 of RFC 8894.

SCEP supports the following functions:

- CA public key distribution

- Certificate enrollment and issue

- Certificate renewal

- Certificate query

- CRL query

There is no database of per user information which could be used to simplify the process of creating a SubjectDN. Such database could also allow the user information to be centrally managed and preapproved for a given organization.

It is possible to add an SCEP server to any Certification Authority, and many already support it. There are various SCEP clients and APIs for adding SCEP support to applications or devices that require certificates. There are both commercial and open source implementations of SCEP clients and servers.

EST (Enrollment over Secure Transport)

EST is specified in IETF RFC 7030, "Enrollment over Secure Transport," October 2013. It was created to allow clients to request and obtain TLS Client Certificates and the associated "CA" Certificates (Root and Intermediate Certs) from a CA. It was intended to replace SCEP (see previous). It is implemented over HTTPS. It uses certain Uniform Resource Identifiers (URIs) from RFC 8615, "Well-Known Uniform Resource Identifiers (URIs)," May 2019. Well-Known URIs can be registered at www.iana.org/assignments/well-known-uris/.

EST has a limited number of operations:

- Distribution of CA certificates

- Enrollment of client certificates

- Re-enrollment of client certificates

- Full CMC (Certificate Management over CMS)

- Server-side key generation (creation of public/private key pair on EST server)

- Request list of attributes expected or desired in a request by the CA

It does not appear to support requesting TLS Server Certs, Document Signing Certs, or Code Signing Certs. An S/MIME Certificate is a minor variation of a TLS Client Cert, so it should be supported (depending on implementation).

Bouncy Castle cryptographic API includes open source implementations of client-side EST for both Java and C#.

To use EST, you do the following:

- Create a public/private key pair, either on the client (e.g., using OpenSSL or Bouncy Castle) or on the EST server, using RSA or various ECC asymmetric key algorithms. If the key pair is created on the EST server, you must obtain the private key and certificate via CMC.

- Create a PKCS #10 Certificate-Signing Request (CSR) on the client or optionally on the EST server.

- Submit the CSR to a Certification Authority (CA). This would be done by CMC (Certificate Management over CMS). Many implementations of EST are done by CAs, which provide a way to submit the CSR to their own CA and pay for the certificate.

- Retrieve the generated client certificate, again via CMC (or the server could email it to you).

The following commercial CAs have confirmed support for server-side EST:

- DigiCert

- GlobalSign

- Entrust

ACME (Automated Certificate Management Environment)

ACME (Automated Certificate Management Environment) (v2) is specified in IETF RFC 8555, "Automated Certificate Management Environment (ACME)," March 2019. It is heavily used by Let's Encrypt which is a non-profit Certificate Authority that issues free TLS Server Certificates for use in securing websites and email servers. Many "casual" websites use Let's Encrypt certificates via automation plug-ins such as Really Simple SSL for the WordPress content management system. Real commercial websites still tend to use "real" certificates from commercial Certification Authorities.

ACME was designed to automate the process of requesting a TLS Server Certificate, including establishing ownership of the relevant domain name. There are various plug-ins for content management systems such as WordPress that implement ACME (e.g., Really Simple SSL). If you run a website on WordPress, this can simplify obtaining and installing a TLS Server Cert for your site, at no cost (at least when using the base-level Really Simple SSL).

ACME is not capable of requesting TLS Client Certificates, S/MIME Certificates, Document Signing Certificates, or Code Signing Certificates. It only supports requesting TLS Server Certificates and only from Let's Encrypt. I don't believe any commercial CAs support it (there would be no financial incentive to do so).

IRP (Identity Registration Protocol)

IRP is a proprietary, patented Certificate Management Protocol created at Sixscape Communications Pte Ltd. It is used in many of Sixscape's certificate automation products. It allows embedding certificate management in any network application or device. Unlike most of the other Certificate Management Protocols, it maintains a user database, with per user information and good authentication (username/password or Strong Client Authentication with a TLS Client Certificate). It is secured with explicit TLS over TCP (not over HTTP). It supports the following operations:

- Create and manage a user account with considerable information for each user, including all information needed to create a Subject Distinguished Name in a CSR. This can simplify the process of creating a CSR, and optionally the per user information can be managed or vetted by the server operator (simplifying auto-RA or even eliminating the RA process entirely).

- Obtaining CA certificates from a CA (Root and Intermediate Certs for any supported certificate hierarchy).

- Submit a PKCS #10 Certificate-Signing Request (CSR) to a CA. This can be for TLS Server Certs, TLS Client Certs, S/MIME Certs, Document Signing Certs, or Code Signing Certs. Normally, the asymmetric key pair is created on the client and never leaves it. The key pair can even be created inside a hardware cryptographic token if desired (not recommended if the key pair is used for encryption as there is then no way to back up the key material). This can be used for initial certificate request or for certificate renewal.

- Retrieve the issued certificate to reassociate it with the private key to create full key material.

IRP can be implemented as part of a CA (as we did in our IDCentral CA), or it can be grafted onto any existing CA (and we have grafted it only several existing CAs, including GlobalSign, Entrust, EJBCA, and MS Certificate Services. In this usage, IRP is similar to ODBC for databases. Every Database Manager has a unique API and implementation of SQL. ODBC allows you to write clients to a single "standardized" API, and an ODBC *connector* maps the ODBC API calls to any supported Database Manager. This makes it easy to use any Database Manager from a given client rather than having to modify it heavily to change to another Database Manager. Many CAs have unique RESTFUL APIs. If you graft an IRP "Front End" onto a CA, any IRP-enabled client can now do full certificate management with that CA with no rewriting required.

Our IRP implementation has a unique feature with Strong Client Authentication (SCA). Most servers secured with TLS only allow turning SCA on for all users or off for all users. It can allow SCA to be "allowed" vs. "required," but until it is "required," a hacker could attack username/password authentication (UPA) for any user. We allow you to enable SCA on a per user basis (some users can require SCA while others still use UPA). This allows a gradual phase in of SCA. You can start with all users using UPA, and as each user obtains their TLS Client Certificate, our IRP server can automatically disable UPA for them. You can even provide a timeout after which only SCA is allowed for all users (e.g., give users two weeks to enable SCA). If a given user loses their client cert, the administrator can re-enable UPA (or even automatically re-enable it if the user can answer security questions), either for some period of time or until they obtain a client cert. This eliminates the possibility of hackers attacking the UPA scheme except for users who have had UPA temporarily enabled, while still allowing a gradual deployment of SCA.

Example of Certificate Request and Retrieval Using IRP

This demo is done using SixWallet, a native Windows application that implements IRP. The IRP server, in this case the Sixscape IDCentral CA, deployed in AWS.

The main window of SixWallet looks like the "Certificate Manager" in Internet Explorer, with some additions (Figure 9-1):

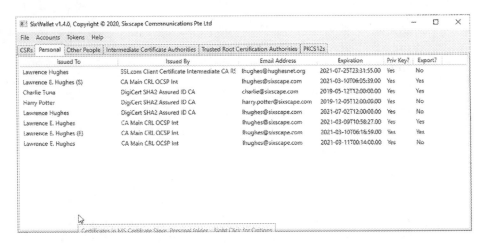

Figure 9-1.   *The main window of SixWallet looks like the "Certificate Manager" in Internet Explorer*

If you double-click (or right-click View Certificate) a certificate in the Person, Other People, Intermediate Certificate Authorities, or Trusted Root Certification Authority tabs, it will display the cert, as shown in Figure 9-2.

Figure 9-2. *Double-click (or right-click View Certificate) a certificate to display cert*

The other tabs allow viewing details of the certificate and the Certification Path (trust chain).

The CSRs tab (not found in the Internet Explorer Certificate Manager) allows you to create a CSR, optionally with the help of IRP (e.g., to get the IRP user's Subject Distinguished Name fields), as shown in Figure 9-3.

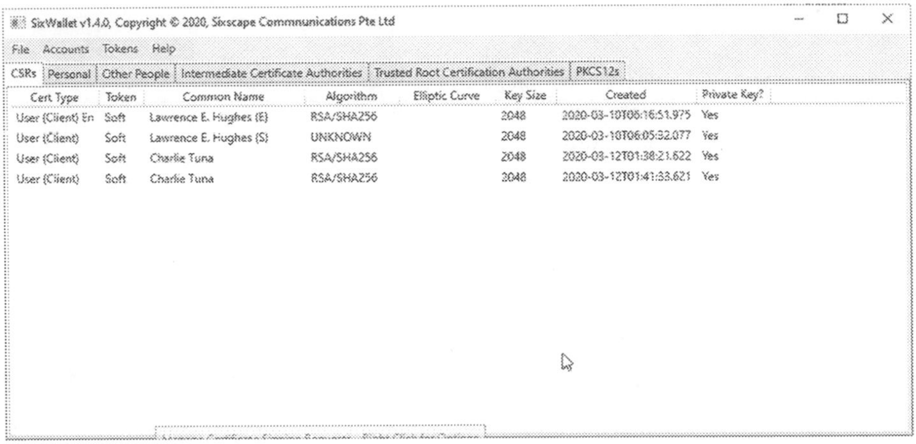

Figure 9-3. *The CSRs tab allows you to create a CSR, optionally, with the help of IRP*

The *Cert Type* column will indicate the certificate type being requested. Possible values currently are

- User Cert (Strong Client Auth, Email S/MIME, XMPP S/MIME, MS Network Logon)

- User Signing Cert (for digital signing with dual key pairs)

- User Encrypting Cert (for encryption with dual key pairs)

- Node Cert (enable SSL/TLS on a server, provide server-to-client auth, key exchange

The *Token* column indicates whether this is for a *soft token* (private key kept in MS Certificate Store) or a hard token (hardware crypto token, e.g., smart card). SixWallet allows you to create key material directly in a hardware token, even remote from the CA. This is the highest level of security, but if you do this, there is no backup of your private key possible. This is fine for Strong Client Authentication or digital signatures but is risky for encryption. If you lose the private key needed to open encrypted files, there is no way to decrypt those files.

The *Common Name* column contains the CommonName (CN) field from the CSR Subject Distinguished Name:

- For a Node Cert, this is the fully qualified node name of the node for which this CSR was created.

- For a User Cert, this is the full name of the person for which this CSR was created.

The *Algorithm* column specifies the cryptographic algorithms used to create the key pair and cert. The first part, before the slash (e.g., *RSA*), indicates the public key algorithm of the generated key pair and of the public key part of the signing algorithm. The second part, after the slash (e.g., *SHA256*), indicates the HASH part of the signing algorithm. After 2016, nobody should be using SHA1 (it has been deprecated).

If the algorithm uses ECC (Elliptic Curve Cryptography), for example, ECDSA, then the *Elliptic Curve* column contains the name of the specific Elliptic Curve used in this CSR (there are many possible).

The *Key Size* column contains the length in bits of the key. For RSA, this is usually some multiple of 1024. For ECC, this may be various lengths, for example, 112, 160, 224, 256, etc. The curve selected determines the key length in this case. Note that 256-bit ECC is about as strong as 2048-bit RSA.

The *Created* column contains the date and time this CSR was created. It helps in reassociating the retrieved certificate with the correct private key and makes each CSR unique in the local DB and on the CA. The syntax for this timestamp is ISO 8601 (yyyy-mm-ddThh:mm:ss:fff).

The *Private Key* column indicates whether there is a private key corresponding to this CSR in the local DB. Normally, if you create a CSR, a private key is created at the same time. If you import a CSR without importing a private key, you could have a CSR with no private key. Private keys in the local DB are always kept encrypted. When you export a CSR, if there is a private key associated with it, it will also be exported.

If you right-click the CSR page, the context menu has the following options. For some menu items, you right-click a listed CSR to view/delete/whatever and then select the option. For others, you just right-click anywhere the CSR page.

CSR page right-click menu options:

- Create New CSR

- View/Modify CSR

- Reassociate Cert

- View CSR in PEM Format

- Export CSR and Key

- Import CSR

- Delete CSR

- Refresh

CSRs (Create/Manage CSR)

With CSRs, the viewer is a bit different from the certificate viewer (note that the public key and private key are not shown). You can also modify the fields in the Subject DN to create a new CSR. You cannot change anything in a certificate once it is signed, but you can create a new CSR (and private key) based on an existing CSR. This viewer allows you to see the contents of an existing CSR (right-click a CSR and select View/Manage CSR, or double-click a CSR). You can also modify the fields and create a new CSR based on an existing one. See Figure 9-4.

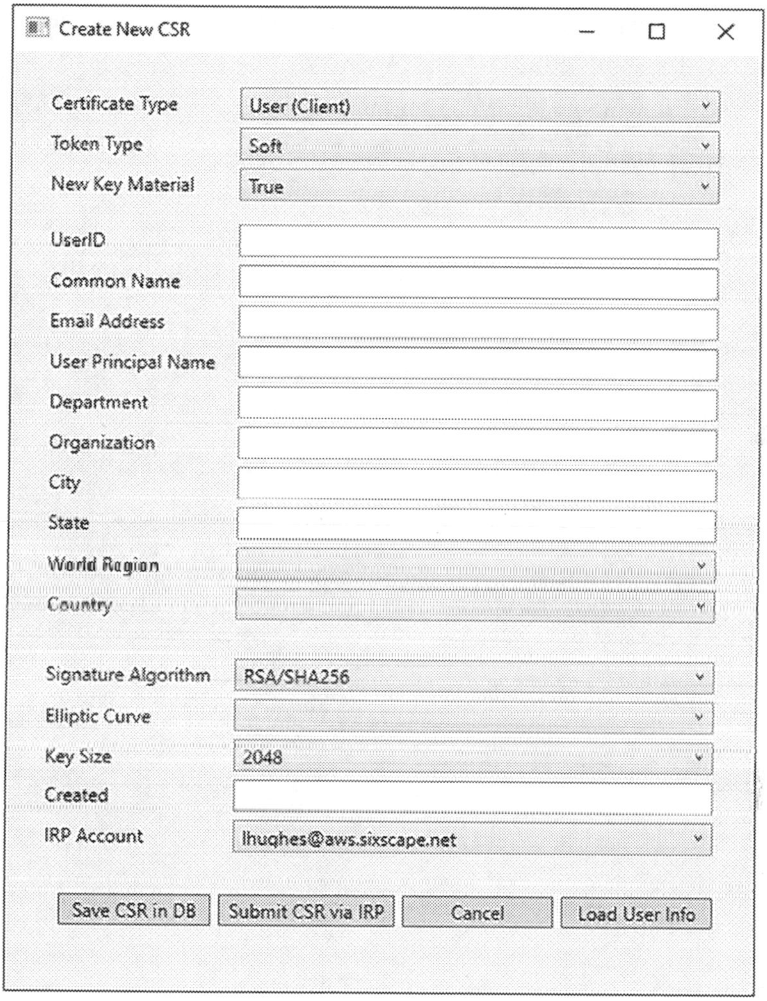

Figure 9-4. *Viewer that allows you to see the contents of an existing CSR*

When you are viewing an existing CSR, you can save it as a new CSR in the local database or submit it to a CA via IRP.

The Certificate Type can be

- **User (Client)** Cert (Strong Client Auth, Email S/MIME, XMPP S/MIME, MS Network Logon)

- **User (Client) Signing** Cert – cert used for signing with dual key pairs

- **User (Client) Encrypting** Cert – cert used for encryption with dual key pairs

- **Node (Server)** Cert – enable SSL/TLS on a server, provide server-to-client auth, and key exchange

If you select Certificate Type as *Node (Server)*, the form changes as in Figure 9-5.

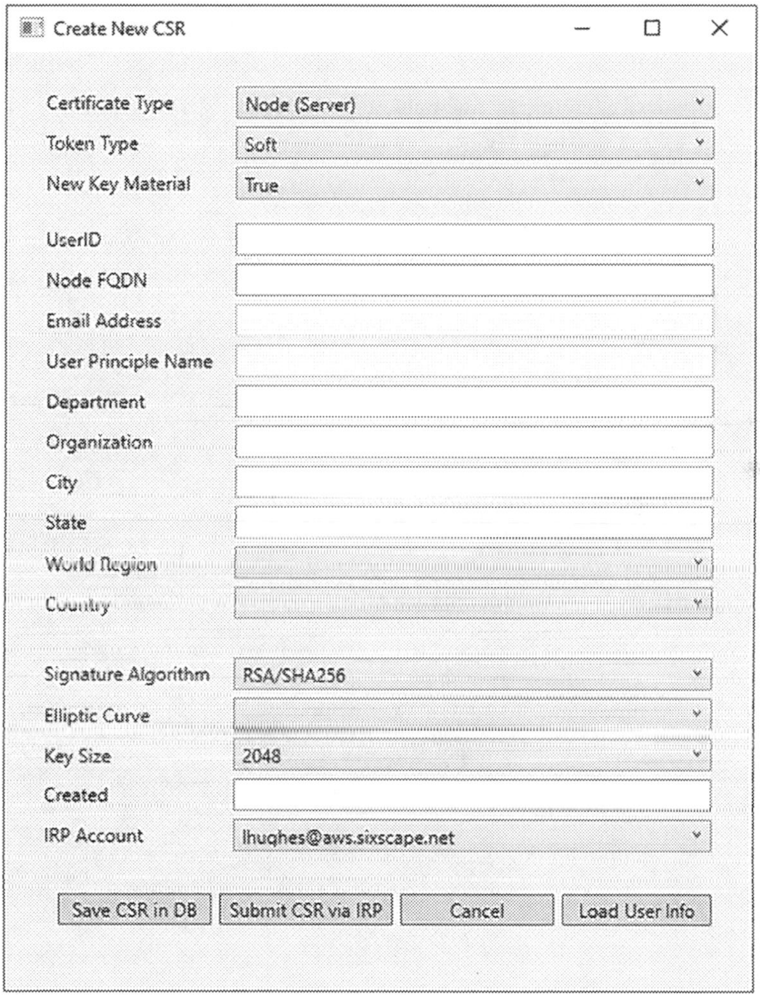

Figure 9-5. *Select Certificate Type as Node (Server) and the form changes*

Note that the Email Address and User Principal Name fields are cleared and disabled. These fields are not normally included in a node (server) cert. Also, the label for the first field (CommonName) changes from *User's Name* to *Node FQDN* (for Fully Qualified Domain Name).

Assuming you have created an IRP account and that account has user info (the information used to create a Subject Distinguished Name in the CSR) defined for it, you can load that information into the CSR form by clicking *Load User Info* (see Figure 9-6).

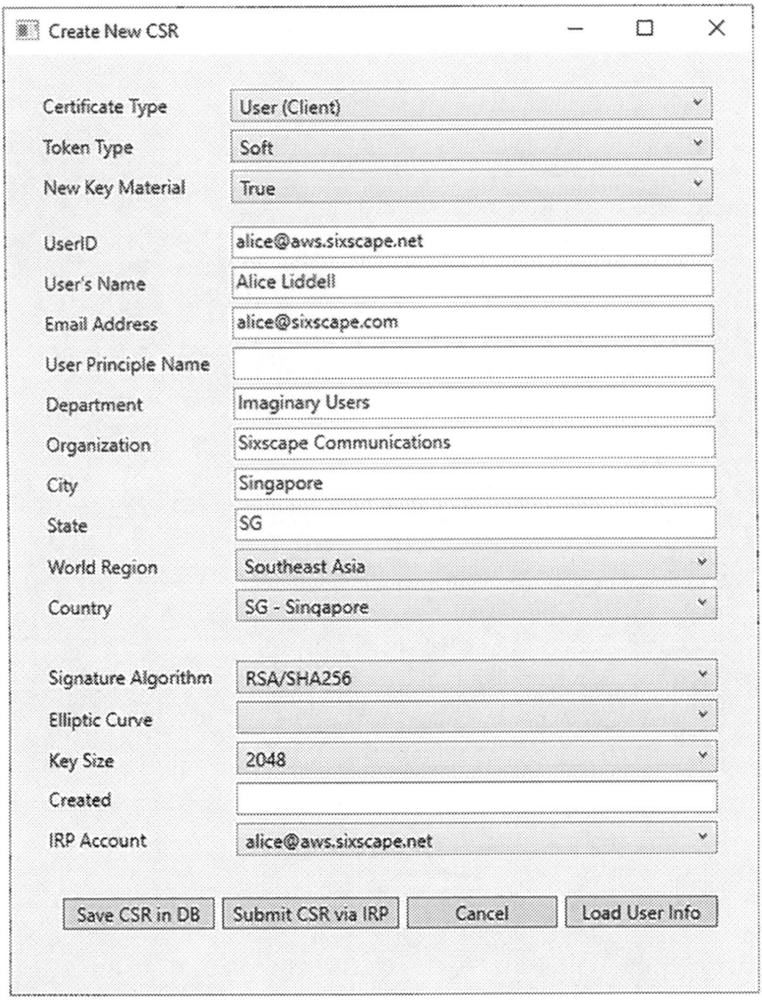

Figure 9-6. *Load information into the CSR form by clicking Load User Info*

The IRP account for this user is *alice@aws.sixscape.net*. When you click *Load User Info*, it connects via IRP and downloads Alice's user info and loads it into the fields of the CSR form.

This helps you create a CSR quickly and accurately. You can create or update an IRP account via *Main Menu/Accounts/IRP/*(right-click) *Create New Account* and view or manage the user info via *Main Menu/Accounts/IRP/*(right-click an IRP account) *Connect To Server*. You can allow users to create and manage their own IRP accounts, or they can be controlled centrally by a Security Admin.

In any case, you fill in the Subject DN attributes or load it via IRP and then click *Submit CSR via IRP*. That will

- Generate a public/private key pair (using the selected algorithm and key size).

- Create a PKCS10 CSR object containing the specified SubjectDN and public key.

- Digitally sign the CSR with the generated private key.

- Ask for a passphrase to protect the private key in the local DB.

- Store the preceding information, the new CSR, and the new private key (encrypted with AES and a key derived from the passphrase you supply) in the local DB.

You will be asked to enter a passphrase that is used to protect the private key in the local database until needed. See Figure 9-7.

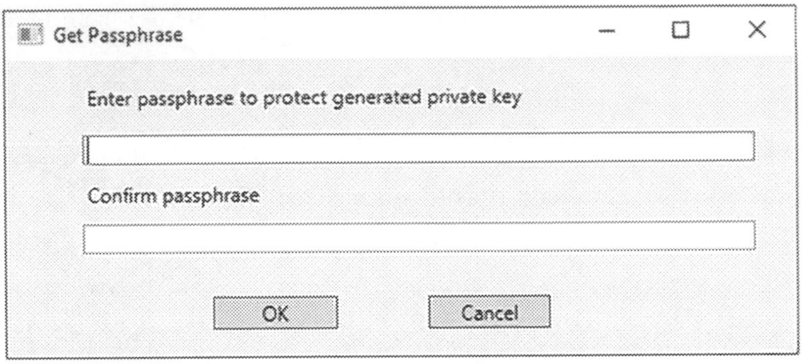

Figure 9-7. *Enter a passphrase that is used to protect the private key*

Assuming everything works, you will see the following (Figure 9-8).

Figure 9-8. *The confirmation of the CSR*

You can view the CSR details at any time, but not the private key or the public key. You can view the CSR in PEM format in order to cut and paste it into a web form at a CA. You can also submit the CSR to a CA that supports IRP via that protocol (this requires access to a CA that supports IRP and an IRP account on that CA). This is done with the *Submit CSR via IRP* button.

If you submit a CSR to a CA that supports IRP, the RA (Registration Authority) will review the request and approve or deny it. This involves verifying that all the information in the Subject Distinguished Name is accurate and current and that you have the right to request a certificate using the fields in the submitted Subject DN. They can also remove any item from the submitted Subject DN that they can't verify, before approving the CSR for signing.

If the RA approves the request, then the CA (Certification Authority) will create a signed digital certificate from the CSR, using the specified algorithm. You can then use SixWallet to retrieve that certificate, reassociate it with the private key (from when the CSR was created), and store the resulting key material in your local MS Certificate Store (in the *My Certs* folder). This is done with the *Reassociate Cert* option on the CSR page (right-click the CSR used to request the cert and select *Reassociate Cert*) and then clicking the *Get Cert via IRP* button in the Reassociate Cert dialog.

CSRs (Reassociate Cert)

This is the most complex function. It assumes you have somehow received notification that the new cert is ready from the CA. You can download the new cert via IRP from a CA that supports IRP during this function. This cert should be a file in PEM or DER format (e.g., .crt or .cer file type). This cert is created by the CA and does not currently have an associated private key. That is the point of this function – to reassociate the new cert with the private key generated when you created the CSR.

IRP will find the cert automatically and download it for you. When you click *Open*, the following things happen:

- The new cert is loaded into an X.509 certificate object.

- A "crypto challenge" is done to verify that the new cert corresponds to the private key.

- The private key is loaded into the same X.509 certificate object – you will be asked to enter the passphrase used to protect the private key when the CSR was created.

- The resulting combined key material is stored in the MS Certificate Store (it shows up under *Personal*). You are asked to specify whether the private key will be exportable or not and to choose the protection level in the MS Certificate Store.

- You are asked to enter a passphrase that will protect the key material in a PKCS #12 object which is saved in the local DB (it appears under *PKCS12s*). Note if the private key is in a hardware token, the private key cannot be loaded into the PKCS #12 – only the cert.

When you right-click a CSR and select *Reassociate Cert*, you should see the information from the CSR as follows (Figure 9-9).

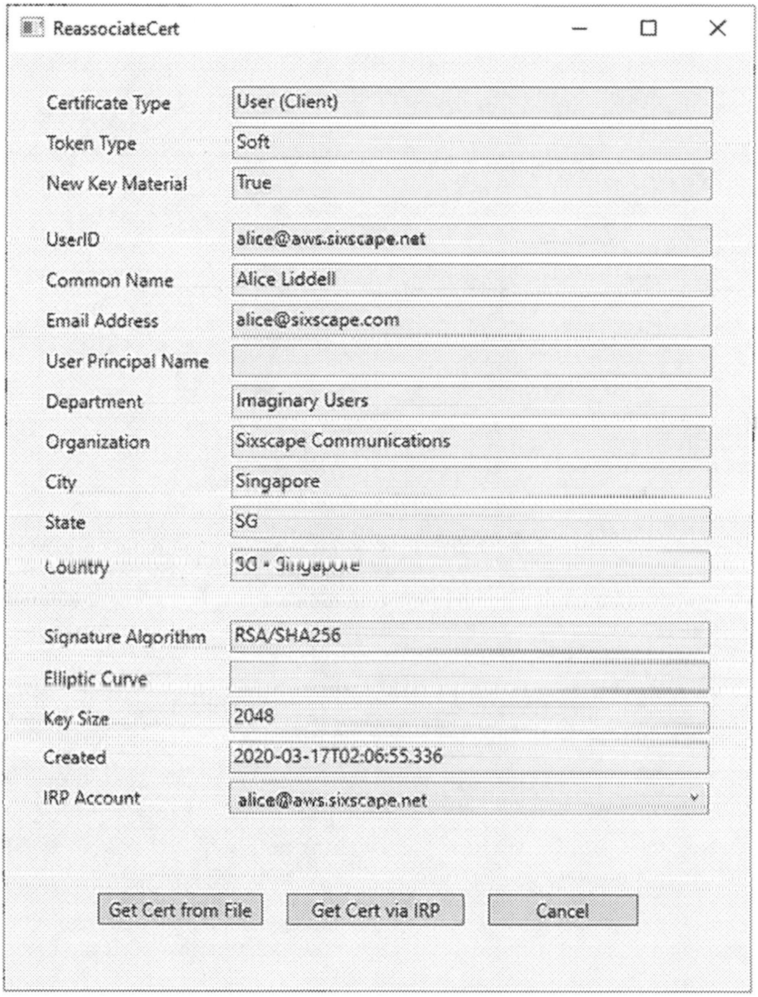

Figure 9-9. *When you select Reassociate Cert, you should see the information from the CSR*

If you are using IRP, you can select the account to use with the *IRP Account* ComboBox at the bottom of this form. This should be the same IRP account you used to submit the CSR (and will be loaded for you). Just to remind you, IRP accounts are created with *IRP: Create New IRP Account.*

You can't change any fields in the cert at this point. Whichever scheme you use, you will need to provide the passphrase that was used to protect the private key in the local database (Figure 9-10).

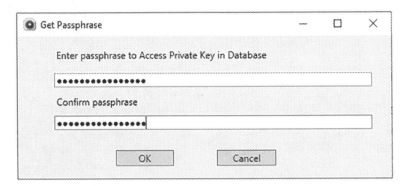

Figure 9-10. *Provide the passphrase that was used to protect the private key*

Enter the passphrase, confirm it, and click *OK*.

You can now choose whether the private key will be exportable and the protection level (Figure 9-11).

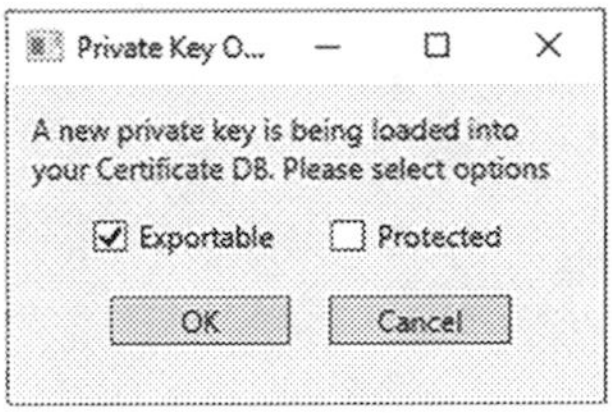

Figure 9-11. *Make your selections for the private key*

If you chose *Protected*, then you can choose medium- or high-level protection. If you chose high level, then you will need to enter a passphrase that you will need to enter every time you access that private key.

Select preferred private key options, and click *OK*.

If you are using IRP, shortly, the following box will display (Figure 9-12).

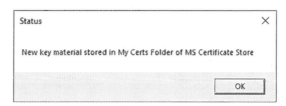

Figure 9-12. *View if you are using IRP*

Dismiss this by clicking *OK*.

You will then get to enter a passphrase to protect a new PKCS #12 (Figure 9-13).

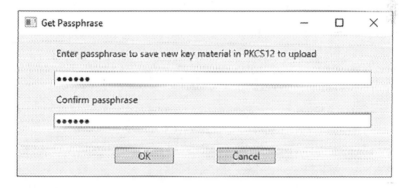

Figure 9-13. *Enter passphrase to protect a new PKCS*

Enter passphrase to protect the automatically generated PKCS #12, and click *OK*. You will then see the following (Figure 9-14).

Figure 9-14. *Enter passphrase to protect the automatically generated PKCS #12*

143

Dismiss this with *OK*. You will then see the following (Figure 9-15).

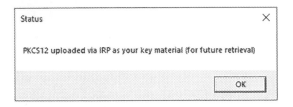

Figure 9-15. *Dismiss this with OK*

Three things have happened:

1. Your new key material is in your Cert DB (My Certs).

2. The PKCS #12 has been written to the local DB.

3. The PKCS #12 has been uploaded to your IRP account.

If you look in the *Personal* page, you will see the new certificate (Figure 9-16).

Issued To	Issued By	Email Address	Expiration	Priv Key?	Export?
Lawrence Hughes	SSL.com Client Certificate Intermediate CA R!	lhughes@hughesnet.org	2021-07-25T23:31:55.00	Yes	No
Lawrence E. Hughes (S)	CA Main CRL OCSP Int	lhughes@sixscape.com	2021-03-10T06:05:39.00	Yes	Yes
Charlie Tuna	DigiCert SHA2 Assured ID CA	charlie@sixscape.com	2019-05-12T12:00:00.00	Yes	Yes
Harry Potter	DigiCert SHA2 Assured ID CA	harry.potter@sixscape.com	2019-12-05T12:00:00.00	Yes	No
Lawrence Hughes	DigiCert SHA2 Assured ID CA	lhughes@sixscape.com	2021-07-02T12:00:00.00	Yes	No
Lawrence E. Hughes	CA Main CRL OCSP Int	lhughes@sixscape.com	2021-03-09T10:58:27.00	Yes	Yes
Lawrence E. Hughes (E)	CA Main CRL OCSP Int	lhughes@sixscape.com	2021-03-10T06:16:59.00	Yes	Yes
Lawrence E. Hughes	CA Main CRL OCSP Int	lhughes@sixscape.com	2021-03-11T00:14:00.00	Yes	No
Alice Liddell	CA Main CRL OCSP Int	alice@sixscape.com	2021-03-17T02:07:03.00	Yes	Yes

Figure 9-16. *The new certificate appears on the Personal page*

Now select the PKCS12s tab to see the new PKCS #12 in the local DB. See Figure 9-17.

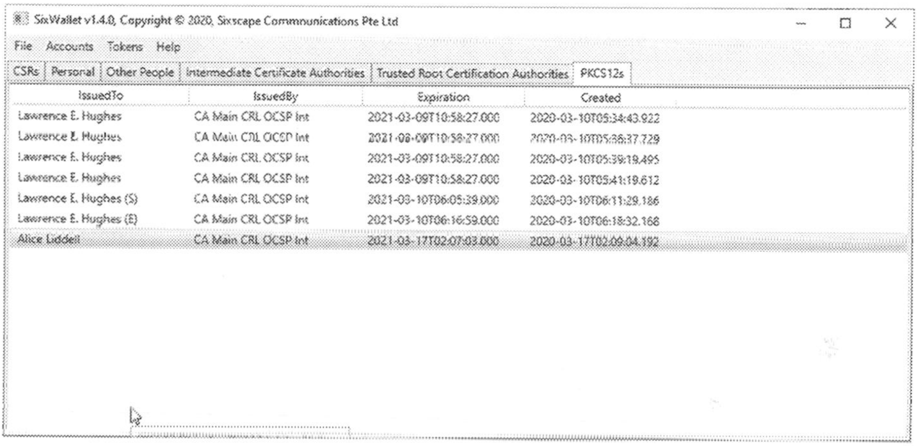

Figure 9-17. *Select the PKCS12s tab to see the new PKCS #12*

SixWallet is basically a manual client for IRP. It is also possible to implement the IRP protocol in any client application or device that has network connectivity and automate the earlier steps to hide all the complexity from the user.

Sixscape has a plug-in for Microsoft Outlook that fully automates the management of S/MIME Certificates using IRP. The first time you use an account that does not currently have an S/MIME Certificate, it will obtain one for you and install it in Outlook, ready to use (in about ten seconds). This can be done from any CA that supports IRP.

CHAPTER 10

Public Key Infrastructure (PKI)

You now have seen all the pieces that make up a PKI, so it is time to put the pieces together and understand where each piece fits into the overall picture.

A Public Key Infrastructure consists of the following components:

- A Registration Authority that reviews Certificate-Signing Requests (CSRs) and either rejects the request or approves it and hands it off to the Certification Authority for issuance. This includes some way for users to submit CSRs, either by a web page or some protocol.

- A Certification Authority that can actually issue various kinds of digital certificates once approved by the Registration Authority.

- A mechanism for generating *Certificate Revocation Lists* (CRLs) periodically for relying parties to determine the current revocation status and servers (HTTP and LDAP) to publish the CRLs.

© Lawrence E. Hughes 2022
L. E. Hughes, *Pro Active Directory Certificate Services*,
https://doi.org/10.1007/978-1-4842-7486-6_10

- An Online Certificate Status Protocol (OCSP) Server that can provide the current revocation status for an individual certificate.

- Management tools that allow the operators to monitor and approve requests.

- Secure storage for the Root and Intermediate Private Keys, typically a Hardware Storage Module (HSM).

- A legal framework, including a Certification Practices Statement.

- A physically secure location, with biometric access controls, multiple access layers, and video logs of all secure areas.

- A secure, trusted network for the servers to run in, which still allows access by end users. There should be very experienced network security engineers involved in locking down the network.

- Trusted personnel to deploy and manage the RA and CA.

- Periodic audits of the network, servers, and services, possibly including formal reviews such as SAS-70 for things like obtaining WebTrust certification. For an internal PKI, some audits would be highly recommended, but not as extensive or expensive as for a commercial public CA.

The trusted personnel who operate the CA require considerable training, skill certification, and background checks. It is highly recommended that external groups do network security reviews ("white hat hacking") to find possible vulnerabilities before any criminals (including state actors) do.

Developers creating applications using the digital certificates will typically require training in use of cryptography, digital certificates, and applications of TLS and S/MIME.

A Certification Authority can host any number of *certificate hierarchies*. They might have several hierarchies for servers (e.g., domain validated, domain and company validated, and extended validation) and several hierarchies for client certs (e.g., only email validated, email and name validated, and full SubjectDN).

A certificate hierarchy consists of the following items:

- A Trusted Root Certificate (widely published, self-signed) and corresponding Root Private Key (very securely stored, e.g., offline in a cryptographic token in a safe). The Root Private Key is needed only to sign the top-level Intermediate Cert, maybe once every five years.

- One or more Intermediate Certificates (widely published, signed by Parent Private Key, and corresponding Intermediate Private Keys) (typically stored in an HSM). The lowest-level Intermediate Private Key is needed to sign End-Entity Certs in this hierarchy.

- A potentially large number of End-Entity Certs, usually distributed to the applicant at the time of creation.

- A periodically published CRL (published via HTTPS and/or LDAPS) for this hierarchy.

- An OCSP server that can provide revocation information from the hierarchy database or possibly CRLs.

- A database containing various items related to the hierarchy, for example, all issued certs, revocation status of each cert, etc.

- Management tools that allow review of certificate requests (by an RA) and signing of approved certificates, revocation of certs, etc.

- Automated email generation to notify certificate owners of imminent expiration, etc.

Each certificate includes one or more *CRL Distribution Points* which contain URLs where a user can obtain the current CRL for that certificate, as well as an Authority Information Access (AIA) that indicates where to obtain OCSP connections.

There are two kinds of certificate hierarchies: public and private (this has nothing to do with public and private asymmetric keys).

A public hierarchy has been approved by WebTrust as operating in a secure and reliable manner. The Trusted Root Cert is periodically provided to OS and device vendors to install in the Root folder of their Certificate Store. This means that certificate in that hierarchy will be trusted by all relying parties with no further effort. See Figure 10-1.

Issued To	Issued By	Expiration
Copyright (c) 1997 Microsoft Corp.	Copyright (c) 1997 Microsoft Corp.	1999-12-30T23:59:59.00
Microsoft Authenticode(tm) Root A:	Microsoft Authenticode(tm) Root Authority	1999-12-31T23:59:59.00
NO LIABILITY ACCEPTED, (c)97 VeriS	NO LIABILITY ACCEPTED, (c)97 VeriSign, Inc.	2004-01-07T23:59:59.00
UTN-USERFirst-Object	UTN-USERFirst-Object	2019-07-09T18:40:36.00
AddTrust External CA Root	AddTrust External CA Root	2020-05-30T10:48:38.00
Microsoft Root Authority	Microsoft Root Authority	2020-12-31T07:00:00.00
Thawte Timestamping CA	Thawte Timestamping CA	2020-12-31T23:59:59.00
Thawte Premium Server CA	Thawte Premium Server CA	2020-12-31T23:59:59.00
QuoVadis Root Certification Authori	QuoVadis Root Certification Authority	2021-03-17T18:33:33.00
Microsoft Root Certificate Authority	Microsoft Root Certificate Authority	2021-05-09T23:28:13.00
DST Root CA X3	DST Root CA X3	2021-09-30T14:01:15.00
GlobalSign	GlobalSign	2021-12-15T08:00:00.00
GeoTrust Global CA	GeoTrust Global CA	2022-05-21T04:00:00.00
Security Communication RootCA1	Security Communication RootCA1	2023-09-30T04:20:49.00
SG-WS3-CA	SG-WS3-CA	2025-04-24T06:01:16.00
SG-WS3-CA	SG-WS3-CA	2025-04-24T06:01:16.00

Figure 10-1. *Trusted Root Cert*

Trust Chains

You can view the trust chain (aka "certification path") from a given certificate to a Trusted Root (assuming the complete path exists) (Figure 10-2).

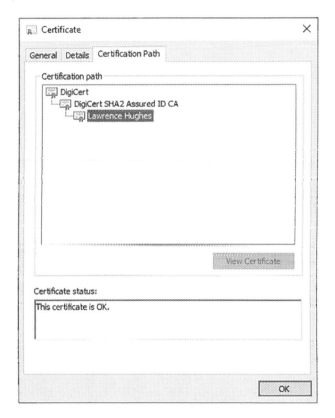

Figure 10-2. *View of the trust chain*

Here, "Lawrence Hughes" is the End-Entity Cert, "DigiCert SHA2 Assured ID CA" is the Intermediate Cert, and "DigiCert" is the Trusted Root Cert. That is a complete certification path. You can double-click any of those certs to view them. The Issuer Distinguished Name of each cert is the same as the Subject Distinguished Name of its parent cert, until the Trusted Root Cert (which is self-signed) where the Issuer Distinguished

Name and Subject Distinguished Name are the same. That is how you chase a trust path when validating a certificate.

The IssuerDN for any cert is the same as the SubjectDN of its parent, until you reach the Trusted Root Certificate, where the SubjectDN and IssuerDN are the same.

For example:

End-Entity Certificate SubjectDN:

> *E = lhughes@sixscape.com, CN = Lawrence Hughes, OU = Administration, O = Sixscape Communications, Pte. Ltd., L = Singapore, C = SG*

End-Entity Certificate Issuer DN:

> *CN = DigiCert SHA2 Assured ID CA, OU = www.digicert.com, O = DigiCert Inc, C = US*

Intermediate Certificate SubjectDN:

> *CN = DigiCert SHA2 Assured ID CA, OU = www.digicert.com, O = DigiCert Inc, C = US*

Intermediate Certificate IssuerDN:

> *CN = DigiCert Assured ID Root CA. OU = www.digicert.com, O = DigiCert Inc, C = US*

Root Certificate SubjectDN:

> *CN = DigiCert Assured ID Root CA. OU = www.digicert.com, O = DigiCert Inc, C = US*

Root Certificate IssuerDN:

> *CN = DigiCert Assured ID Root CA. OU = www.digicert.com, O = DigiCert Inc, C = US*

To build a trust chain, you start with the End-Entity Certificate and then find a certificate in the Certificate Store whose SubjectDN is the same as the End-Entity's certificate IssuerDN (it will be in the Intermediate CAs folder). You repeat this process until you find a certificate where the SubjectDN and IssuerDN are the same which is the Root Certificate (it will be in the Trusted Root CAs folder). A trust chain can be as short as two certificates or as long as four or five certificates. Most trust chains are three certificates long (End-Entity, Intermediate, and Root).

SixWallet Certificate Status

SixWallet allows you to check the current status of any certificate in any of the folders (right-click cert, choose *Check Certificate Status*) (Figure 10-3).

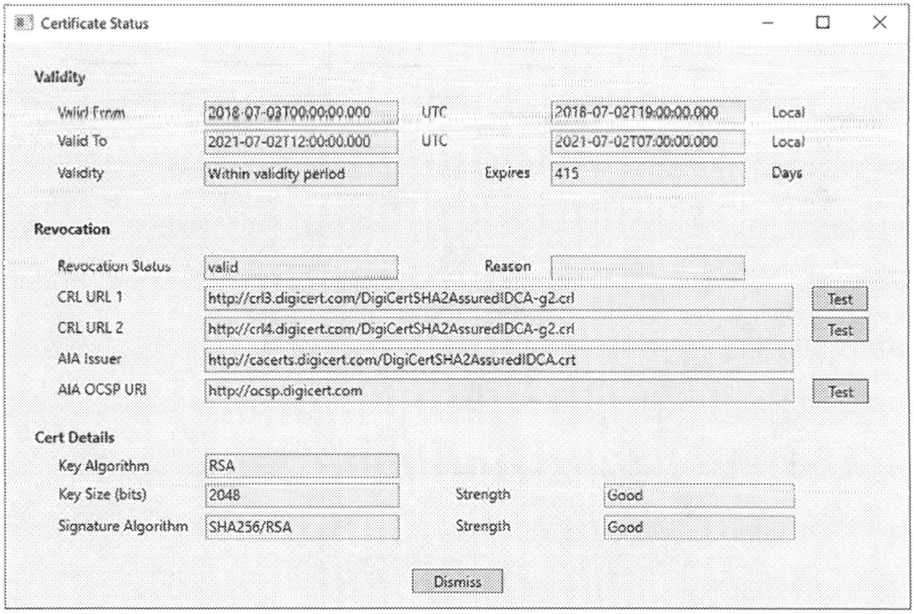

Figure 10-3. *Check the current status of any certificate*

You can even check the CRL(s) and OCSP.

CHAPTER 11

SSL and TLS

Years ago, Netscape Communications created some of the basic products and protocols that have largely defined the Second Internet (the one based on IPv4). These included the first commercially viable browser (Netscape Navigator), the first commercially viable web server (Netscape Web Server), and SSL (Secure Sockets Layer).

Originally, SSL was a proprietary protocol owned and controlled by Netscape. It became so widely used that it was released to the IETF, who renamed it TLS for *Transport Layer Security* (which is curious because it exists within the *Application Layer* or more specifically a *shim* between the *Application Layer* and the *Transport Layer*). It definitely does not live in the *Transport Layer*, as then it would be in Kernel Space, a part of the operating system. SSL/TLS is part of each *Application*, hence lives in User Space, in the *Application Layer*.

Adding TLS to an application is a very complex process that involves modifying all network I/O to work via the Secure Sockets Layer rather than directly through the Socket API. Both the server and the client must be heavily modified. I have implemented several servers that use TLS so I understand exactly what this involves. On the server side, you must also provide support for installing a TLS Server Certificate and the corresponding private key. If you support Strong Client Authentication, you must incorporate support for this on both client and server, this time including support for TLS Client Certificates on the client side. It is also necessary to install any relevant CA certificates so that all certificates will be trusted.

© Lawrence E. Hughes 2022
L. E. Hughes, *Pro Active Directory Certificate Services*,
https://doi.org/10.1007/978-1-4842-7486-6_11

When you surf to a site over *HTTPS*, that is HTTP over TLS. To be more precise, it is HTTP over TLS over TCP over IP over some Link Layer protocol (like Ethernet). See Figure 11-1.

Figure 11-1. *When surfing to a site over HTTPS, that is HTTP over TLS*

The padlock icon indicates that this site is secured with TLS. If I click it, I can view information about the TLS Server Certificate used, including viewing the TLS Server Certificate itself. See Figure 11-2.

Figure 11-2. *Information about the TLS Server Certificate*

While SSL was originally designed just for the Web (HTTP), it is now used with many protocols, including SMTP, IMAP, LDAP, etc. When you connect securely to an email server with *SMTPS*, that is SMTP over TLS. TLS itself runs over TCP (from the TCP/IP Transport Layer). There is a similar protocol that works over UDP, called DTLS (Datagram Transport Layer Security – RFC 6012), for connectionless traffic.

SSL was designed for an Internet based on IPv4 with Network Address Translation (NAT). A node behind NAT (most nodes on the IPv4 Internet today) can only make an *outgoing connection* to an external node via a NAT gateway. A NAT gateway maps the node's private address onto a public address, which can connect to a server that has a public address. NAT forces us to use client/server architecture with a few (mostly static) centralized nodes that have public addresses and many decentralized clients that have private addresses. DNS is sufficient for publishing the node names and IP addresses of those centralized servers.

Netscape released SSL v2.0 to fix a number of problems with the initial implementation and later released SSL v3.0 to fix even more issues and add Strong Client Authentication. Due to its overwhelming popularity and widespread deployment, Netscape released all IP rights to SSL and turned it over to the IETF in 1999. There it was renamed Transport Layer Security (TLS) and has been through several major revisions. You can think of TLS 1.0 as SSL 3.1.

- RFC 2246, "The TLS Protocol Version 1.0," January 1999

- RFC 4346, "The Transport Layer Security (TLS) Protocol Version 1.1," April 2006

- RFC 5246, "The Transport Layer Security (TLS) Protocol Version 1.2," August 2008

- RFC 8446, "The Transport Layer Security (TLS) Protocol Version 1.3," August 2018

These revisions were made by several very talented network engineers from multiple organizations, scrutinized by peer review, and approved by consensus. The result is far stronger and more resistant to hacking attacks than SSL ever was.

TLS normally only needs one TLS Server Certificate, which is installed on the centralized server used by possibly millions of clients. That server certificate identifies the server by *Fully Qualified Domain Name* (node name with domain name, e.g., `www.pkiedu.com`). To get a TLS Server Certificate, you have to convince a CA that you have rights to use the domain name (e.g., *pkiedu.com*) and typically also the organization name (e.g., *PKIEdu Inc.*). You might include other fields such as locality (city), state, and country. This certificate enables SSL/TLS encryption and provides server-to-client authentication. If only a server certificate is used (very common), then some other scheme (e.g., username/password) must be used to authenticate the user (client) to the server, once the encrypted session has begun.

Implicit TLS vs. Explicit TLS

When SSL was first created for HTTP (and for several other protocols, such as FTP, SMTP, IMAP, and LDAP), it used two separate *ports* (e.g., port 25/tcp is assigned to SMTP) for each protocol: one port for unsecured (e.g., 80/tcp for HTTP) and a different port for secured (e.g., 443/tcp for HTTPS). If you connect on the nonsecure port, there was no TLS and no option to start it. If you connect on the secure port, it does a TLS handshake immediately upon connection – no option for nonsecure. This is called *implicit TLS*. Whether or not to use TLS depends on the port you connect to. This was using up a lot of port numbers – two port numbers for every protocol, and ports are a scarce resource.

So, *explicit TLS* was created. This allows both nonsecure and secure operation on a single port number. The idea is to connect first in nonsecured mode (no TLS), and the server advertises support for TLS during a negotiation phase ("I support TLS"). If the client *also* supports

TLS, it can then initiate a switch to secured mode by requesting a TLS handshake. Assuming the handshake goes well, both client and server are now working in secured mode over the same port.

Since HTTP does not have a negotiation mechanism, it still uses intrinsic TLS – by default port 80/tcp for nonsecure and 443/tcp for secure. You can always use other ports (e.g., 8080/tcp for nonsecure and 8443/tcp for secure), but then the client has to know which port is secure and which port is nonsecure.

Initially, SMTPS, POP3S, IMAPS, LDAPS, and FTPS were all implemented in implicit mode.

Protocol	Nonsecure port	Secure port
SMTP	25/tcp	465/tcp
POP3	110/tcp	995/tcp
IMAP	143/tcp	993/tcp
LDAP	589/tcp	636/tcp
FTP control	21/tcp	990/tcp
FTP data	20/tcp	989/tcp

The use of implicit TLS with all protocols except HTTP has now been deprecated (it is not supposed to be used anymore). If you propose a new protocol to IANA, they require support of *only* explicit TLS (they will only assign one port number to a given protocol). This means your protocol must support a negotiation mechanism. I know this for a fact, as I have had two protocols approved by IANA (IRP, port 4604/tcp, and SixID, port 4606/tcp), and they required me to support explicit TLS. You can still find a few servers that support implicit TLS, but usually in addition to explicit TLS on the basic port number. This is mainly to allow legacy clients to still be able to connect securely. At some point, the IETF will probably recommend that all use of implicit TLS be discontinued, even for legacy apps.

Microsoft has caused some confusion in their documentation and configuration by using the term "SSL/TLS" to mean *implicit TLS* and "STARTTLS" to mean *explicit TLS*. In reality, no one should be using *any* version of SSL today (or for that matter, TLS 1.0 or TLS 1.1), and both SSL and TLS can be implemented with either implicit or explicit operation. They should use the terms from the IETF RFCs which are *implicit TLS* and *explicit TLS*. See Figure 11-3.

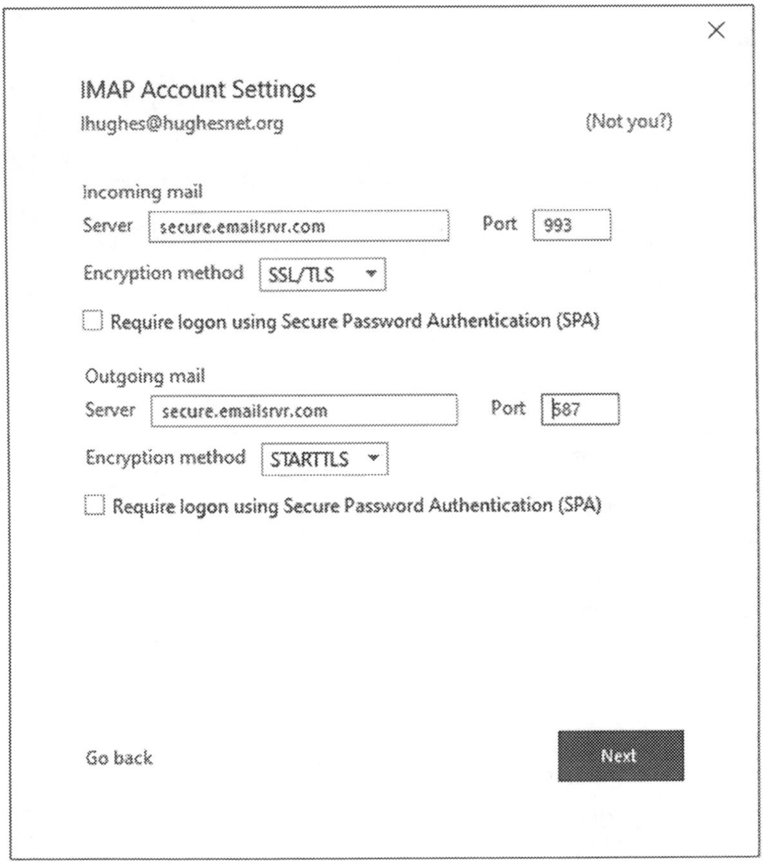

Figure 11-3. *SSL and TLS can be implemented with either implicit or explicit operation*

TLS with Other Protocols (in Addition to HTTP)

SSL was designed for just HTTP. It has been so useful; we have used it to secure many other widely used protocols, including SMTP, POP3, IMAP, FTP, and LDAP.

- RFC 2487 "SMTP Service Extension for Secure SMTP over TLS," January 1999

- RFC 2595, "Using TLS with IMAP, POP3 and ACAP," June 1999

- RFC 4217, "Securing FTP with TLS," October 2005

- RFC 4511, "Lightweight Directory Access Protocol (LDAP): The Protocol," June 2006

- RFC 4513, "Lightweight Directory Access Protocol (LDAP): Authentication Methods and Security Mechanisms," June 2006

You can add TLS to *any* network protocol that meets certain requirements:

- It is layered over *Transmission Control Protocol* (TCP), not *User Datagram Protocol* (UDP), that is, should be *connection oriented*, not *connectionless*.

- It is a text-based query-response protocol (not a binary protocol like DNS).

- It has a negotiation mechanism on initial connection to allow the server to advertise support for TLS and for the client to initiate the handshake ("STARTTLS").

If you are implementing a TLS-secured client/server application, there are a number of toolkits available (e.g., SecureBlackBox from nSoftware) that provide the necessary code to do this (on both server and client sides). Some toolkits include support for implementing Strong Client Authentication with a TLS Client Certificate. I will be providing sample source code in C#.Net on the website for this book with example code for both server and client side (for a trivial "echo" protocol). For C#.Net programmers, this will help them understand TLS in depth and can even be used as a starting point for your own TLS clients and servers.

Note that the problems with a browser "latching onto" a TLS Client Certificate (until all instances of that browser are killed) are a problem with the *implementation* of browsers, not with TLS or Strong Client Authentication, or even with HTTPS. It would be trivial for the browser vendors to provide a way to turn loose of a previously used TLS Client Certificate if those chose to, but for some reason, all browser vendors refuse to do this (I have contacted several of them with no results). Many mobile-based browsers do not support Strong Client Authentication at all.

HTTP is inherently a "single-link" protocol. One browser connects to one server – period. If I click a hyperlink on a web page, the server does not make a second or an ongoing connection to another web server, the current link is dropped, and a new single-link connection to the new URL is made. If you use a web proxy, your browser makes a single-link connection to the proxy, and the proxy makes a second (completely new) single-link connection to the actual server. Proxies really complicate the use of TLS. In this case, the TLS Server Certificate needs to be installed on the proxy, not the actual server. You are actually securing the link from your client to the *proxy*, not all the way to the actual server. Whether the link from the proxy to the actual server is secured or not is a separate issue. Some proxies allow transparent forwarding of the single-link connection to the actual server but cannot do any monitoring or control over the connection (other than blocking the entire connection) as the traffic is encrypted while going through such a proxy.

The *real* problem is with using TLS to secure protocols other than HTTP, which are *normally* multi-link, like email. When Alice sends an email message to Bob, there are several single-link connections involved:

- From Alice's email client to Alice's email server (via SMTP or sometimes IMAP).

- From Alice's email server to Bob's email server (via SMTP), these are potentially the same server if both Alice and Bob happen to have accounts on the same email server.

- From Bob's email client to Bob's email server (via IMAP or possibly POP3 [not recommended]).

Each of these connections can be independently secured with TLS (SMTPS, IMAPS, etc.). Each connection secures a single link from one node to another (e.g., from Alice's email client to Alice's email server), and the traffic is in plaintext (possibly unencrypted) on all intermediary nodes (the email servers). Furthermore, there is no way to ensure that all connections involved are secured. Alice only has control over the connection from her email client to her email server, and Bob only has control over the connection from his email client to his email server. The connection between email servers is only under the control of the people who operate those servers. It is possible to secure server-to-server links with SMTPS, but most people would not even be aware of this. It would be handy to have an SMTP message header that says, "only forward this message if the ongoing connection is secured with TLS – otherwise return it as undeliverable." Or in the case of IMAP, "only allow retrieval of this message over IMAPS." Unfortunately, no such message header exists, and no existing email servers or clients use them. You *can* determine whether or not each link *was* secured with TLS by examining the "Received" headers added by each server along the way (these headers indicate the

IP address of the sender and whether the connection was over TLS). Not many people ever bother to check these headers or are even aware of their existence. Most email clients do not make them easy to view.

Here are typical message headers for an SMTP/IMAP message:

```
Delivered-To: lhughes@pkiedu.com
Return-Path: <lhughes@hughesnet.org>
Delivered-To: lhughes@pkiedu.com
Received: from director7.mail.ord1d.rsapps.net ([172.31.255.6])
      by backend17.mail.ord1d.rsapps.net with LMTP
      id eGNNHWhQSWC+ewAAZbIBGg
      (envelope-from <lhughes@hughesnet.org>)
      for <lhughes@pkiedu.com>; Wed, 10 Mar 2021 18:04:08 -0500
Received: from proxy15.mail.iad3b.rsapps.net ([172.31.255.6])
      by director7.mail.ord1d.rsapps.net with LMTP
      id OE9AHWhQSWBjZwAAovjBpQ
      (envelope-from <lhughes@hughesnet.org>)
      for <lhughes@pkiedu.com>; Wed, 10 Mar 2021 18:04:08 -0500
```
Received: from smtp26.gate.iad3b ([172.31.255.6])
      (using TLSv1.2 with cipher ECDHE-RSA-AES256-GCM-SHA384
      (256/256 bits))
      by proxy15.mail.iad3b.rsapps.net with LMTPS
      id yI+lFmhQSWAJbwAAhyf7VQ
      (envelope-from <lhughes@hughesnet.org>)
      for <lhughes@pkiedu.com>; Wed, 10 Mar 2021 18:04:08 -0500
```
Return-Path: <lhughes@hughesnet.org>
X-Spam-Threshold: 95
X-Spam-Score: 0
X-Spam-Flag: NO
X-Virus-Scanned: OK
X-Orig-To: lhughes@pkiedu.com
X-Originating-Ip: [146.20.161.115]
```

Authentication-Results: smtp26.gate.iad3b.rsapps.net;
iprev=pass policy.iprev="146.20.161.115"; spf=pass smtp.
mailfrom="lhughes@hughesnet.org" smtp.helo="smtp115.iad3b.
emailsrvr.com"; dkim=none (message not signed) header.d=none;
dmarc=none (p=nil; dis=none) header.from=hughesnet.org
X-Suspicious-Flag: NO
X-Classification-ID: eb056ece-81f4-11eb-af3b-5254001088d3-1-1
Received: from [146.20.161.115] ([146.20.161.115:58598]
helo=smtp115.iad3b.emailsrvr.com)
**   by smtp26.gate.iad3b.rsapps.net (envelope-from <lhughes@**
**   hughesnet.org>)**
**   (ecelerity 4.2.38.62370 r(:)) with ESMTPS (cipher=DHE-**
**   RSA-AES256-GCM-SHA384)**
**   id EB/6A-31372-86059406; Wed, 10 Mar 2021 18:04:08 -0500**
X-Auth-ID: lhughes@hughesnet.org
Received: by smtp15.relay.iad3b.emailsrvr.com (Authenticated
sender: lhughes-AT-hughesnet.org) with ESMTPSA id B1041C01A4
        for <lhughes@pkiedu.com>; Wed, 10 Mar 2021 18:04:07
        -0500 (EST)
From: <lhughes@hughesnet.org>
To: <lhughes@pkiedu.com>
Subject: test mail via SMTPS
Date: Wed, 10 Mar 2021 17:06:06 -0600
Message-ID: <54c56e01d71601$f3e9e790$dbbdb6b0$@hughesnet.org>
MIME-Version: 1.0
Content-Type: multipart/alternative;
        boundary="-----=_NextPart_000_54C56F_01D715CF.A94F9EA0"
X-Mailer: Microsoft Outlook 16.0
Thread-Index: AdcWAfNb+vOXoAYpQz2zJqiily4OEA==
Content-Language: en-us

In this example, two links were secured with TLS. There is no
indication of whether it was retrieved over IMAPS.

Securing FTP with TLS

FTP has a different challenge when securing it with TLS. FTP normally uses not just *one* port, but *two*. One port is for data and the other for control. This complicates firewall rules, but it also complicates TLS. Both ports can be secured with TLS (in either implicit or explicit mode). Since the node name is the same for both connections, only a single TLS Server Certificate is required on the server. A better solution in both cases (firewalls and TLS) is to force your TLS connection to use *passive mode*. This makes it use the same port (the data port, 21/tcp) for both data and control.

For example, to configure WinSCP to connect to a TLS secured FTP server (e.g., in IIS), the following will work (Figure 11-4).

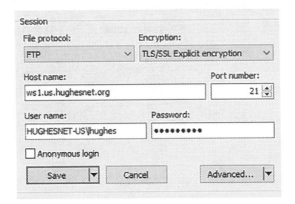

Figure 11-4. *Configure WinSCP to connect to a TLS secured FTP server*

Note that WinSCP uses the correct terms (implicit or explicit TLS/SSL encryption).

If you connect with this setting, the protocol information will look like this (Figure 11-5).

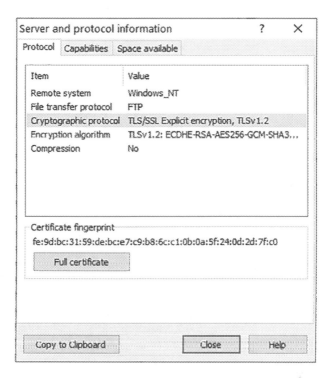

Figure 11-5. The protocol information

Strong Client Authentication with a TLS Client Certificate During the TLS Handshake

Most TLS secured servers only use a TLS Server Certificate. Authentication of the client to the server is done *after* the TLS handshake is complete, using username/password authentication, possibly with some kind of "Two-Factor Authentication," such as an SMS OTP or an OTP token (physical or app based). This is because it is complicated and expensive to issue individual TLS Client Certificates to every user of an online system. This is an excellent reason to deploy Microsoft Certificate Services for Strong Client Authentication by users within an organization.

TLS (since SSL v3.0) also supports using a *TLS Client Certificate* for client-to-server authentication that happens *during* the handshake before the encrypted session begins. If you use SCA, the server must be configured to support Client Authentication (options are "require certificate" or "allow certificate"). When you configure this option, once the server-to-client authentication is done, the server sends a request to the client to upload a TLS Client Certificate. Each user requires a unique TLS Client Certificate that identifies *them* (not their node). This is much more difficult to provide than a single TLS Server Certificate, regardless of how many people use that server. Each user's identity must be validated by the TLS Client Certificate issuer (which can be a public hierarchy CA like GlobalSign or a private hierarchy CA run by an organization, e.g., using Microsoft Certificate Services or EJBCA).

Strong Client Authentication (SCA) using a TLS Client Certificate is far stronger than any username/password scheme, even with Two-Factor Authentication. There is no need for a password. However, you probably still need to know *who* connected (a username or UserID) to user the correct user's information and determine what if anything they are allowed to see or do. If the application can see the contents of the TLS Client Certificate, there is ample information on who connected in the Subject Distinguished Name. That may contain the user's full name (in the CN field), their email address (in the E field), a UserID (in the UID field), or even a User Principal Name (in the UPN field). This information is readily available to any web application. It is particularly easy to get this in PHP scripts (with Apache or NGINX web servers). When you connect using SCA, the system variable $_SERVER('SSL_CLIENT_VERIFY') is true. The fields from the SubjectDN of the TLS Client Certificate are available in other system variables, such as $_SERVER('SSL_CLIENT_S_DN_Email'). The "S_DN" is for Subject Distinguished Name. You can also check the IssuerDN from the TLS Client Certificate to be sure that the supplied certificate is from an issuer you trust (e.g., $_SERVER('SSL_CLIENT_I_DN_CN')) which would be the CN field from the IssuerDN. Therefore, if SCA is used, there is no need to ask for either a username or a password. Upon successful TLS connection, you can go directly into the web application, knowing who made the connection.

TLS Cryptosuites

A *cryptosuite* is a combination of algorithms for

- Symmetric session key exchange

- Public key algorithm (e.g., RSA)

- Symmetric key algorithm used for encryption (c.g., AES256)

- Symmetric key encryption mode (e.g., CTR)

- Message digest algorithm (e.g., SHA2-256)

Every TLS connection negotiates the strongest cryptosuite supported by both the server and the client. Each release of TLS until v1.2 has included more supported cryptosuites. A typical cryptosuite might be *ECDH_RSA_AES256_GCM_SHA384*. TLS v1.3 provides a simpler scheme for negotiating these cryptographic algorithms that is considerably faster.

Older versions of TLS exchanged the symmetric session key by having the client create a random session key, then encrypting it with the server's public key (from the server-to-client authentication phase) and sending it to the server. The server would then decrypt that using its private key. Someone could capture all traffic between the client and server and not be able to capture the symmetric session key.

More recent versions of TLS include cryptosuites that support Diffie-Hellman Key Agreement to securely agree upon a symmetric session key (e.g., ECHD mentioned earlier). Since DH Key Agreement uses no asymmetric key encryption or decryption, it is significantly faster than the old scheme.

TLS Only Secures One Client/Server Network Link

TLS provides only a few things and does these for a single network link (or connection):

- Server-to-client authentication

- Optional client-to-server authentication

- Exchange of a symmetric session key to support encryption between client and server

- Encryption of all traffic after TLS handshake is complete, but only while the data is in transit

For Web (HTTP), this is not a problem. All web connections involve only *one* link (from web browser to web server). If I click an HTTP hyperlink, the server I was using doesn't make an ongoing connection; my browser makes a new one-link connection to a new server (which might also be secured with TLS or not).

For email, there are a minimum of *two* links (if both parties have accounts on the same email server) or more commonly *three or more* links:

- Alice's client to Alice's email server (using SMTP or IMAP).

- Alice's email server to Bob's email server (using SMTP) – note these could be the same node if Alice and Bob's accounts are on the same email server.

- Bob's client to Bob's email server (using IMAP).

Each of these links must be secured independently with TLS, and even then, the traffic is in plaintext on the server(s). This is *not* end-to-end encryption.

Each server authenticates itself to the corresponding client (Alice's mail server assumes the client role when it relays the message to Bob's mail server). There is no original sender to final recipient authentication, let alone mutual authentication, even if Strong Client Authentication is used.

You can provide end-to-end encryption and sender-to-recipient authentication for email with S/MIME, which is entirely based on the clients – servers are transparent to S/MIME. The encrypted and/or signed messages flow right through them – they aren't even aware this is happening. S/MIME does involve issuing an S/MIME certificate to every user and providing a shared address book that supports digital certificates.

The Splintered IPv4 Internet (Public vs. Private Addresses)

Prior to the mid-1990s, the IPv4 Internet had a flat (monolithic) address space with only public, globally routable IP addresses. Any node in the world could connect directly to any other node, unless the path between them was blocked by a router or firewall.

About 1995, the IETF realized that at the rate addresses were being allocated, by 2000, they would all be gone. So, they created Network Address Translation and RFC 1918 "Addresses for Private Internets" as a temporary stopgap to extend the life of the IPv4 address space to roughly 2010. This is similar to a business telephone system Private Branch Exchange (PBX). A public IPv4 address is like a real telephone number, while a private IPv4 address is like an internal extension behind a PBX. This has allowed connecting some 20 billion nodes to the IPv4 Internet, but at the cost of creating millions of private Internets, each of which is hiding behind one public IPv4 address. Unfortunately, we are now in 2022, and only about 38% of the traffic on the global Internet is over IPv6.

If the address of your node begins with 10, or 172.16 to 172.31, or 192.168, you have a *private IP address* behind a NAT gateway. You can make *outgoing connections* through your NAT gateway to external nodes that have a public IP address, but no external node (outside of your private subnet) can (directly) connect *to you*. Once an outgoing connection is made, traffic can flow in both directions. But you can't run a server in your private subnet or do a real peer-to-peer connection to any node outside of your private Internet. If you *also* have an IPv6 address, that is public, and you can make outgoing connections *to* any other IPv6 node and accept incoming connections *from* any other IPv6 node. That is called *Dual Stack*. Eventually, most of us will be running *only* IPv6 and accessing external legacy (IPv4-only) nodes via NAT64/DNS64 gateways.

IPv4 Address Exhaustion

In 2011, IANA allocated the final five unallocated "/8" blocks of IPv4 public addresses to the Regional Internet Registries (RIRs): APNIC, ARIN, RIPE, LACNIC, and AfriNIC. There are no more blocks of IPv4 public addresses left at IANA and no way to create more. Over the next few years, all five RIRs reached "end of normal allocation" of IPv4 public addresses. Now many ISPs are deploying Carrier Grade NAT (CGN) which has *two* layers of NAT – one at the ISP and another in the home or business. This is like a PBX behind another PBX.

Note: some ISPs still use the old term "static address" when they mean "static public address." This goes back to dial-up access days, when all addresses were public, but many ISPs would reuse the same address pool over and over again for a large number of dial-in users. When one person hung up, that address became available for another customer, which was called "dynamic IP address." You could get a dedicated address just for you, at higher cost. Those were called "static IP addresses." You can assign a static private IP address to a node, but that doesn't make that address routable on the global Internet.

Public IPv4 addresses include all addresses that are not private addresses (RFC 1918), or assigned as multicast or experimental addresses, or any other special purpose, like 127/8, which is the loopback address (yes, all 16.7 million addresses in that block are loopback addresses – try using 127.1.2.3, works the same as 127.0.0.1).

With IPv4 + NAT, you can't have real peer-to-peer connections, except within a single private Internet. Skype *looks* like it is peer to peer, but it does this using NAT Traversal. This uses an external STUN server to accept connections on behalf of the private client. The client makes an outgoing connection to the STUN server and allows traffic from the accepted connections to come back down the outgoing connection to the STUN server. This is actually a big security risk, as the client bypasses your firewall. It's like having an "inside man" on a bank robbery. Even with a STUN server, there is not a single uninterrupted connection from my node to yours – it all goes through an intermediary server (the STUN server), which interrupts the TLS security.

PeerTLS

I have created a new version of TLS, which I call **PeerTLS**. It is really just a new way of *using* TLS. All connections are only one link (possible with all nodes having public addresses and no NAT between them). Both nodes use a TLS Client Certificate (no TLS Server Certificate is used), which identifies the users, not their nodes. When I exchange a message with someone, I'm not interested in what node they happen to be using at the time; I am interested in who *they* are. Since there is only one link between the two nodes, TLS can provide end-to-end encryption for any protocol, as well as mutual strong authentication (both parties know for certain who they are exchanging messages with). This is possible only when both ends have IPv6 addresses or for two nodes within the same IPv4 private Internet. PeerTLS does away with intermediate servers. Every node has both a client (which can initiate outgoing connections) and a server (which can accept incoming connections). This is called a *User Agent*. I had to create a new directory service (SixID) to allow any node to securely register and update their IPv6 address (and other identifying information, including their digital certificate) and allow others to securely retrieve that information. DNS is not adequate for end-to-end direct messaging.

Interestingly enough, all TLS toolkits that I have tried so far work fine with PeerTLS, although they were all designed for traditional client/server TLS (where one end has a TLS Server Certificate). If they support checking that the node name you connect to matches the CN field in the TLS Server Certificate, you need to disable this function (all toolkits I've tried allow this).

All existing IPv4+NAT-based mobile applications are client only. Since all mobile nodes with IPv4 have only private addresses, there is no way for a mobile node to accept incoming connections (either run a server or do real peer-to-peer messaging). Again, amazingly enough, all TLS toolkits I have tried for both Android and iOS support accepting incoming connections. It just isn't very useful for IPv4, as it works only within a private subnet (will not cross a NAT gateway). With IPv6, there are no private addresses (not in the same sense as IPv4 RFC 1918 addresses) and no NAT to block incoming connections. Therefore, PeerTLS works fine on all mobile devices (of course you must have IPv6 data service). You can check your mobile device now for IPv6 (it is probably already there), on Android and iOS.

It is possible to make end-to-end direct connections over PeerTLS for several protocols, including

- VoIP – Voice over Internet Protocol, including Chat over IP (SIP Messaging)

- FTP – File Transfer Protocol (FTP)

- SMTP – Simple Mail Transfer Protocol

As IPv6 is more widely deployed, PeerTLS will allow far more secure messaging and file transfer directly between nodes. Many cellular service providers have found it very cost effective (and simpler to deploy) with IPv6 than with IPv4+NAT, so most phones today support IPv6. As 5G is rolled out, *all* 5G phones will support IPv6.

It may sound strange to have an FTP or SMTP server running on your phone that other people can connect directly to, but that is possible with IPv6, and PeerTLS allows it to be extremely secure.

CHAPTER 12

S/MIME Secure Email

Years ago, there were a variety of incompatible schemes for attaching files to emails. The IETF created a standard for email attachments which is now universally used, not just in email, but in web pages and other places. It is called MIME. It is specified in several RFCs.

MIME

RFC 2045, "Multipurpose Internet Mail Extensions (MIME) Part One: Format of Internet Message Bodies," November 1996

RFC 2046, "Multipurpose Internet Mail Extensions (MIME) Part Two: Media Types," November 1996

RFC 2047, "Multipurpose Internet Mail Extensions (MIME) Part Three: Message Header Extensions for Non-ASCII Text," November 1996

RFC 2048, "Multipurpose Internet Mail Extensions (MIME) Part Four: Registration Procedures," November 1996

RFC 2049: "Multipurpose Internet Mail Extensions (MIME) Part Five: Conformance Criteria and Examples," November 1996

There are various body parts described (e.g., text, html, etc.), plus numerous attachment types (images, audio, video, binary, Microsoft Office documents, etc.). You can even have nested MIME messages.

© Lawrence E. Hughes 2022
L. E. Hughes, *Pro Active Directory Certificate Services*,
https://doi.org/10.1007/978-1-4842-7486-6_12

S/MIME – MIME with Security

Some additional extension types were defined as S/MIME (Secure MIME), which is currently specified in RFC 8551, "Secure/Multipurpose Internet Mail Extensions (S/MIME) Version 4.0 Message Specification," April 2019.

S/MIME defines several new MIME extensions related to encryption and digital signatures. You can use neither, either, or both features.

A **digital signature** signs the entire message (body parts and other attachments, but not the message headers) adding a new attachment that holds the signature. This provides *sender-to-recipient authentication* and detection of tampering with the message (*message integrity*).

A **digital envelope** encrypts the entire message (body parts and other attachments, but not the message headers). This provides *privacy*.

There is also a "signed receipt" message that allows a recipient to return a digitally signed message that acknowledges receipt of a message and provides *recipient-to-sender authentication*.

I discuss MIME and S/MIME at length in my book, *Internet E-mail: Protocols, Standards, and Implementation* (Artech House, 1998).

S/MIME Implementations

All Internet email clients I am aware of support MIME, and most support S/MIME.

S/MIME is designed to be implemented in thick "native" email clients, not in webmail. A few vendors (e.g., Microsoft) have released webmail that supports S/MIME, but there are some very serious problems with this:

- If the sender is using webmail, the message is not secure all the way from the sender, but only from the web server running the webmail application. Likewise, if the recipient is using webmail, the message is not secure all the way to the recipient, but only to the web server running the webmail application. If both sender and recipient are using webmail, the message is only secure between the two web servers. Even if the sender and/or recipient is accessing their webmail via HTTPS, you don't have true sender-to-recipient security.

- The private key needed for opening a digital envelope or creating a digital signature does not normally exist on the web server, but on the user's client computer where a thick client would run. Putting everyone's private key on the web server would be a security disaster, and providing web mechanisms (like Active-X) to allow the web server to use your private key on the machine where your browser is running is just as much of a disaster.

- Web servers and browsers and HTTP itself are notoriously difficult to secure. SMTP and IMAP are far better protocols from a security viewpoint.

I strongly recommend against using S/MIME in webmail. If you want truly end-to-end secure email, use a native email client like Microsoft Outlook or Mozilla Thunderbird.

Email servers do not participate in any way with S/MIME – S/MIIME is transparent to them. Secured messages pass through email servers in exactly the same way that unsecured messages do. Unlike TLS, S/MIME-secured messages remain encrypted and/or signed on every intermediate server and even in the recipient's message store. S/MIME is a client-to-client security protocol. The sending client secures the message, and the receiving client allows viewing the message and validating any digital signature.

S/MIME is an *end-to-end* security protocol. It protects the entire message (except for the headers) all the way from original sender to final recipient. Compare this with SSL/TLS which is a *link-oriented* protocol that protects the message only while in transit over a single link between a client and a server. TLS and S/MIME are *complementary* (not competitors) – they address different aspects of security and work well together. Since S/MIME does not encrypt the message headers at the start of an email message (the "To:", "From:", "Subject:", etc.), TLS can provide privacy for those headers between the clients and their servers, as well as making sure that the client is connecting to the correct server. Finally, when retrieving a message over IMAP, the username and password are sent in plaintext without TLS, so a hacker can see your credentials if you don't use IMAPS. It is also possible to use *SMTP authentication*, in which case your credentials again are sent in plaintext if you don't use SMTPS.

It is less common for the server-to-server link(s) in email to be protected by TLS, but it can be done (the sending server does the client role when forwarding messages to another server). The clients have no control over this, although you can check the headers of a received message and see if TLS *was* used on the various links. There is no mechanism to ensure that *all* links in an email path are protected with TLS. It would be nice to have a "minimum security" header that says "if you can't provide at least TLS with 128-bit symmetric and 2048-bit asymmetric, return the message to sender as undeliverable," but there is no such header currently, and of course, no servers enforce that. Even with TLS, the message headers are still in plaintext and unprotected on all intermediate email servers.

S/MIME Digital Certificates

S/MIME does require getting a special client cert for every participant. It is a basic client cert that identifies a person but has some additional content.

The *Subject Alternative Name* field of the certificate must contain the sender's email address. This must match the email address in the *From* message header (the sender) for S/MIME to work. See Figure 12-1.

Figure 12-1. *Subject Alternative Name field of the certificate*

There is also an additional *Enhanced Key Usage* flag, "Secure Email" (OID 1.3.6.1.5.5.7.3.4), not found in a basic client cert used for Strong Client Authentication (Figure 12-2).

Figure 12-2. *Enhanced key Usage*

S/MIME Certificates (aka "Secure Email Certificates") are available from many CAs. Some only contain the subject's email address (E=lhughes@hughesnet.org). Other contain more fields in the Subject Distinguished Name (Figure 12-3).

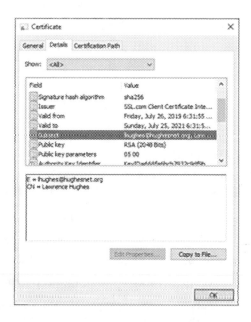

Figure 12-3. *More fields in the Subject Distinguished Name*

The more fields in the *Subject Distinguished Name*, the better the sender is identified, but the certificate issuer will charge you to validate each of the fields contained in a certificate (and of course, you have to provide proof of each field when applying for the certificate). Ideally, an S/MIME Cert should contain at least the CN (sender's name) in addition to the E (email address) field. S/MIME does not require that the SubjectDN of the S/MIME Certificate contain any specific fields.

Public vs. Private Certificate Hierarchies

There are two types of certificates: *public hierarchy* and *private hierarchy*. A public hierarchy certificate chains up to a Trusted Root Cert found in most operating systems. There is an organization called WebTrust that certifies CAs as operating with certain standards. Once certified by WebTrust, your Root Cert will be installed in all operating system.

Technically, WebTrust only certifies CAs for issuing TLS Server Certificates, but they are working on new standards for certifying operation with other certificate types, including S/MIME. In general, if a CA meets WebTrust's standards for TLS Server Certificates, they are probably trustworthy for issuing other certificate types, including S/MIME.

With a private hierarchy certificate, you need to install the Root and Intermediate Certs of the certificate issuer in all relying client nodes (senders and recipients). While this can be done, it is not easy for a typical end user, and without them, they will see security errors in use.

If you are only exchanging secure emails within a closed group, like a company, private hierarchy can work; it's just more effort. For communicating with any possible other user, public hierarchy is much preferred. Most well-known CAs like GlobalSign, Entrust, DigiCert, and Sectigo issue public hierarchy certs. If your company issues your certs on EJBCA or Microsoft Certificate Services, it is almost certainly private hierarchy.

Example: Signed Message

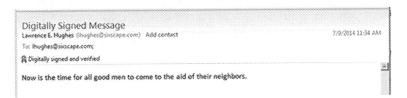

Figure 12-4. *Digitally signed message*

When you open a digitally signed message, it will show that the signature has been checked and whether it is valid or not.

If you click the seal icon, you will see the properties of this message (Figure 12-5).

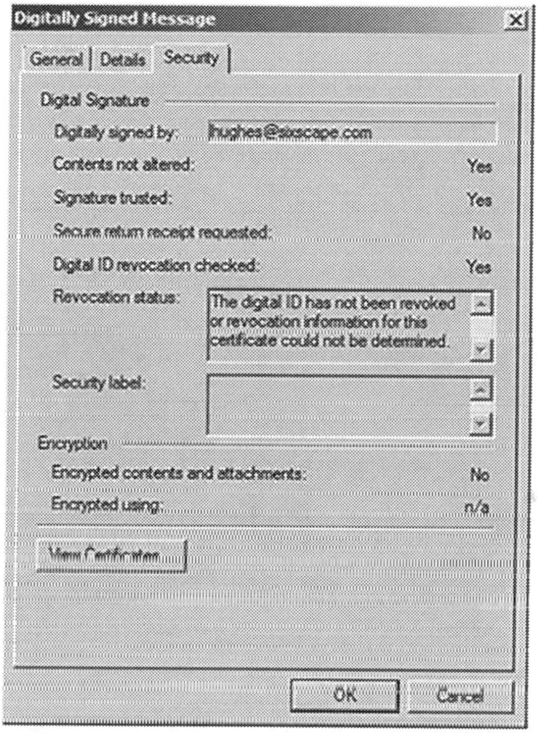

Figure 12-5. *View the properties of the message*

If the message has been tampered with (here, I modified "good men" to "bad men"), you will see the following dire warning when you open the message (Figure 12-6).

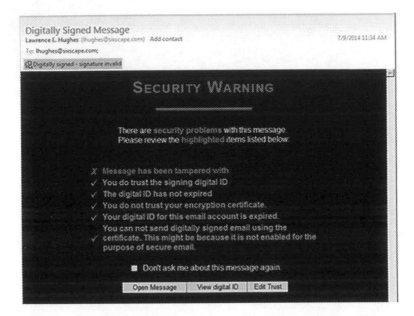

Figure 12-6. *Warning if the message has been tampered with*

And if you tell it to open the message anyway, you will see a warning and the bogus message (Figure 12-7).

Figure 12-7. *Response is a warning and the bogus message*

Example: Encrypted Message

When you view an encrypted message, your email client will decrypt it for you, using your private key. You will see something like the following (Figure 12-8).

Figure 12-8. *View an encrypted message*

If you click the padlock icon, you will see the following (Figure 12-9).

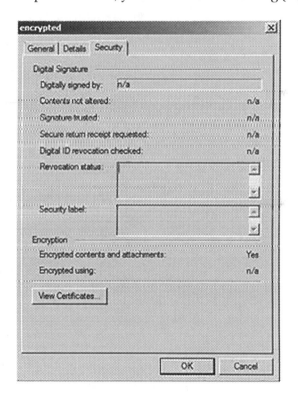

Figure 12-9. *View after you click the padlock icon*

Example: Signed and Encrypted Message

If you open a message that was *both* signed and encrypted, you will see the following (Figure 12-10).

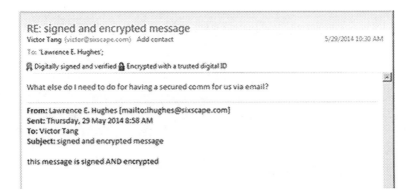

Figure 12-10. *View if you open a message that was both signed and encrypted*

If you click either the seal or padlock icons, you will see the following (Figure 12-11).

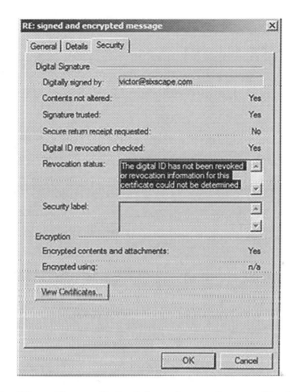

Figure 12-11. *View if you click either the seal or padlock icons*

Installing an S/MIME Certificate in Microsoft Outlook

You can obtain an S/MIME Certificate from various CAs or create your own with MS Certificate Services or EJBCA. So how do you install that certificate in MS Outlook and associate it with a particular email account? In my opinion, Microsoft could have made this easier, but here are the steps for doing this manually.

You first need to install your S/MIME Certificate in the Personal folder of your Certificate Store if it is not already there. This can be as simple as double-clicking a PKCS #12 file containing your certificate and private key (you will need to supply the passphrase used to protect the contents of the PKCS #12 container). See Figure 12-12.

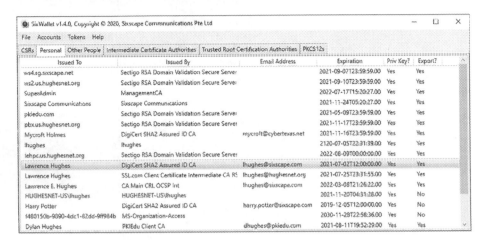

Figure 12-12. *Install your S/MIME Certificate in the Personal folder of your Certificate Store*

Double-click the certificate to view it. See Figure 12-13.

Figure 12-13. *View the certificate*

Note that this certificate "protects email messages," and there is a private key in the Certificate Store corresponding to this certificate.

In this case, the SubjectDN includes the E, CN, OU, O, L, and C fields (Figure 12-14).

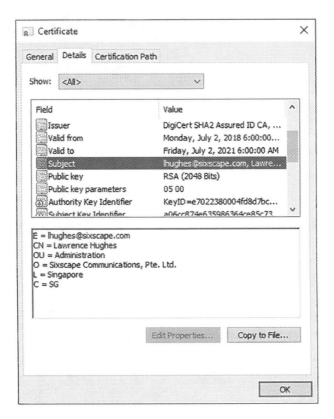

Figure 12-14. *View of the subject*

The *Enhanced Key Usage* flags include *Secure Email* (Figure 12-15).

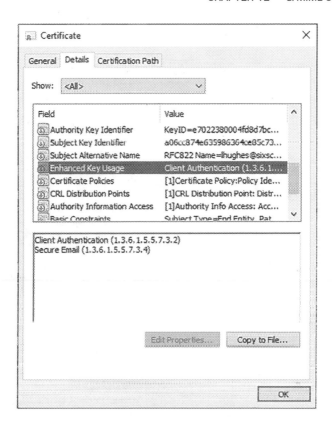

Figure 12-15. *View of the Enhanced Key Usage*

Finally, the *Subject Alternative Name* field contains my email address as *RFC822Name* (Figure 12-16).

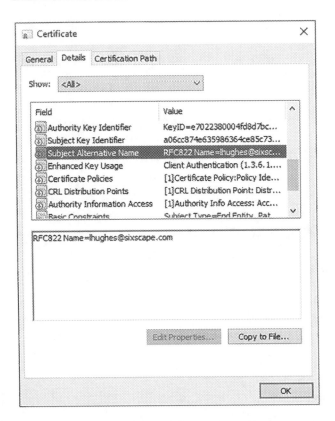

Figure 12-16. *View of the Subject Alternative Name*

The following procedure will work with any recent on-premises (thick-client) version of MS Outlook (since about Office 2010) including ones installed via Microsoft 365. This is *not* applicable to the webmail version of Outlook (OWA).

In Outlook, click the *File* menu header, and select *Options* (Figure 12-17).

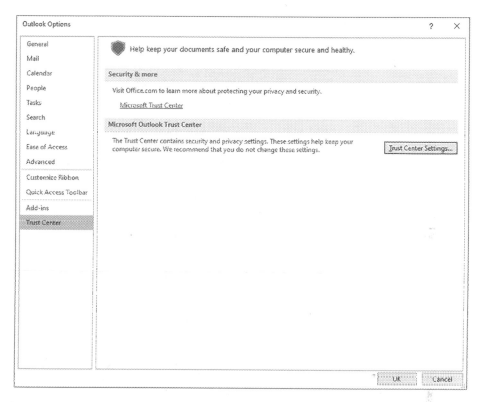

Figure 12-17. *From the File menu header, select Options*

Select *Trust Center,* click the *Trust Center Settings* button, and then select *Email Security* (Figure 12-18).

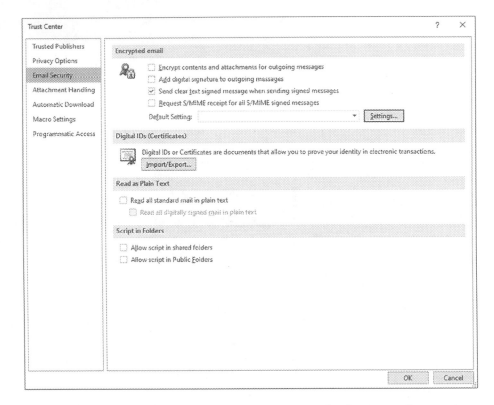

Figure 12-18. *Click Trust Center Settings, and select Email Security*

Under *Encrypted email,* after *Default Setting,* click the *Settings* button
(Figure 12-19).

Figure 12-19. *Click the Settings pull-down menu*

For *Security Settings Name,* enter your email address, for example, *lhughes@sixscape.com.*

Select the two *Default Security Setting* options.

After *Signing Certificate,* click the *Choose* button. You will see a list of certificates in your Certificate Store *Personal* folder. See Figure 12-20.

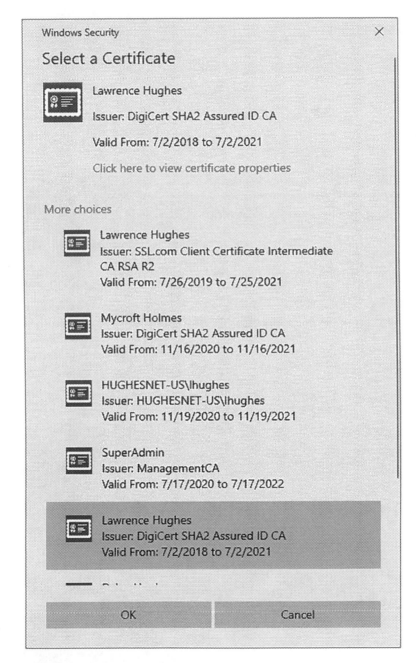

Figure 12-20. *List of certificates in the Certificate Store Personal folder*

Choose your S/MIME Certificate from the list and click *OK*.

Do the same for *Encryption Certificate*.

Set the *hash algorithm* to **SHA256** and *encryption algorithm* to **AES (256-bit)**.

It should now look like that in Figure 12-21.

Figure 12-21. *Set the hash algorithm to **SHA256** and encryption algorithm to **AES (256-bit)***

Now click *OK*. Dismiss the *Trust Center* dialog by clicking *OK*. Dismiss the *Outlook Options* dialog with *OK*.

Now, try sending a signed message to yourself (be sure to select *Sign* under *Options*). See Figure 12-22.

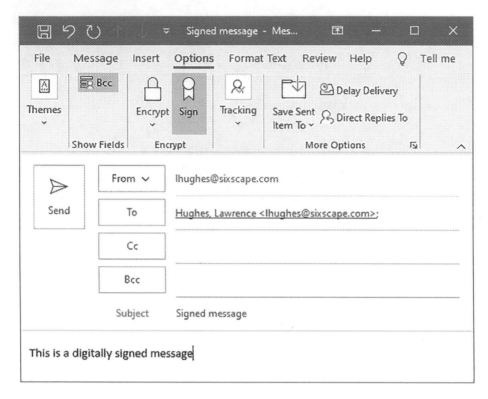

Figure 12-22. *Send a signed message to yourself*

Click *Send*. In a minute, your message should arrive in your Inbox (Figure 12-23).

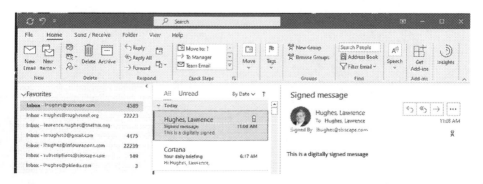

Figure 12-23. *The message appears in your Inbox*

Note that there is a "seal" icon in the message list for the new message, and the reading pane shows a red seal icon and "Signed by lhughes@ sixscape.com".

Note the red seal icon under the message time. Click it to see information on the signature, including whether the signature was valid and trusted (Figure 12-24).

Figure 12-24. *Click the red seal icon under the message time*

Now click the *Details* button. Click the *Signer* item (Figure 12-25).

Figure 12-25. *Signer item highlighted*

This shows that the signer was *lhughes@sixscape.com* using RSA/
SHA256 and the date and time it was signed.

Click the *View Details* button, as shown in Figure 12-26.

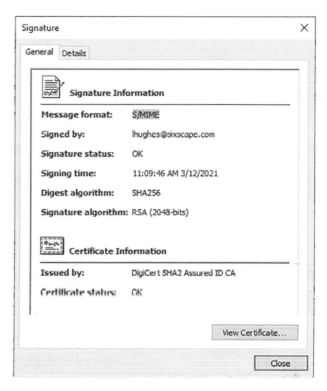

Figure 12-26. *The View Details*

This shows additional information about the signed message.
Click the *View Certificate* button (Figure 12-27).

Figure 12-27. *View Certificate Information*

Click the *Details* tab and select *Subject* (Figure 12-28).

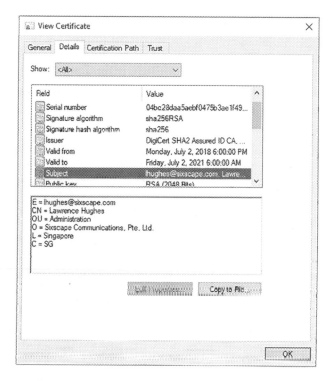

Figure 12-28. *Select Subject*

This is our S/MIME Certificate since we were the sender. Had someone else sent this message, this would show *their* S/MIME Certificate, not ours.

Now send yourself another message, and this time select the *Encrypt* option (Figure 12-29).

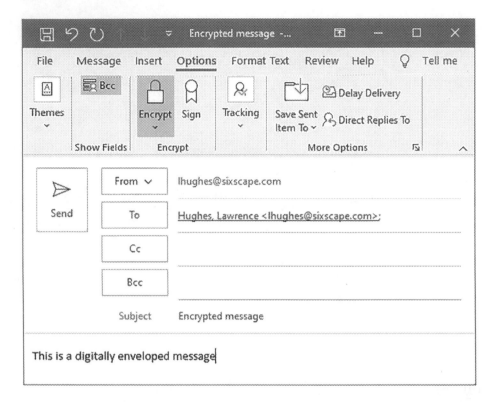

Figure 12-29. *Send a second message to yourself*

In a minute, the message will appear in your Inbox, as show in Figure 12-30.

Figure 12-30. *Message appears in your Inbox*

Note that there is a padlock icon in the message list, but not in the reading pane. Oddly enough there is no icon you can click to view the encryption properties. I believe this is a bug in Outlook. You will have to add a signature to view the encryption properties.

Note that if you are sending someone else an encrypted message, you will need to have *their* digital certificate in your address book. There are various ways of accomplishing that. One way to is have them send you and signed message, then right-click the recipient and add them (and their certificate) into one of your address books.

Finally, send yourself a message that is both signed and encrypted (Figure 12-31).

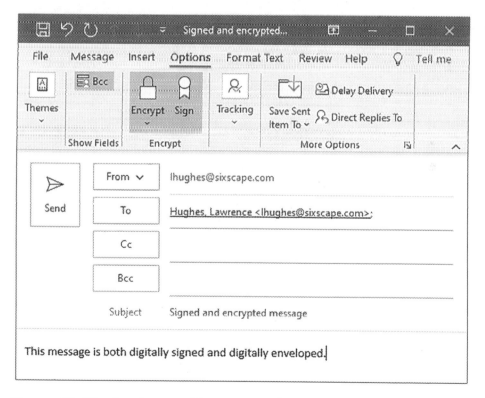

Figure 12-31. *Send yourself a message that is signed and encrypted*

Click *Send*. In a minute, the message will arrive in your Inbox. See Figure 12-32.

Figure 12-32. *The message arrives in the Inbox*

Now note that the reading pane has both padlock and red seal icons. Click either of them (Figure 12-33).

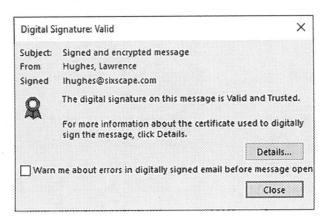

Figure 12-33. *Click either the padlock or red seal icon to see this*

Click the *Details* button. Select the *Encryption Layer* item. See Figure 12-34.

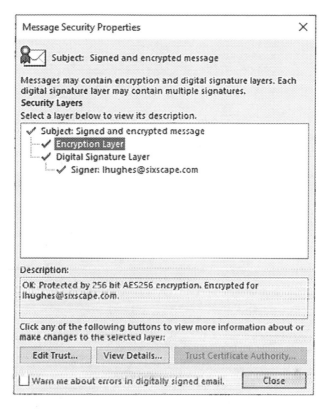

Figure 12-34. *Select the Encryption Layer item*

Note that it was encrypted with AES256, for lhughes@sixscape.com.
Click the *View Details* button (Figure 12-35).

Figure 12-35. *View Details*

To view the certificate it was encrypted with, click *View Certificate*. See Figure 12-36.

Figure 12-36. *After clicking View Certificate, the Certificate Information appears*

Again, this is our own S/MIME Certificate. If it was sent by someone else, it would still show our S/MIME Certificate. For them to send you an encrypted message, they would need *your* S/MIME Certificate in their address book at the time they send the message.

S/MIME with Applications Other Than Email

Just as SSL was originally created for Web and later found to be useful on other protocols (email [SMTP], file transfer [FTP], LDAP/AD, etc.), it is possible to use S/MIME with applications other than email. You can send an S/MIME-protected message over FTP or FTPS or via file sharing apps like Dropbox, Onebox, etc. As with S/MIME email, this provides very strong end-to-end security and sender authentication for files, and the intermediary servers do not need to know anything about S/MIME (as with email, S/MIME-secured messages are just funny-looking regular messages to the servers).

PART II

Deploying and Using Active Directory Certificate Services

CHAPTER 13

Deploy Microsoft Certificate Services

Microsoft Windows Server includes several powerful optional subsystems, such as Active Directory, DNS, and DHCP. One of those subsystems is not widely known or deployed because it requires considerable knowledge and expertise in cryptography and Public Key Infrastructure. It is a full-blown *Certificate Authority*, which is a software system for creating and managing digital certificates, such as a "TLS Server Certificate" required to deploy HTTPS on a web server.

Many people depend on commercial "public" Certification Authorities, for example, DigiCert, Entrust, GlobalSign, and Sectigo (formerly Comodo) to issue and manage their certificates.

However, there are many situations, especially in corporate or government networks, that might require being able to issue and manage *your own* ("in-house") digital certificates. Unlike public CAs, you can issue as many of these as you want for free, and they can be integrated with your in-house Active Directory.

Microsoft *Active Directory Certificate Services* (AD CS) is one product that allows you to do this. There are other products on the market, such as the Open Source EJBCA that can also be used. Microsoft Certificate Services runs only on Windows Server and is normally tightly integrated with Active Directory (although you can deploy it as a "Stand-alone" CA without AD integration). If you already have deployed a network with

© Lawrence E. Hughes 2022
L. E. Hughes, *Pro Active Directory Certificate Services*,
https://doi.org/10.1007/978-1-4842-7486-6_13

Active Directory running, then Certificate Services is an additional service you can deploy in-house. There is no cost (other than one or two copies of Windows Server, if you don't already have suitable Member Servers), to do this.

We will be deploying an *Enterprise CA*, rather than a *Stand-alone CA*. This will integrate with your network Active Directory.

One major difference with certificates issued by an in-house CA (called "private hierarchy") is that the Root Cert of that hierarchy is not automatically installed in all operating systems (the Root Certs of major public CAs are already installed in most operating systems). That means you must manually install the Root (and maybe Intermediate) Certs on every relying node. AD CS does that for you for all Windows nodes that are part of your AD Domain. You can still provide copies of your Root and Intermediate Certs for other people to install on their nodes so they can use your certs (you can publish copies of those certs on your website so people can download and install them just by clicking them).

You can deploy everything on *one* Windows Server, which results in a two-level hierarchy – Root Cert and then End-Entity Certificates (TLS Server, TLS Client, S/MIME, etc.). The End-Entity Certs are signed by the Root Private Key. In this case, the Root Private Key must be online all the time to sign new End-Entity Certs. This is a major security risk. If the Root Private Key is compromised, every End-Entity Cert is compromised.

Two-Level Hierarchy

Root Cert (self-signed) + Root Private Key (online)

End-Entity Certs (signed by Root Private Key) + End-Entity Private Keys

I recommend deploying AD CS on *two* Windows Servers, one for your Root CA and one for your Subordinate CA.

The Root CA holds the Root Certificate and Root Private Key, which is used to sign the Intermediate Certificate (this is the only certificate signed by the Root Private Key).

The Subordinate CA holds the Intermediate Certificate and Intermediate Private Keys, which are used to sign End-Entity Certs (server certs, client certs, etc.)

Your Root Private Key is the most sensitive part of the entire system. If it is compromised, you must start over from scratch and reissue all Intermediate Certificates and all End-Entity Certificates. Ideally, you should leave the Root CA server offline (and possibly even powered off and stored securely in a safe). If you are not going to support revocation checking, that is easy. Unfortunately, if the Root CA is offline, the normal process for checking revocation status of all certificates in a trust chain (including the Root Certificate) will fail. This means you cannot use the generated TLS Server Certificates in web servers.

So, if you are going to support revocation checking, you either need to leave the Root CA online (which is a security risk) or go through a complex process of moving the Root Certificate revocation information to the Intermediate CA, at which point you can take the Root CA offline and revocation checking will still work. This process is outside of the scope of this book, but there are two websites that provide all the details of how to do this:

https://social.technet.microsoft.com/wiki/contents/
articles/2900.offline-root-certification-authority-ca.aspx
https://marckean.com/2010/07/28/build-an-offline-root-ca-
with-a-subordinate-ca/

In a three-level hierarchy, the Root Private Key is used to sign the Intermediate Cert, and the Intermediate Private Key is used to sign the End-Entity Certs. It is typical for the Root Cert to have a lifetime of 25 years or so, the Intermediate Cert to have a lifetime of 5 years, and End-Entity Certs to have a lifetime of 1–2 years.

Three-Level Hierarchy

Root Cert (self-signed) + Root Private Key (offline except when creating Intermediate Cert)

Intermediate Cert (signed by Root Private Key) + Intermediate Private Key (online)

End-Entity Certs (signed by Intermediate Private Key) + End-Entity Private Keys

With an offline Root CA deployment, once the Intermediate CA is created, you don't need the Root CA again until the Intermediate Cert expires (once every five years) or is compromised (which could happen at any time). The Root CA can be left in an offline state (powered down, not connected to your network) or even secured in a locked safe (complete with the Root Private Key) until it is needed again. If the Intermediate Private Key is compromised, every End-Entity Cert signed by it is compromised, but you can create a new Intermediate Cert (with a new Intermediate Private Key) and reissue the End-Entity Certs. The old Root Cert which may be deployed in many places will still work. Even if you deploy the Intermediate CA on a hardware server, you can still deploy the Root CA on a VM and put it away securely until it is needed again. If the Root Private Key is compromised, you must start over again from scratch, including updating all installed copies of the old Root and Intermediate Certs *and* all End-Entity Certs.

We will install a *Root CA* and a *Subordinate CA* on two Windows Servers, using Microsoft *Active Directory Certificate Services* (AD CS). I have two physical Windows Servers running WS 2019 in my network, which are both domain controllers (DCs). However, you are not supposed to install AD CS on a DC. So, I will deploy Certificate Services on two *virtual* Windows 2019 Member Server deployments (in the following labs, using VirtualBox, although you can use VMWare Workstation if you prefer). The same steps work pretty much the same way if you are installing on hardware servers.

We will support revocation checking (with CRLs and OCSP), so we will leave the Root CA online. You can protect the Root Private Key in an HSM (Hardware Security Module), which reduces the chance of Root key compromise. That is out of scope of this book. The Root Private Key is not used to validate trust chains; only the Root Certificate is needed.

Neither server will require significant RAM (4096 MB is sufficient) or CPU power (one CPU or core is sufficient). If you are deploying a large Enterprise CA (many thousands of certificates), you might need more CPUs and/or RAM on the Subordinate CA. Check CPU and memory utilization and upgrade your server as needed.

You will need to have an *Active Directory Domain* deployed in your network. I happen to have two Windows Server 2019 servers (*ws1. us.hughesnet.org* and *ws2.us.hughesnet.org*) running Active Directory for the domain HUGHESNET-US (us.hughesnet.org), with two domain controllers. **Do not try to install Certificate Services on domain controllers**.

It is important that your virtual machines have the same system time as your domain controllers. Even ten-minute difference can cause certain things to fail. You can use NTP to make them have exactly the same time.

First, we will deploy the Root CA.

Deploy Root CA

Install a copy of Windows Server 2019, **Desktop Experience** on VirtualBox:

- Recommended VirtualBox settings: 50GB drive, 4GB RAM, 1–2 CPUs, and Bridged Adapter.

- Install the *VirtualBox Guest Additions*.

- Run *Windows Update* until you are "Up to Date" **after clicking** ***Check for Updates***. This will require several iterations.

You're up to date
Last checked: Today, 8:31 AM

- Set your time zone.

- Activate Windows Server with a valid license key.

I named my first virtual server *RootCA.us.hughesnet.org*.

You need to assign **static** IP addresses for both IPv4 and IPv6. Your node name should be added to your local DNS with both A and AAAA records. My IPv4 subnet is *172.20/16*. My IPv6 subnet is *2001:470:b863:1000::/64*. I chose the following settings for IPv4 and IPv6 for the Root CA server. If your network does not have IPv6, set only the IPv4 (and please join the 21st century soon). Ask your network admin for unused IP addresses you can assign.

IPv4 Settings:

```
        IP Address:          172.20.111.1
        Subnet Mask:         255.255.0.0
        Default Gateway:     172.20.0.1

        DNS Server 1:        172.20.0.11
        DNS Server 2:        172.20.0.12
```

IPv6 Settings:

```
        IP Address:          2001:470:b863:1000::111:1
        Prefix Length:       /64
        Default Gateway:     determined automatically via Router
                             Discovery

        DNS Server 1:        2001:470:b863:1000::11
        DNS Server 2:        2001:470:b863:1000::12
```

Join this server to your domain as a **Member Server** (do not install Active Directory on this node). In my case, that is to domain *us.hughesnet. org* (NetBIOS name *Hughesnet-US*). Once you've joined the domain, login as Administrator of your domain (not of the local PC). In my case, that is *HUGHESNET-US\Administrator*.

You may wish to install Chrome. That is the browser used in these notes.

Add Active Directory Certificate Services Role

The next step is to add the *Active Directory Certificate Services* role to Windows Server 2019. Certificate Services is an optional part of Windows Server 2019. There is no need for any additional license. It is covered by the main Windows Server 2019 license.

In Server Manager, click *Add Roles and Features*. You can ignore the *Before you begin* screen. See Figure 13-1.

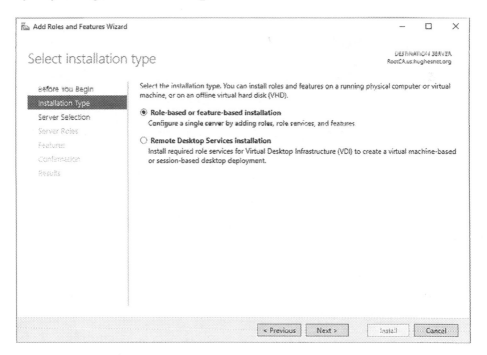

Figure 13-1. *Select role-based or feature-based installation. Click Next*

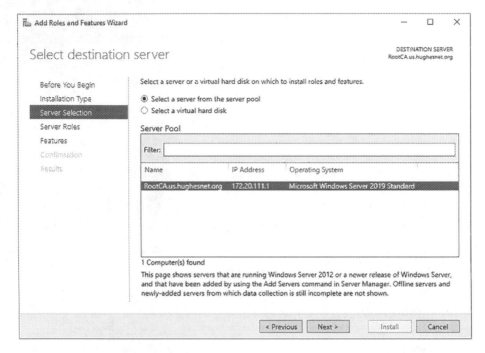

Figure 13-2. *Select the RootCA server as the destination (use your RootCA server name). Click Next*

You will now see the *Select server roles* screen (Figure 13-3).

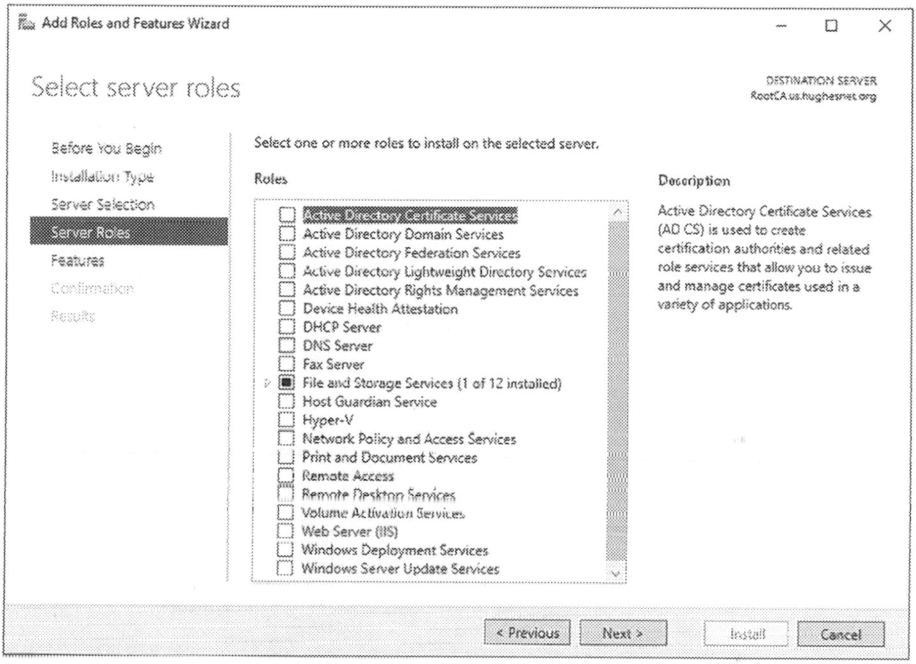

Figure 13-3. *Select "Active Directory Certificate Services." Click "Next"*

Select *Active Directory Certificate Services* role – it will show some additional required tools (Figure 13-4).

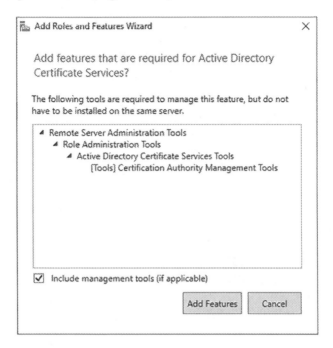

Figure 13-4. *Click "Add Features." Click "Next"*

You will now see the *Select features* screen, shown in Figure 13-5.

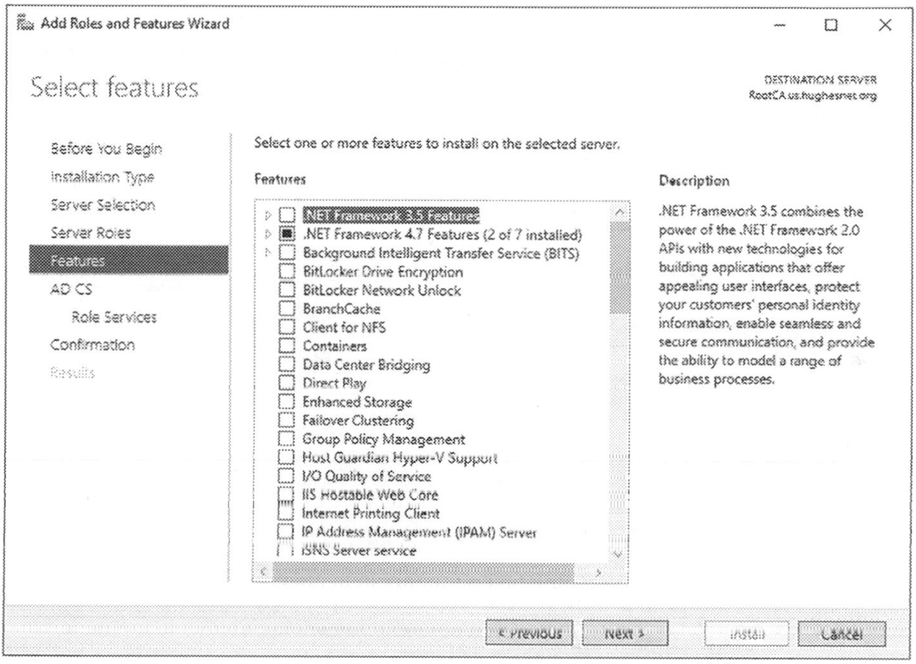

Figure 13-5. *Click "Next"*

You will now see the *Active Directory Certificate Services* screen
(Figure 13-6).

Figure 13-6. Click "Next"

Under *Role Services,* select *Certification Authority Web Enrollment –*
it will show some additional required tools. Don't worry about *Online
Responder* at this point. We will add that later. See Figure 13-7.

Figure 13-7. *List of additional tools*

You will now see the *Select role services* screen (Figure 13-8).

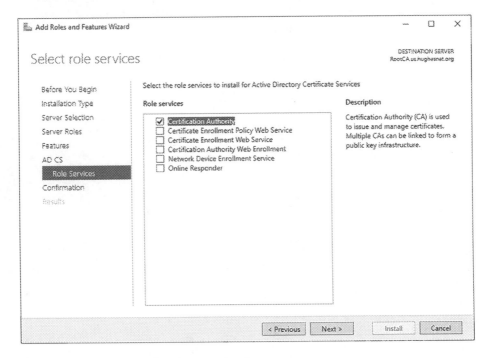

Figure 13-8. *Select "Role Services"*

By default, only *Certification Authority* is selected. That is the only role we want on the root server.

Click *Next*.

You will then see the *Confirm installation selections* screen. See Figure 13-9.

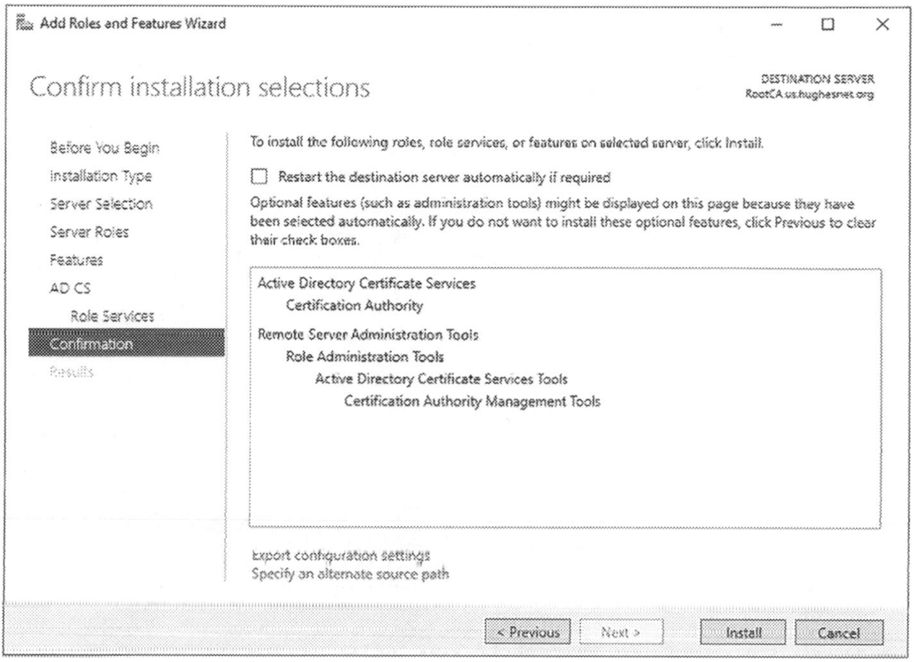

Figure 13-9. *Click "Install"*

You will see the *Installation progress* screen.

It will then install AD CS and additional items needed by it
(Figure 13-10).

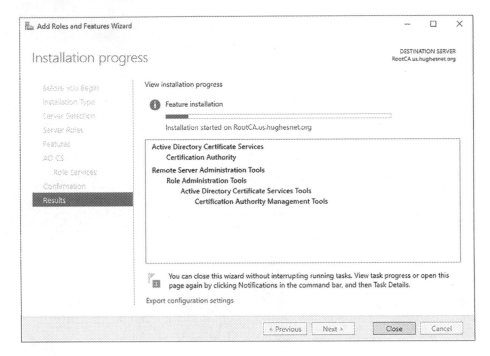

Figure 13-10. *When it has done installing, click "Close"*

In Server Manager, there will be a yellow triangle with an exclamation point at the top of the screen, as shown in Figure 13-11.

Figure 13-11. *Click on the yellow triangle*

You will see *Post-deployment Configuration.* Click *Configure Active Directory Certificate Services on the destination server.* That will start the AD CS Configuration wizard. See Figure 13-12.

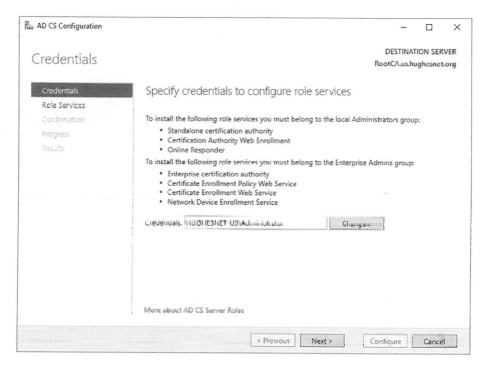

Figure 13-12. *Credentials for configuring role services*

Enter the domain administrator account name (in my case, *HUGHESNET-US\Administrator*). Click *Next.*

The *More about AD CS Server Roles* is a link to the following web page. This may help you understand the bigger picture (e.g., Stand-alone CAs, etc.).

`https://docs.microsoft.com/en-us/previous-versions/windows/`
`it-pro/windows-server-2012-R2-and-2012/hh831740(v=ws.11)?redire`
`ctedfrom=MSDN`

You will see the *Role Services* window (Figure 13-13).

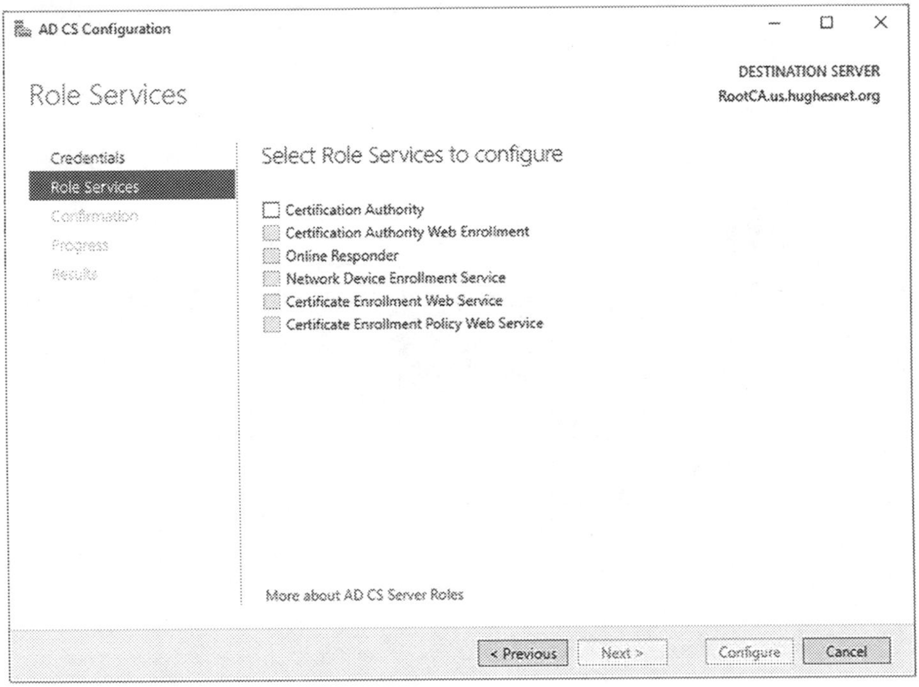

Figure 13-13. *Select "Certification Authority"*

It will now look like this (Figure 13-14).

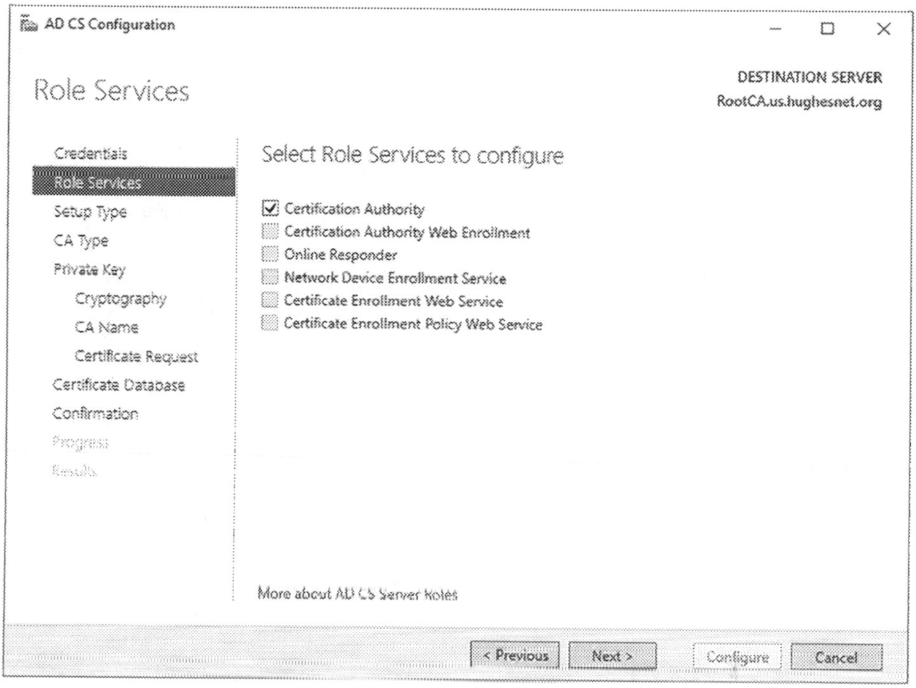

Figure 13-14. *Click Next*

You will see the *Setup Type* window. See Figure 13-15.

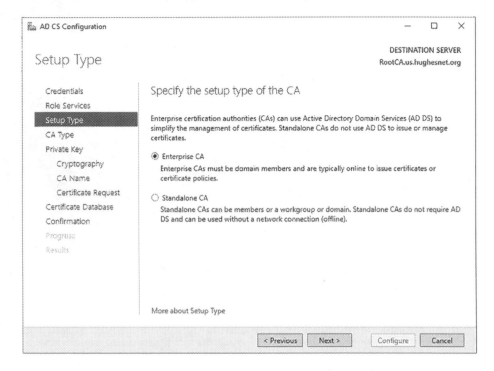

Figure 13-15. *Setup Type window*

We want to integrate our CA with the network *Active Directory,* so select *Enterprise CA*. Click *Next*.

You will see the *CA Type* window. See Figure 13-16.

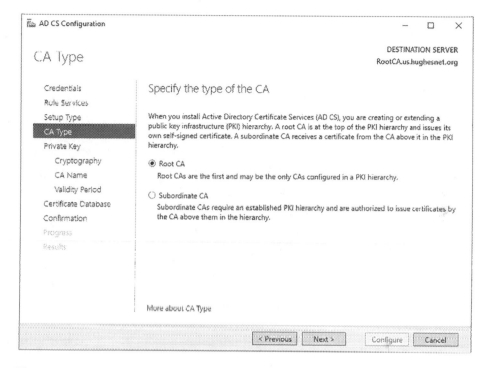

Figure 13-16. *CA Type*

By default, it will select *Subordinate CA*. **Select *Root CA*.** Click *Next*.

You will see the *Private Key* window. See Figure 13-17.

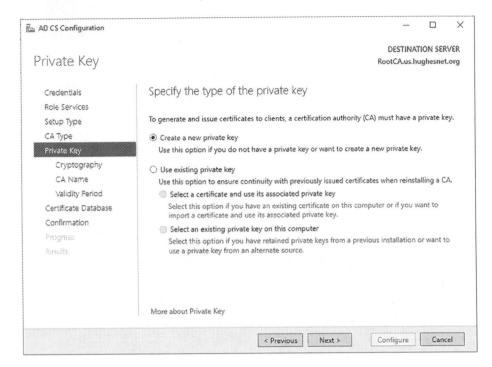

Figure 13-17. *Select "Create a new private key." Click "Next"*

You will see the *Cryptography for CA* window (Figure 13-18).

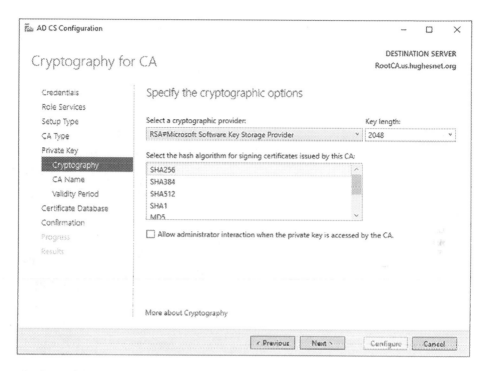

Figure 13-18. Cryptography for CA window

Select cryptographic provider as **RSA#Microsoft Software Key Storage Provider**, *Key length* as **2048**, and *hash algorithm* as **SHA256**.

For really secure implementation, you can deploy an HSM (Hardware Security Module), which would require selecting the appropriate cryptographic provider for the HSM. That is beyond the scope of this book. This would create the key material in the HSM and use it only remotely via PKCS #11. It is extremely difficult for anyone to compromise the Root Private Key in an HSM.

A "real" HSM might run $5000 to $10000. There are versions that plug into your computer backplane and external ones that are accessed via Ethernet. You can actually use a hardware USB token as a "poor man's" HSM (cost about $15). One token that would work here is the ePass2003 PKI Token from Feitian. It uses the same PKCS #11 protocol as a real HSM, and since the Root Private Key is not used very often, the USB version has sufficient performance for this. It has the advantage that you can remove the USB token and store it in a safe when not using the private key. You may need a security consultant to help you set up either a real HSM or a USB token.

See `https://en.wikipedia.org/wiki/Hardware_security_module` for details on HSMs. The HSM must be accessible from the root server (this can be difficult in Cloud deployments).

Click *Next*.

You will see the CA Name window (see Figure 13-19). Enter the name for your Root CA in the *Common name for this CA* field. In my case, that is *PKIEdu Root CA*. You won't be able to change this later. The default for *Distinguished name suffix* should be OK. It is based on your domain name (in my case, us.hughesnet.org).

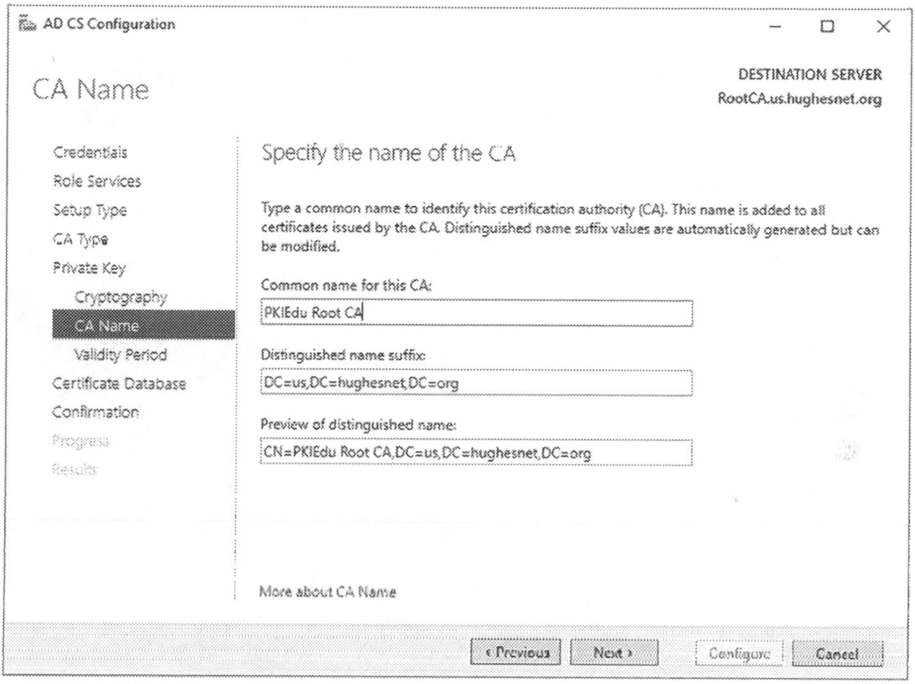

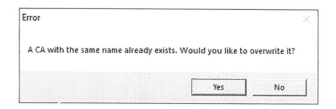

Figure 13-19. *CA Name*

Click *Next*. If you are reinstalling, it may display the following
(Figure 13-20).

Figure 13-20. *If it does, click Yes*

You will now see the *Validity Period* window (see Figure 13-21). **I use
25 years for the Root Certificate**.

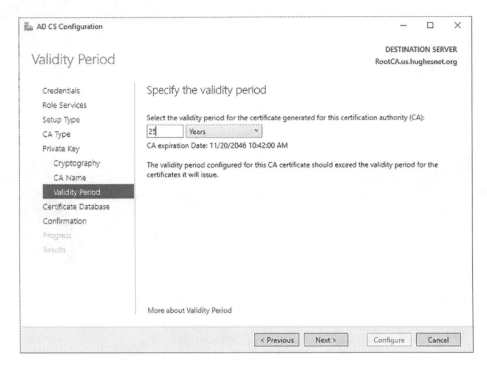

Figure 13-21. *Click Next*

You will now see the *CA Database* window. The defaults should be fine. See Figure 13-22.

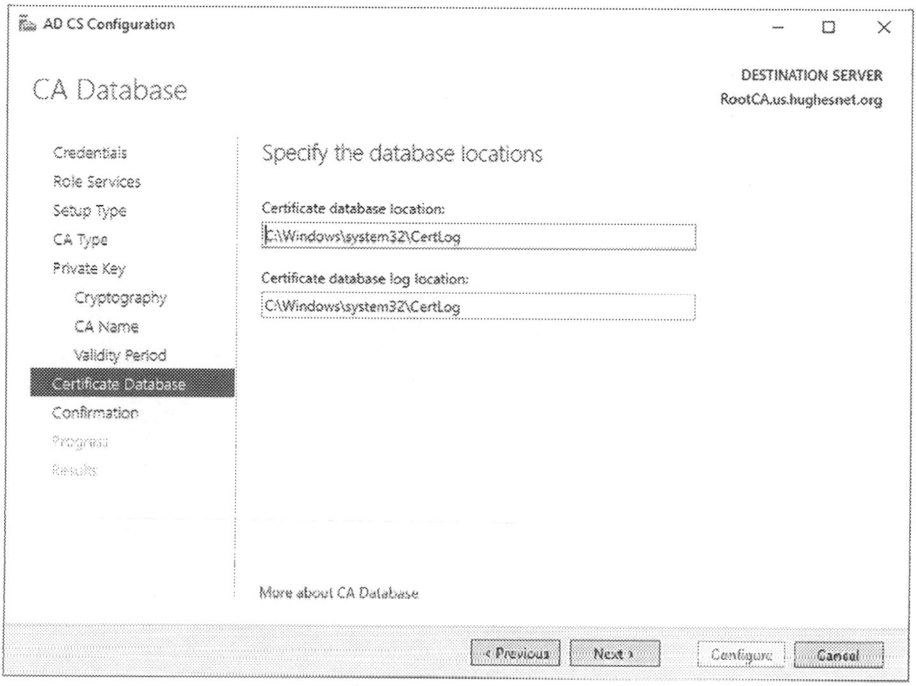

Figure 13-22. *Click Next*

You will now see the *Confirmation* window (Figure 13-23). Review all settings.

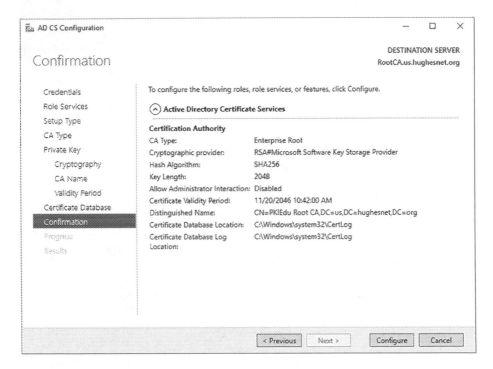

Figure 13-23. *Assuming everything looks OK, click Configure*

If everything went OK, you will see the following (Figure 13-24).

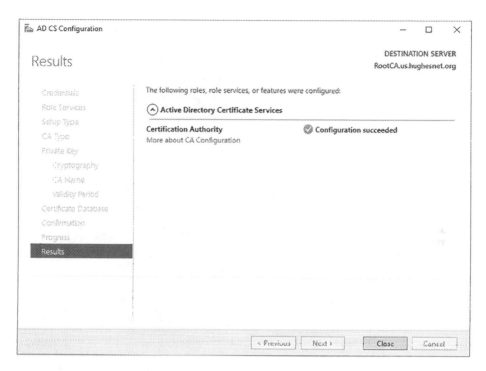

Figure 13-24.   *Results window*

Congratulations! The basic deployment of your Root CA is now complete. Click *Close*.

Deploy Subordinate CA for Intermediate and End-Entity Certificates

Install a second copy of Windows Server 2019, **Desktop Experience** on VirtualBox. Optionally, you can deploy the Intermediate CA on a physical machine. The steps are pretty similar to those as follows:

- Recommended VirtualBox settings: 50GB drive, 4GB RAM, 1–2 CPUs, and Bridged Adapter.

- Install the *VirtualBox Guest Additions*.

- Run *Windows Update* until you are "Up to Date." This may require several iterations.

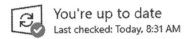

You're up to date
Last checked: Today, 8:31 AM

- Set your time zone.

- Activate Windows Server with a valid license key.

I named my second virtual server *IntCA.us.hughesnet.org*. Its purpose is to issue Intermediate Certs and End-Entity Certs such as TLS Server Certificates for web (and other) servers, TLS Client Certificates, S/MIME certificates, and Windows Smart card Logon certificates. It is a subordinate CA that chains up to *PKIEdu Root CA*.

You need to assign **static** IP addresses for both IPv4 and IPv6. My IPv4 subnet is *172.20/16*. My IPv6 subnet is *2001:470:b863:1000::/64*. I chose the following settings for IPv4 and IPv6 for the Intermediate CA server. If you don't have IPv6 on your network, you can configure only the IPv4 part, but you should soon join the 21st century by deploying IPv6!

IPv4 Settings:

```
        IP Address:          172.20.111.2
        Subnet Mask:         255.255.0.0
        Default Gateway:     172.20.0.1

        DNS Server 1:        172.20.0.11
        DNS Server 2:        172.20.0.12
```

IPv6 Settings:

```
        IP Address:          2001:470:b863:1000::111:2
        Prefix Length:       /64

        DNS Server 1:        2001:470:b863:1000::11
        DNS Server 2:        2001:470:b863:1000::12
```

Join this server to your domain as a *Member Server*. In my case, that is to *us.hughesnet.org* (or *Hughesnet-US*). Don't do this until you have activated your license.

Once you've joined the domain, log in as Administrator of your domain (not of the local PC). In my case, that is *HUGHESNET-US\Administrator*.

Add Active Directory Certificate Services Role

The next step is to add the *Certificate Services* role to this Windows Server.

In *Server Manager/Dashboard*, click *Add roles and features*. This will start the *Add Roles and Features Wizard*.

You will see the *Before you begin* screen (Figure 13-25).

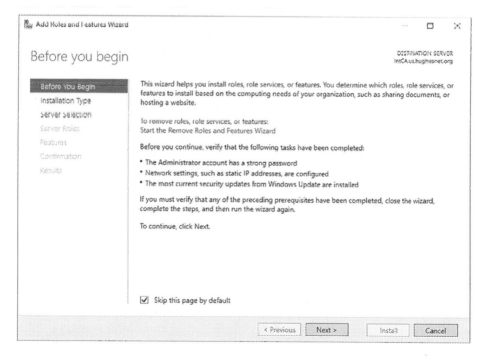

Figure 13-25. *Before you begin window*

You can ignore this (and skip it by default in the future). Click *Next*.

You will see the *Select installation type* window, as shown in
Figure 13-26.

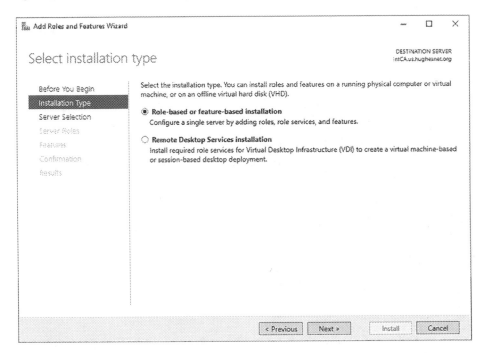

Figure 13-26. *Select role-based or feature-based installation.*
Click Next

You will see the *Select destination server* window in Figure 13-27.

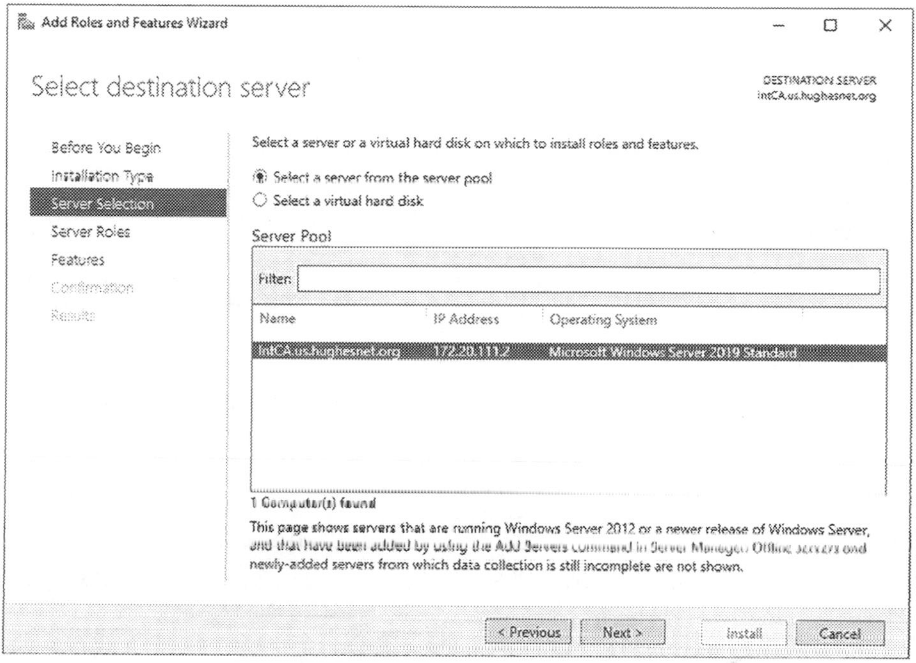

Figure 13-27. *Select* IntCA.us.hughesnet.org *(or your second server name). Click Next*

You will see the *Select server roles* window in Figure 13-28.

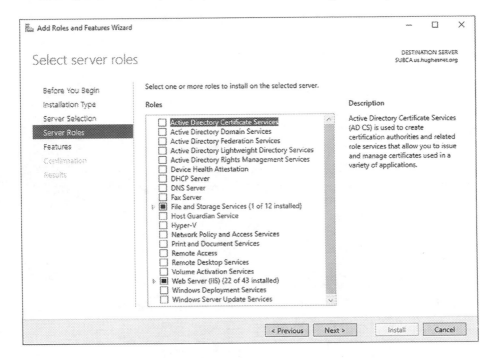

Figure 13-28. *Select Active Directory Certificate Services*

You will see a list of additional tools needed (Figure 13-29).

Figure 13-29. *Click Add Features*

The *Select server roles* window will reappear with *Active Directory Certificate Services* checked. Click *Next*.

You will see the *Select features* window (Figure 13-30.)

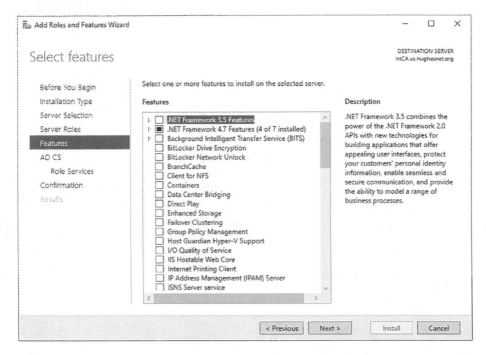

Figure 13-30. *The default (.NET Framework 4.7 or later) should be selected. Click Next*

You should see the *Active Directory Certificate Services* window (Figure 13-31).

Figure 13-31. *Click Next*

You should see the *Select role services* window. See Figure 13-32.

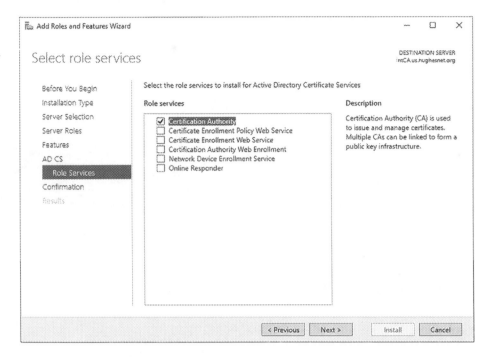

Figure 13-32. *Select role services*

By default, only *Certificate Authority* is selected. Select *Certification Authority Web Enrollment*.

This will make the Int CA handle Web Enrollment requests. The requested certs will be signed by the Int CA private key instead of the Root CA key. This will create a *three-level hierarchy*:

Root Certificate/Root Private Key (kept on Root CA server)

Int Certificate/Int Private Key (kept on the Int CA Server)

End-Entity Certs/End-Entity Private Keys (kept on requesting node)

When you select *Certification Web Enrollment,* it will ask for additional features. See Figure 13-33.

Figure 13-33. Click Add Features

It will now look like this (Figure 13-34).

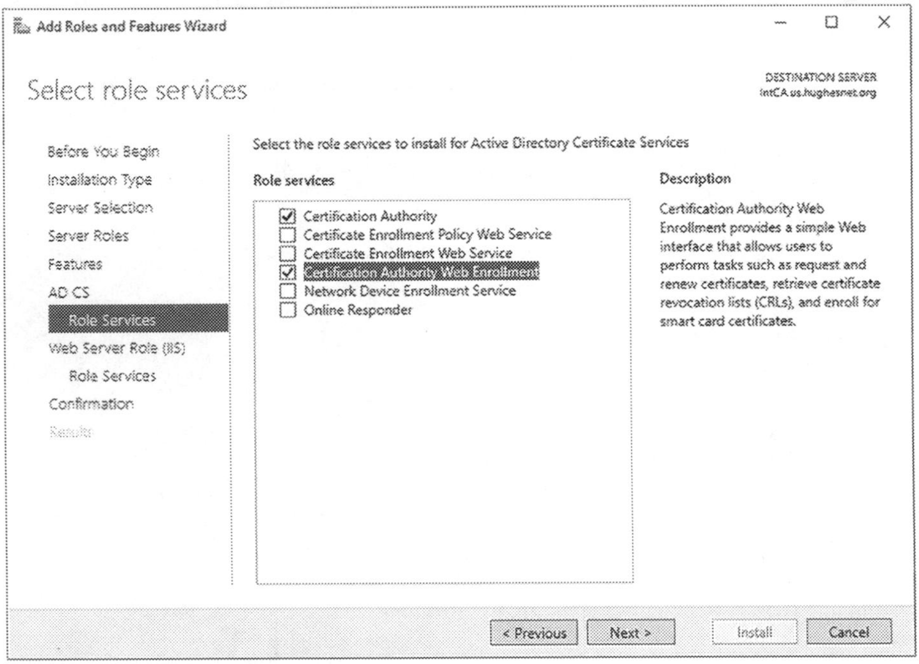

Figure 13-34. *Click Next*

You will now see the *Web Server Role (IIS)* screen (Figure 13-35).

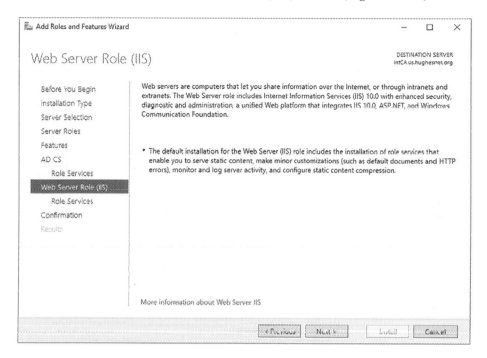

Figure 13-35. *This role is required for the Int CA to handle web enrollment. Click Next*

You will now see the *Select role services* screen (Figure 13-36).

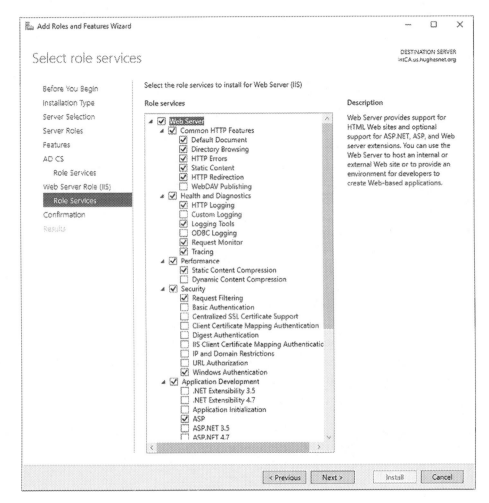

Figure 13-36. *Add Basic Authentication. Click Next*

You will now see the *Confirm installation selections* screen
(Figure 13-37).

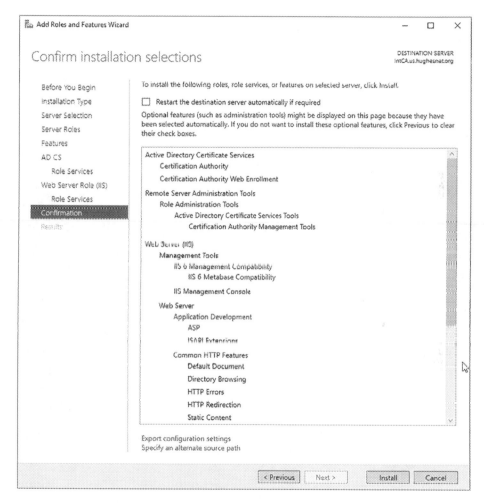

Figure 13-37. *Click Install*

It will take a few minutes to install the Certificate Authority roles, Remote Server Administration Tools, and IIS (Figure 13-38).

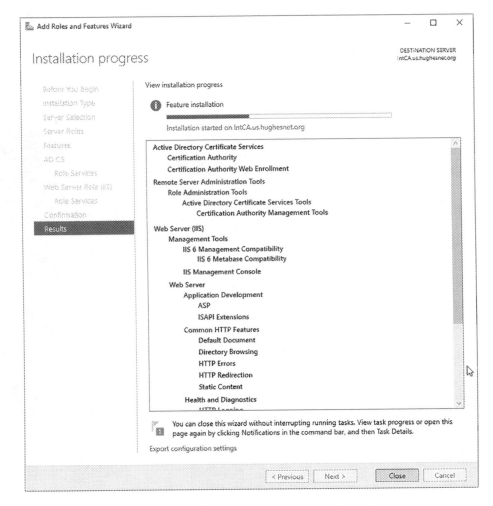

Figure 13-38. *When installation is complete, click Close*

In *Server Manager*, there will be a yellow triangle with an exclamation point at the top of the screen. See Figure 13-39.

Figure 13-39. *Click the yellow triangle*

You will see *Post-deployment Configuration*. Click *Configure Active Directory Certificate Services on the destination server*. That will start the *AD CS Configuration* wizard.

You will see the *Credentials* screen in Figure 13-40.

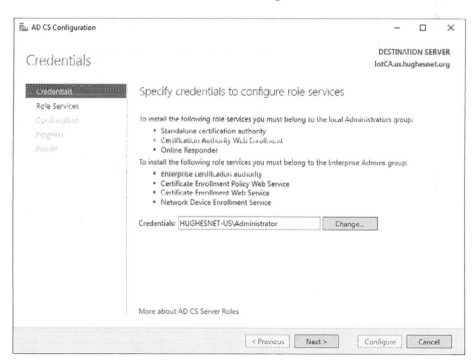

Figure 13-40. *Credentials screen*

Enter your domain administrator account (in my case, *HUGHESNET-US\Administrator*). Click *Next*.

You will now see the *Role Services* window (Figure 13-41).

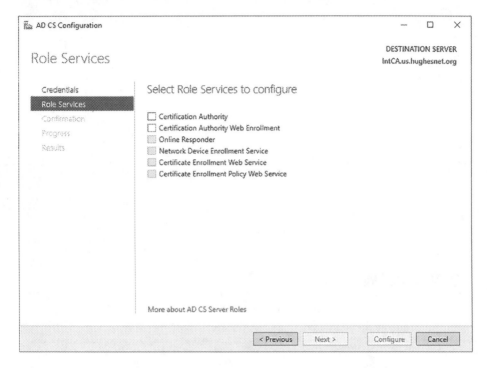

Figure 13-41. *Select both services: Certification Authority and Certification Authority Web Enrollment*

It will now look like this (Figure 13-42).

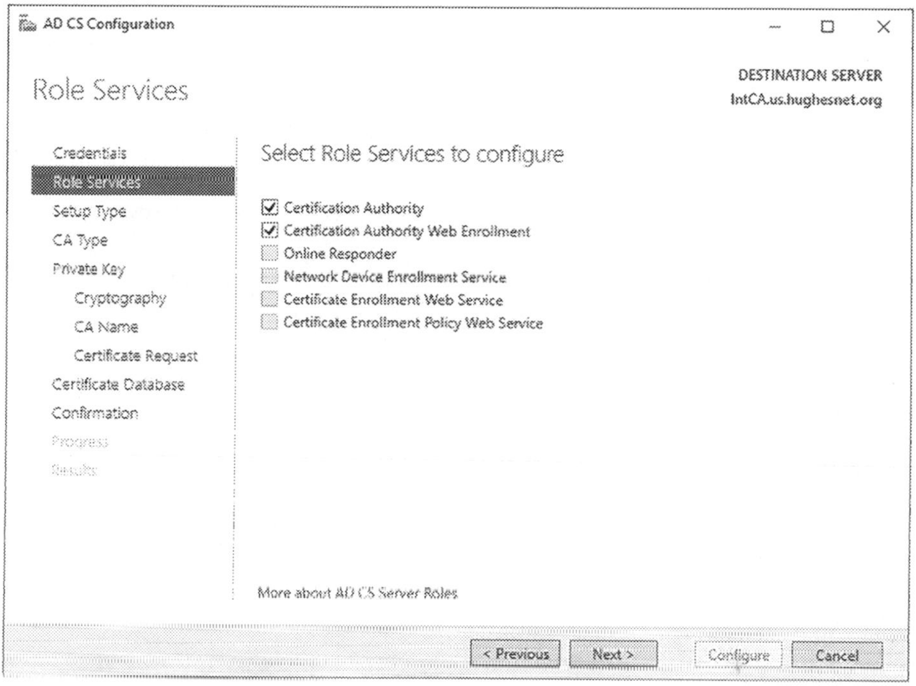

Figure 13-42. *Click Next*

You will now see the *Setup Type* window (Figure 13-43).

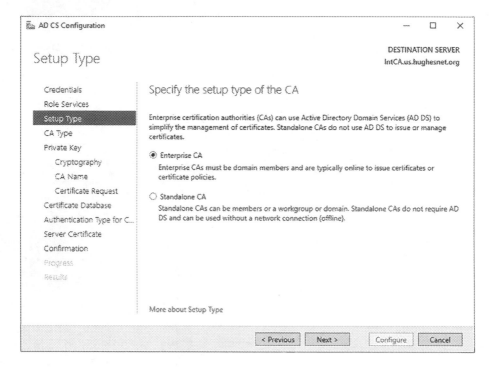

Figure 13-43. *Select Enterprise CA since we want this CA to be integrated with Active Directory Click Next*

You will now see the *CA Type* window (Figure 13-44).

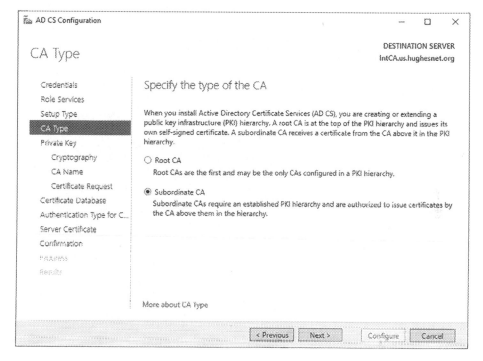

Figure 13-44. *CA Type window*

This time, we *do* want to deploy a Subordinate CA. Select that and click *Next*.

You will now see the *Private Key* window. See Figure 13-45.

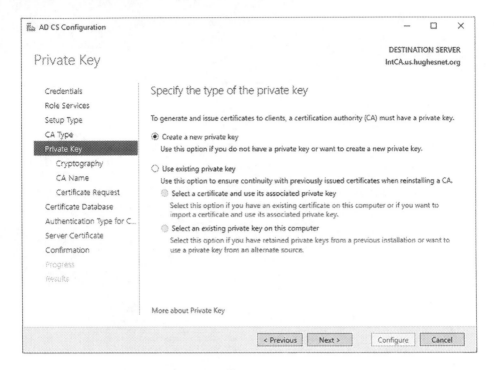

Figure 13-45. *Private Key window*

Select *Create a new private key*. This will create a private key for the Subordinate CA (not the Root CA). Click *Next*.

You will now see the *Cryptography for CA* window (Figure 13-46).

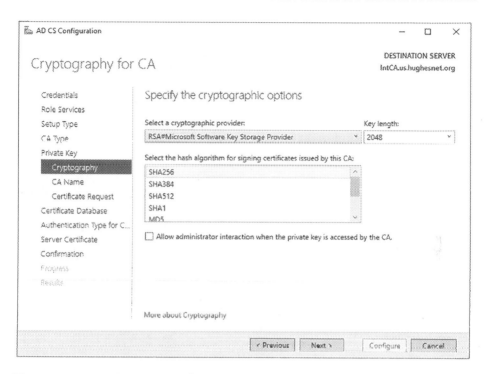

Figure 13-46. *Cryptography options*

Select cryptographic provider as **RSA#Microsoft Software Key Storage Provider**, *Key length* as **2048**, and *hash algorithm* as **SHA256**.

For a *very* secure deployment, you can configure an HSM (Hardware Storage Module) to hold the Intermediate Private Key. This would require selecting the cryptographic provider for your HSM instead of the default MS one. The HSM must be accessible from the Intermediate CA server. With an external HSM (one connected via Ethernet), you could use a single HSM for both the Root and Subordinate CAs. Again, in theory, you could use another USB hardware token for this. This is outside of the scope of this book; you might need to hire a security consultant who is familiar with HSMs for this.

Click *Next*.

You will now see the *CA Name* window (Figure 13-47).

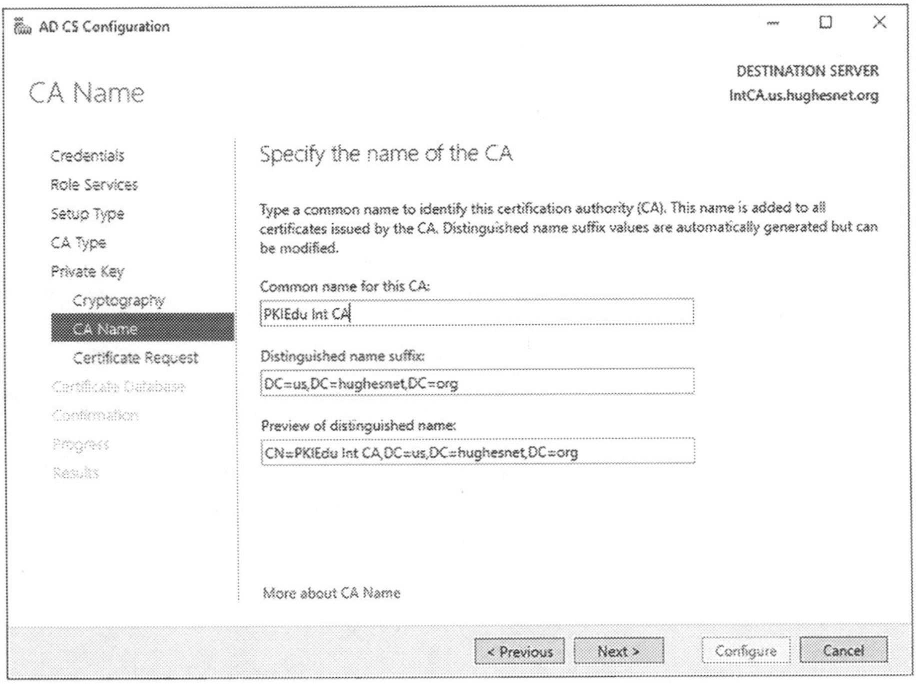

Figure 13-47. *CA Name*

Enter the name you want for the Intermediate CA. In my case, I chose
PKIEdu Int CA. The default for *Distinguished name suffix* should be fine.
In my case, it is **DC=us,DC=hughesnet,DC=org**, which is based on my
domain name (us.hughesnet.org). It is OK for the CA name to have blanks
in it. Click *Next*.

You will now see the *Request a certificate from parent CA* screen. See
Figure 13-48.

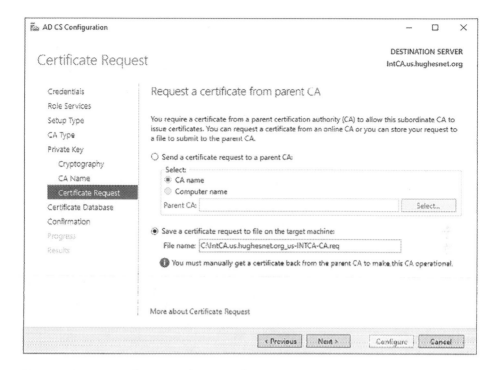

Figure 13-48. *Select Send a certificate request to a parent CA*

Click the *Select* button. You will see a list of CAs (probably only your
Root CA), as shown in Figure 13-49.

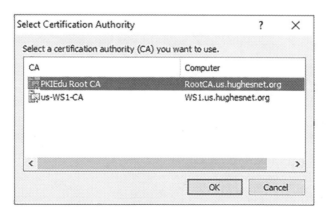

Figure 13-49. *Select your Root CA and click OK*

It will now look like this (Figure 13-50).

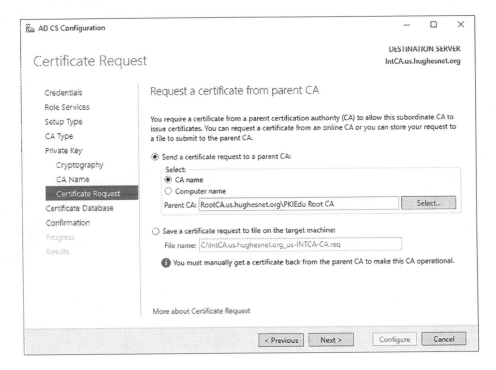

Figure 13-50. *Click Next*

You will now see the *CA Database* window (Figure 13-51).

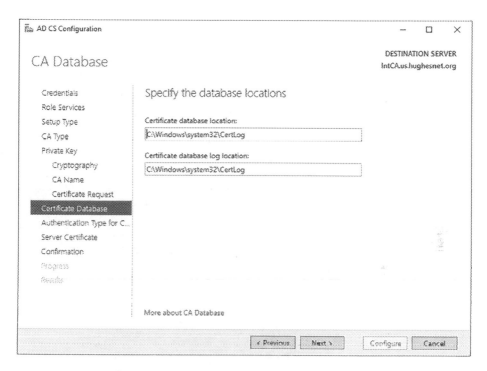

Figure 13-51. *Accept the defaults and click Next*

You will now see the *Confirmation* window. It should look something like this (Figure 13-52).

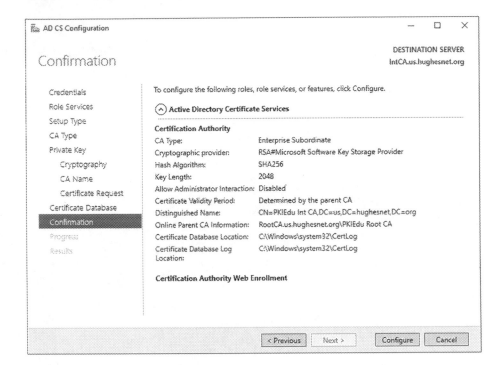

Figure 13-52. *If everything looks good, click Configure*

When configuration is complete (just a few seconds), you should see the following (Figure 13-53).

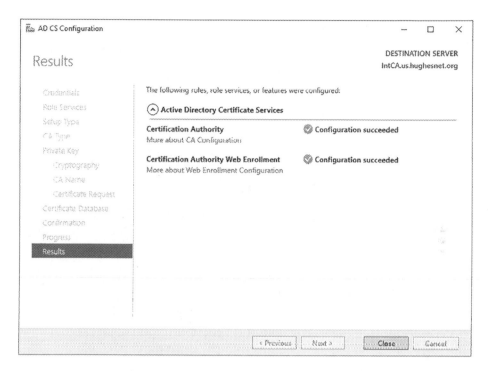

Figure 13-53. *Results*

The *More about CA Configuration* link will take you to the following website:

```
https://docs.microsoft.com/en-us/previous-versions/windows/
it-pro/windows-server-2012-R2-and-2012/hh831574(v=ws.11)?
redirectedfrom=MSDN#CAConfig
```

The *More about Web Enrollment Configuration* link will take you to the following web page:

```
https://docs.microsoft.com/en-us/previous-versions/windows/
it-pro/windows-server-2012-R2-and-2012/hh831649(v=ws.11)?
redirectedfrom=MSDN#WebEnrollConfig
```

Click *Close*.

Congratulations! The basic installation of your Subordinate CAs is complete.

PKIView

There is a handy tool for understanding and troubleshooting your Enterprise CA called PKIView. You can start it by right-clicking Start, then selecting *Run*, and entering *PKIView.msc*. It may take a few minutes after installation for everything to show OK. If you see errors, just wait for a few minutes for things to propagate through *Active Directory*.

PKIView looks something like this (Figure 13-54).

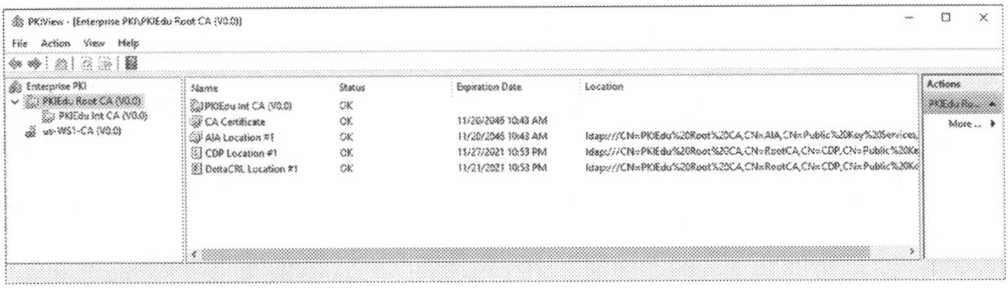

Figure 13-54. *PKIView*

Note that it shows your Root CA (in my case, PKIRoot CA) and subsidiary CA (in my case, PKIEdu Int CA) under it.

You can see that the Root CA Certificate is OK.

The *AIA Location* (for OCSP) and *CDP Location* (for CRL) are also OK. There is also a *DeltaCRL Location*.

Note that the AIA and CDP locations are on the Root CA server. To take your root server offline, you will need to do some complicated configuration to copy the things pointed to by these to the Int CA and change the configuration to point to these (or else revocation checking won't work). This is beyond the scope of this book.

Expand the subsidiary CA now (in my case PKIEdu Int CA). You should see something like this (Figure 13-55).

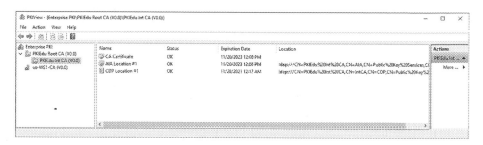

Figure 13-55. *Expanding subsidiary CA*

Again, you can see that the Intermediate CA Certificate is OK, as is the AIA Location (for OCSP) *and CDP Location* (for CRLs).

CHAPTER 14

Issue and Manage TLS Server Certificates

Now that we have deployed Microsoft Certificate Services, we need to configure it to issue various types of certificates. The first type of certificate we will address is called a TLS Server Certificate. This is used to enable TLS on an Internet server, for example, a web server. It also provides server-to-client authentication, which allows the client to know that it is connecting to the server it *meant* to and not some clever fake set up by a hacker. This could be very important if you think you are connecting to your online banking service. If a hacker can trick you into connecting to some server they are running, they can capture your login credentials and empty your bank account.

A TLS Server Certificate contains several important items:

- A *Subject Distinguished Name* (SubjectDN) that identifies the server. It contains a *Common Name* with the fully qualified domain name of the server, for example, *www.mybank.com*. It can include additional information that can include the organization name,

© Lawrence E. Hughes 2022
L. E. Hughes, *Pro Active Directory Certificate Services*,
https://doi.org/10.1007/978-1-4842-7486-6_14

the city, the state, and the country, for example, MyBank Inc., in Frisco, Texas, US. The complete distinguished name in this case would be *CN=www. mybank.com, O=MyBank Inc., L=Frisco, ST=Texas, C=US.*

- An *Issuer Distinguished Name* (IssuerDN) that identifies the Certification Authority that issued this certificate. The IssuerDN for a certificate issued by our CA might be: *CN=PKIEdu Root CA, DC=us, DC=hughesnet, DC=org.* This is used to find the parent certificate (whose SubjectDN is the same as this certificate's IssuerDN). A *Trust Chain* is formed in this manner up to a Trusted Root Certificate that is *self-signed.*

- Various *Usage* flags that determine what this certificate can be used for, for example, *Server Authentication.*

- A *ValidFrom* date that specifies when this certificate's validity period begins, for example, *Wednesday, September 9, 2020, 6:00:00 PM*. If the current date is *before* this date, the certificate will be rejected.

- A *ValidTo* date that specifies when this certificate's validity period ends, for example, *Friday, September 10, 2021, 5:59:59 PM*. If the current date is *after* this date, the certificate will be rejected.

- It may contain one or more *Subject Alternative Names*, like *DNS Name=www.mybank.com*. If present, the node name of the server must match one of these names.

- A *public key* that is unique to this certificate and *bound* to the other identifying information by it. This can be an RSA key with 2048 (or more) bits or an ECC key.

It is half of a matched pair of keys. The other key is the corresponding *private key*, which is typically on the server (but not in the certificate).

- Information on where to check the current revocation status of the certificate, either by *Certificate Revocation List* (CRL) or *Online Certificate Revocation Protocol* (OCSP).

- A *digital signature* that was affixed by the Certification Authority at time of issue and covers all the other fields. The signing is done using the signing CA's private key and validated using the signing CA's public key (from the signing CA's certificate). If anyone changes this signature or any of the other items, the verification will fail and the certificate will be rejected.

Set Up Templates for Root CA

On your Subsidiary CA server (in my case, *IntCA*), in *Server Manager*, click *Tools/Certification Authority*. That will bring up *certsrv*.

Expand your CA name (e.g., PKIEdu Int CA). Expand *Certificate Templates*. You should see the following (Figure 14-1).

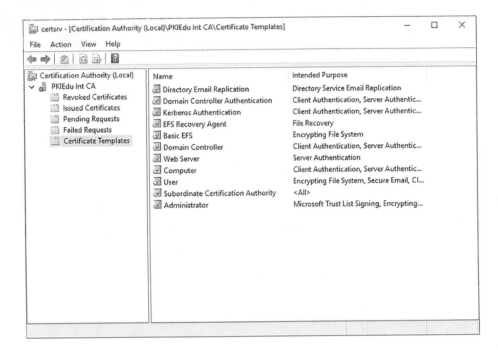

Figure 14-1. *Certificate Templates*

Right-click *Certificate Templates* and choose *Manage*. You should see a list of all default Certificate Templates (Figure 14-2).

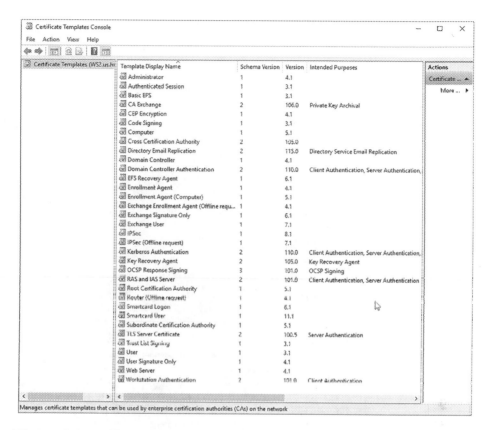

Figure 14-2. *Choose Manage*

In the list of templates, right-click *Web Server* and select *Duplicate Template*. You should see the following (Figure 14-3).

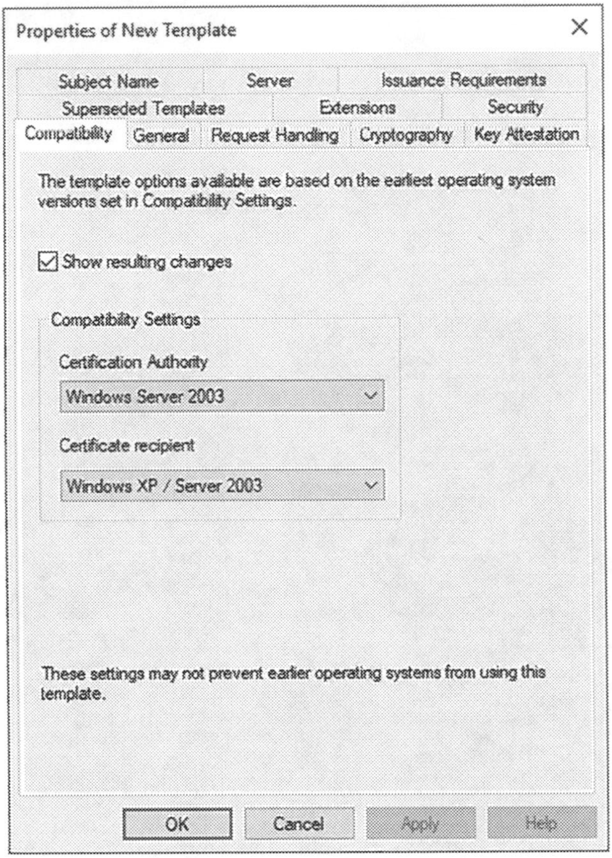

Figure 14-3. *Do not click OK yet*

Click the **General** tab.

Set the *Template Display Name* to **TLS Server Certificate**. That will set the *Template Name* to *TLSServerCertificate*.

Set the Validity period to *two years*.

Select *Publish certificate in Active Directory*.

It should now look like this (Figure 14-4).

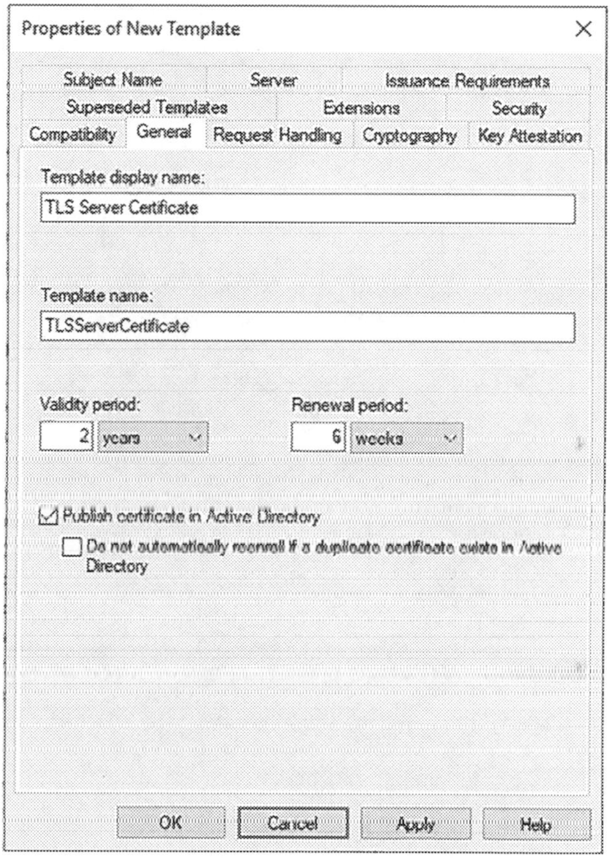

Figure 14-4. *Do not click OK yet*

Select the ***Subject Name*** tab.

Select *Build from this Active Directory information*.

Select *Subject name format* as **Common name**.

Under *Include this information in alternate subject name,* select only **DNS name**.

It should now look like this (Figure 14-5).

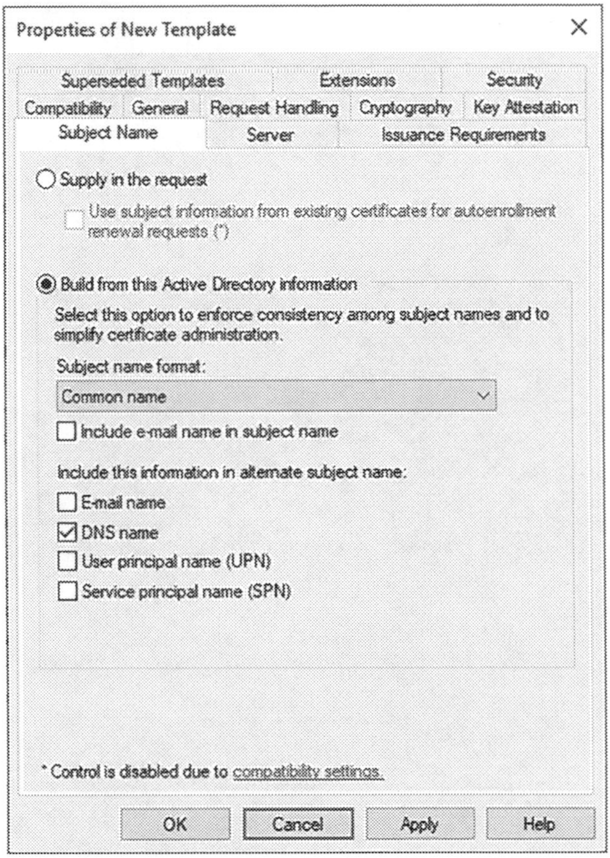

Figure 14-5. *Do not click OK yet*

Select the *Extensions* tab.

You will see that the *Application Policies* is set to **Server Authentication**. See Figure 14-6.

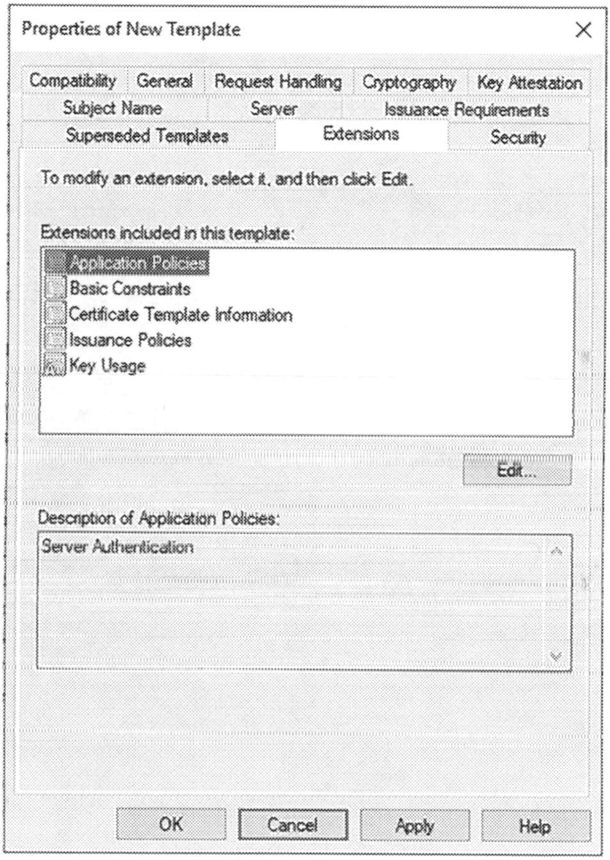

Figure 14-6. *Now you can click OK*

There is now a new template called *TLS Server Certificate*. See Figure 14-7.

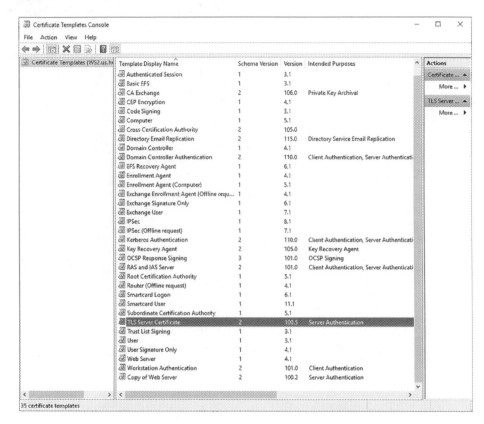

Figure 14-7. *You can dismiss this with the X in upper right*

Prepare for Issuing TLS Server Certs

In *certsrv (Server Manager/Tools/Certification Authority)*, right-click *Certificate Templates* and select *New/Certificate Template to issue*. You will see an *Enable Certificate Templates* window.

From the list of certificate templates, find *TLS Server Certificate*.

Note that if the new template is not yet present in this list, wait until it is replicated to all domain controllers. This may take quite a while, depending on your domain. If it takes too long, try rebooting your Subordinate CA server. See Figure 14-8.

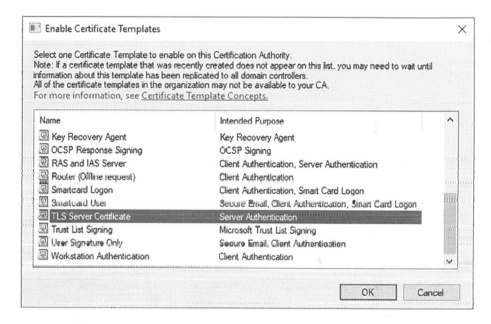

Figure 14-8. *Server Certificates*

Select *TLS Server Certificate* by clicking it, and then click *OK*. This will enable the TLS Server Certificate template for issuing new certs.

Now the available templates include TLS Server Certificate (Figure 14-9).

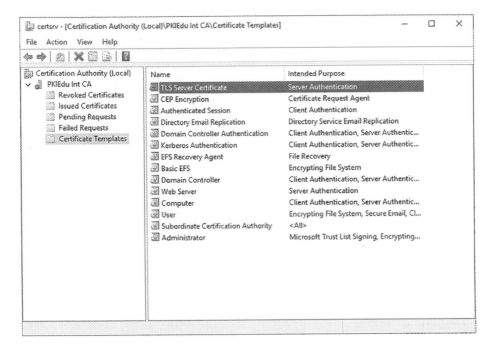

Figure 14-9. *TLS Server Certificate*

Now right-click *Certificate Templates* and select *Manage*. Find
TLS Server Certificate in the list of Templates. Right-click it and select
Properties. Select the *Security* tab.

Select who you want to be able to enroll TLS Server Certificates (e.g.,
Authenticated Users), and select *Read* and *Enroll*. It will now look like this
(Figure 14-10).

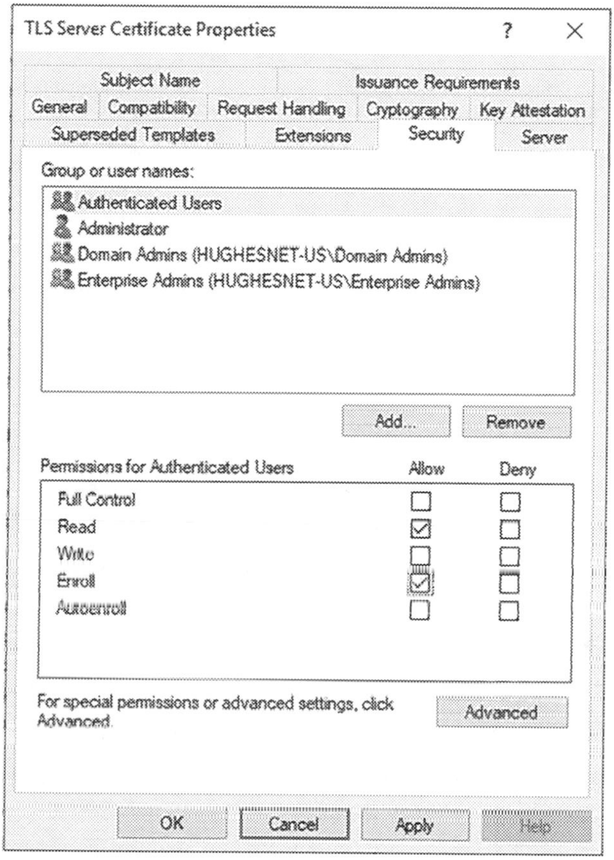

Figure 14-10. *Click OK*

Request and Issue a TLS Server Certificate Using mmc.exe

The next step is to use mmc.exe to request a TLS Server Certificate for PKIEduRootCA.

Start mmc.exe by right-clicking *Start*, selecting *Run*, and entering **mmc.exe**.

You will see an empty mmc shell (Figure 14-11).

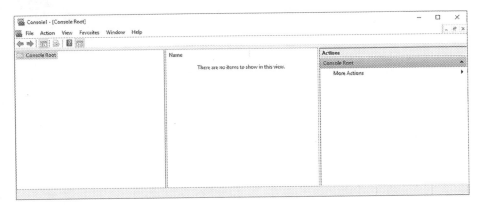

Figure 14-11.   *Empty mmc shell*

Click *File/Add/Remove Snap-in*. Select *Certificates* and then click *Add*. Select *Computer account*. Click *Next*. Select *Local computer*. Click *Finish*. Dismiss the *Add or Remove Snap-ins* dialog with *OK*.

It should now look like this.

In mmc, expand *Certificates*. You will see a list of all certificate folders.

Expand *Personal*. Expand *Certificates*. You should see something like the following (Figure 14-12).

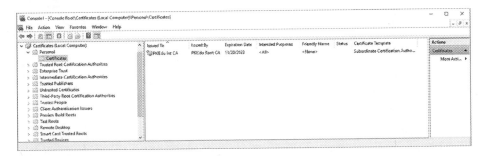

Figure 14-12.   *Certificates window*

Notice that there may already be one or more certs in your Personal/ Local Computer folder. Those were created in the previous exercise.

We now need to create a *TLS Server Certificate* for our Int CA server.

Right-click the middle pane of mmc (Console1) and select *All Tasks/Request New Certificate.*

Ignore the *Before You Begin* page. Click *Next.*

You should now see the following (Figure 14-13).

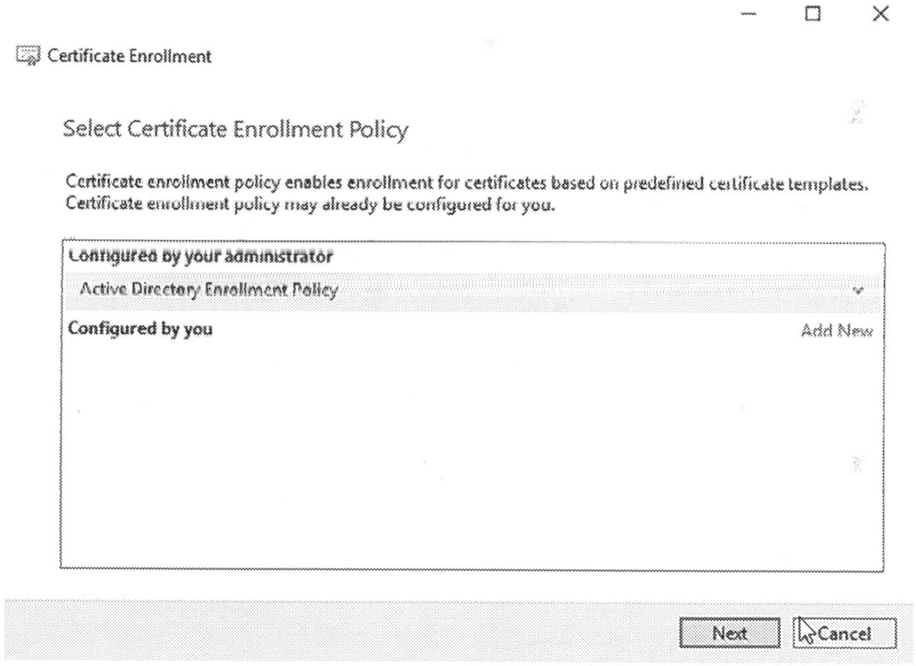

— ☐ ✕

🖳 Certificate Enrollment

Select Certificate Enrollment Policy

Certificate enrollment policy enables enrollment for certificates based on predefined certificate templates. Certificate enrollment policy may already be configured for you.

Configured by your administrator
Active Directory Enrollment Policy

Configured by you   Add New

Next   Cancel

Figure 14-13. *Click Next*

You should now see the following (Figure 14-14)

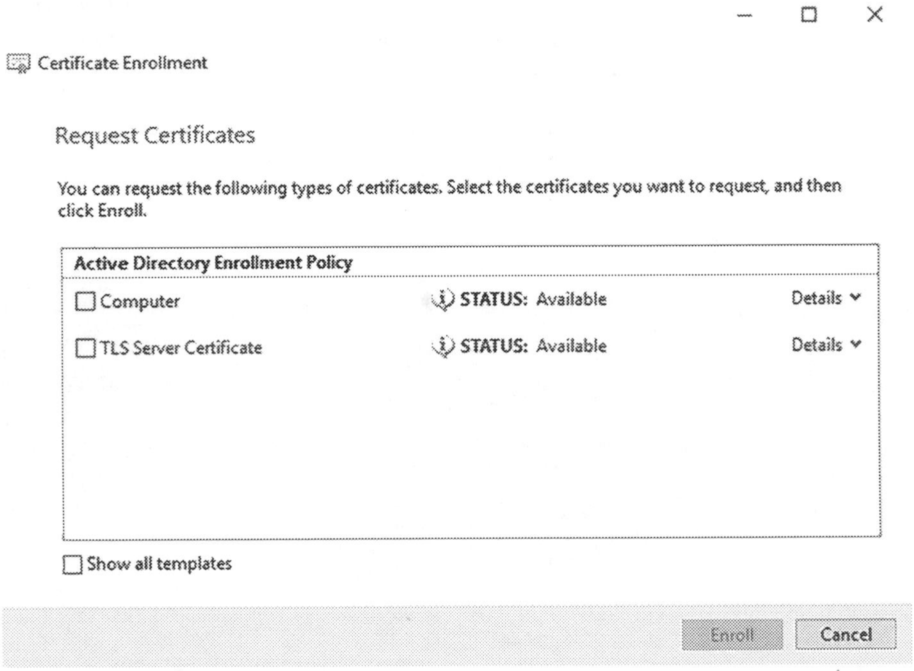

Figure 14-14. *Request Certificates*

Select *TLS Server Certificate.* Click *Details.* It will now look like this (Figure 14-15).

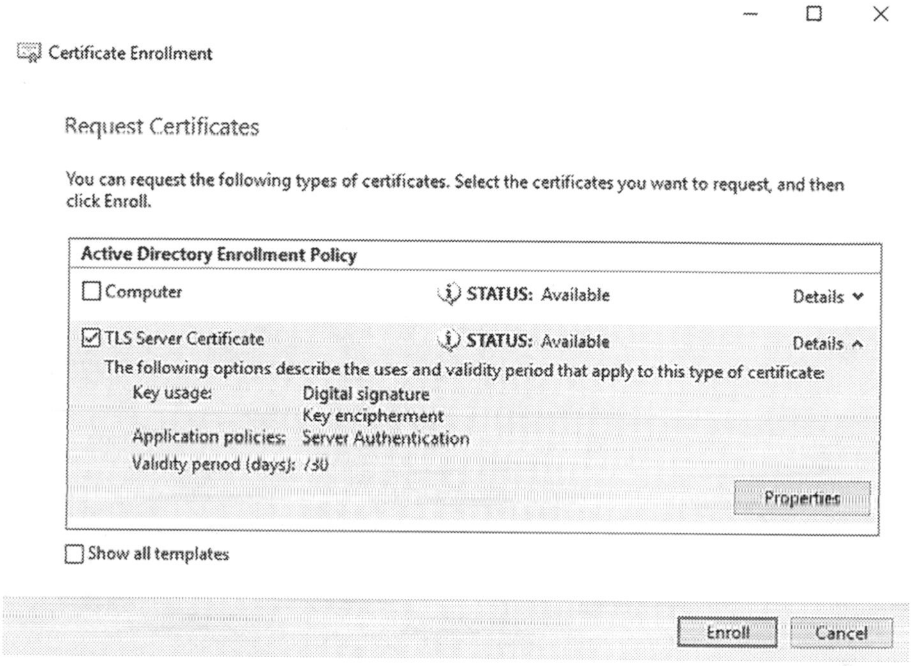

Figure 14-15. Click Properties

In the *Certificate Properties* dialog, select the *Private Key* tab. Expand *Key options.*

Select *Make private key exportable.* See Figure 14-16.

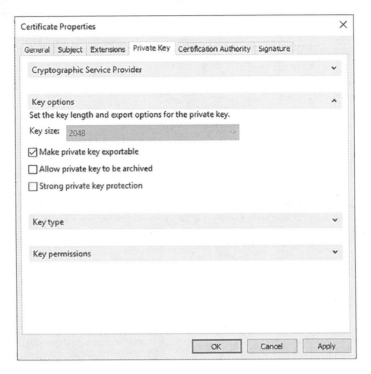

Figure 14-16. *Key options*

This will make the private key for this certificate exportable.
Click *OK* to dismiss the *Certificate Properties* dialog.
Back in the *Certificate Enrollment* wizard, click *Enroll.*

You should now see the following (Figure 14-17).

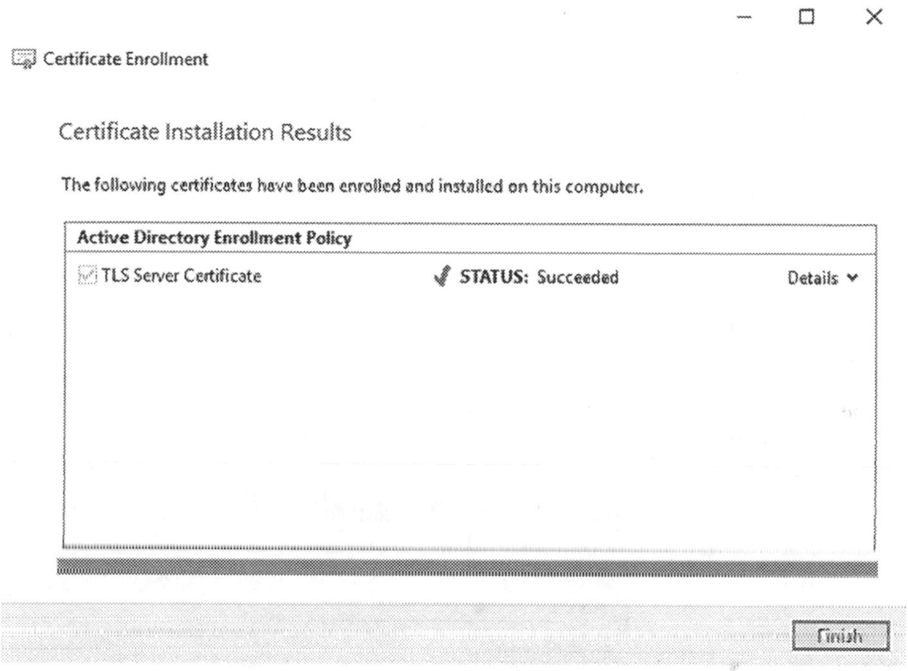

Figure 14-17. *TLS Server Certificate status*

Click the down carat after Details. You should see the following (Figure 14-18).

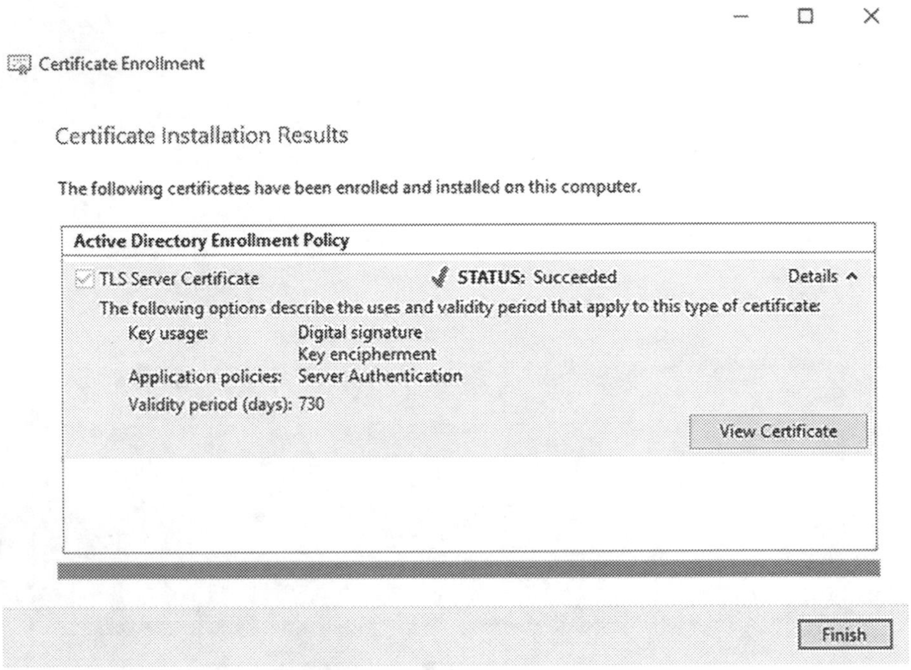

—   □   ×

🖳 Certificate Enrollment

Certificate Installation Results

The following certificates have been enrolled and installed on this computer.

Active Directory Enrollment Policy

☑ TLS Server Certificate   ✓ STATUS: Succeeded   Details ^

The following options describe the uses and validity period that apply to this type of certificate:

Key usage: Digital signature
                      Key encipherment
Application policies: Server Authentication
Validity period (days): 730

[View Certificate]

[Finish]

Figure 14-18. Click Finish

Congratulations, you have just issued a TLS Server Cert for your subsidiary CA server.

In mmc.exe, you should now see the new certificate (Figure 14-19).

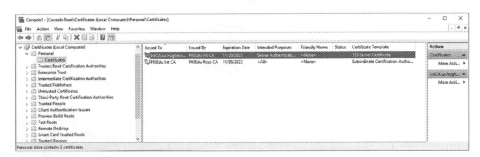

Figure 14-19. New certificate

It was issued using your new *TLS Server Certificate* template and features *Server Authentication*. Double-click the new cert to view its contents (Figure 14-20).

Figure 14-20. *Certificate Information*

Let's explore some more about our new server cert. Click the *Details* tab.

Subject contains

```
CN=IntCA.us.hughesnet.org
```

Issuer contains

```
CN = PKIEdu Int CA
DC = us
DC = hughesnet
DC = org
```

ValidFrom contains the date I issued the cert:

```
Saturday, November 20, 2021 2:14:05 PM
```

ValidTo contains that date plus two years:

```
Monday, November 20, 2023 2:14:05 PM
```

Enhanced Key Usage contains

```
Server Authentication (1.3.6.1.5.5.7.3.1)
```

CRL Distribution Points contains

```
[1]CRL Distribution Point
    Distribution Point Name:
        Full Name:
            URL=ldap:///CN=PKIEdu Int CA,CN=IntCA,
            CN=CDP,CN=Public Key Services,CN=Services,
            CN=Configuration,DC=us,DC=hughesnet,
            DC=org?certificateRevocationList?
            base?objectClass=cRLDistributionP
            oint (ldap:///CN=PKIEdu%20Int%20
            CA,CN=IntCA,CN=CDP,CN=Public%20Key%20Serv
            ices,CN=Services,CN=Configuration,DC=us,D
            C=hughesnet,DC=org?certificateRevocationLi
            st?base?objectClass=cRLDistributionPoint)
```

Authority Information Access (where to connect for OCSP) is

```
[1]Authority Info Access
     Access Method=Certification Authority Issuer
     (1.3.6.1.5.5.7.48.2)
     Alternative Name:
          URL=ldap:///CN=PKIEdu Int CA,CN=AIA,CN=Public
          Key Services,CN=Services,CN=Configuration,
          DC=us,DC=hughesnet,DC=org?cACertificate?
          base?objectClass=certificationAuthority
          (ldap:///CN=PKIEdu%20Int%20CA,CN=AIA,
          CN=Public%20Key%20Services,CN=Services,
          CN=Configuration,DC=us,DC=hughesnet,DC=org?
          cACertificate?base?objectClass=certification
          Authority)
```

Subject Alternative Name contains

```
DNS Name=IntCA.us.hughesnet.org
```

Key Usage contains

```
Digital Signature, Key Encipherment (a0)
```

This is exactly what we need for a TLS Server Certificate.

Now select the *Certification Path* tab. You should see the following (Figure 14-21).

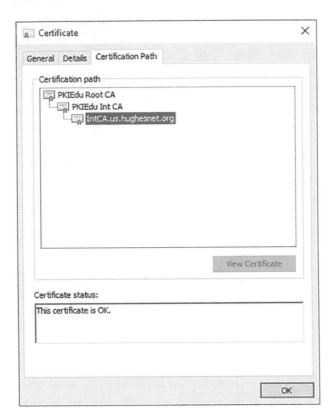

Figure 14-21. *Certificate path*

The new certificate chains up to the PKIEdu Int CA certificate, which chains up to the PKIEdu Root CA certificate, which is a Trusted Root Certificate.

Congratulations! You have just issued a TLS Server Certificate for your Subordinate CA server (in my case, *IntCA.us.hughesnet.org*). Next, we will install it in IIS to test it.

Install Server Cert in Internet Information Server

Now that we have created a TLS Server Certificate for intca.us.hughesnet. org, we need to install it in IIS to enable TLS.

Surf to `http://intca.us.hughesnet.org` (use your own node name). You should see something like this (see Figure 14-22).

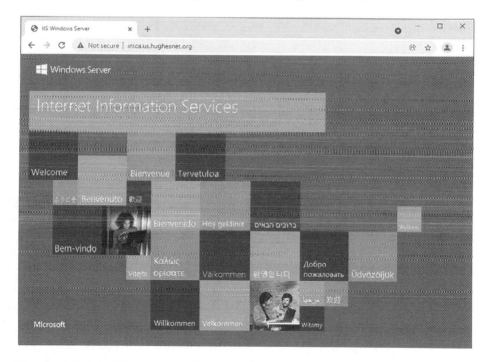

Figure 14-22. *Home page for installing TLS Server Certificate*

Note that it shows "Not secure." There is no TLS Server Certificate installed yet, so HTTPS is not yet working. Let's install the server cert we just created.

Start the IIS Manager on IntCA.us.hughesnet.org. Click *Start/Windows Administrative Tools/Internet Information Services (IIS) Manager*. You should see the following (Figure 14-23).

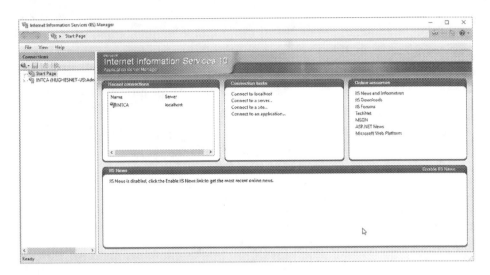

Figure 14-23. *IIS Manager*

Click your server name (in my case, IntCA). Expand it, and then
expand *Sites.* Click *Default Web Site.* You should see the following
(Figure 14-24).

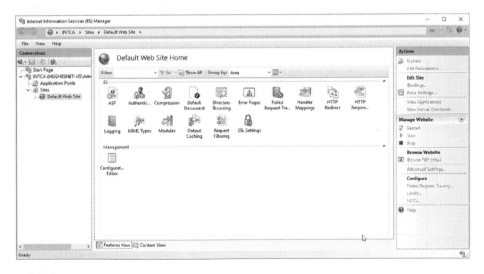

Figure 14-24. *Default Web Site*

Click *Bindings* on the right column. You should see the following (Figure 14-25).

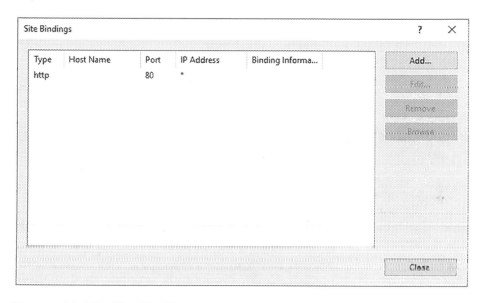

Figure 14-25. *Site Bindings*

The only binding now is for HTTP on port 80/tcp.

Click *Add*.

In the *Add Site Binding* dialog, select *Type* as **https**.

Enter your hostname (e.g., intca.us.hughesnet.org).

Select the SSL Certificate you just created. It should look like this (Figure 14-26).

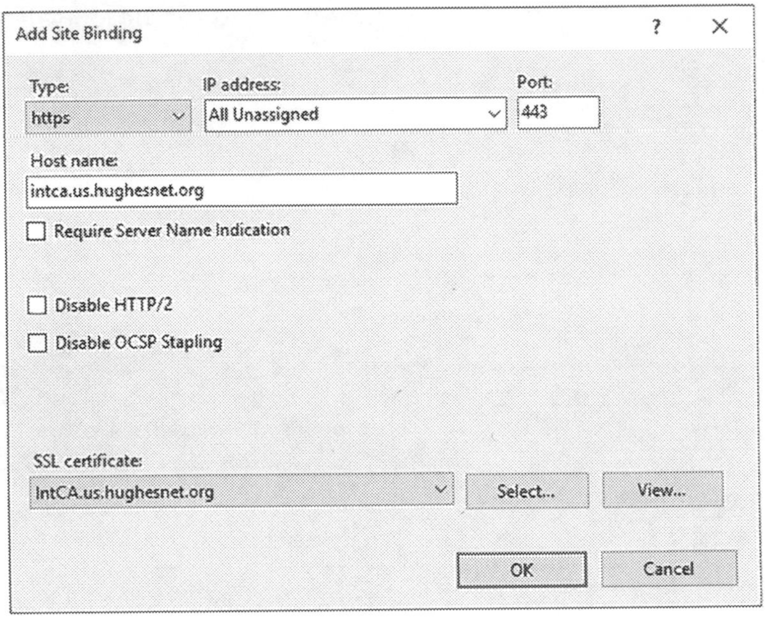

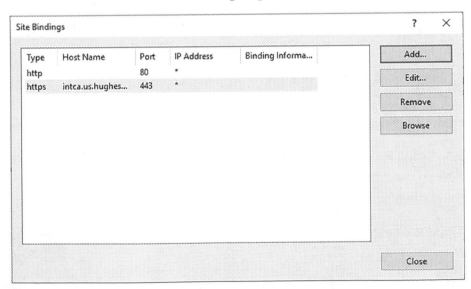

Figure 14-26. *Click OK*

You should now see the following (Figure 14-27).

Figure 14-27. *https support window*

Your IIS now supports https, using the previously created TLS Server Certificate.

Dismiss the preceding dialog by clicking *Close*.

Surf to your website over HTTPS now:

`https://intca.us.hughesnet.org`

You should see something like this (Figure 14-28).

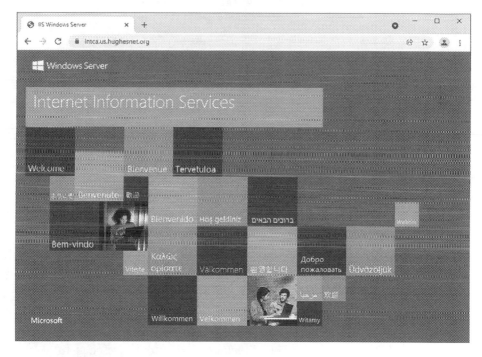

Figure 14-28. *Secure connection enabled*

Note that now there is a padlock before the URL, to indicate that you connected over HTTPS. Click the padlock. It will show "Connection is secure." Click that line. It will show information on the connection, including the line *Certificate is valid* with a link to view the certificate. Click that line.

It will show our TLS Server Certificate (Figure 14-29).

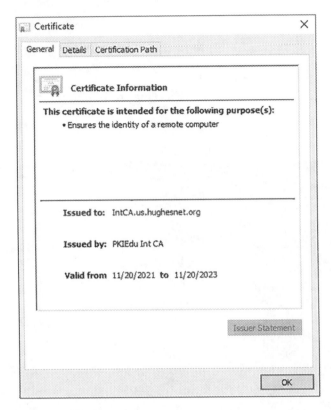

Figure 14-29. *Certificate information*

Congratulations, your new TLS Server Certificate was successfully installed in IIS. HTTPS is working and providing encryption and server-to-client authentication.

If you have other IIS servers in your network, you can try going to those servers and using mmc.exe to request a TLS Server Cert for them as well and install it like we just did for our Subordinate CA server.

Manage Subordinate CA

To manage your Subordinate CA, start certsrv (*Server Manager, Tools, Certification Authority*). Expand your server's name. You should see the following (Figure 14-30).

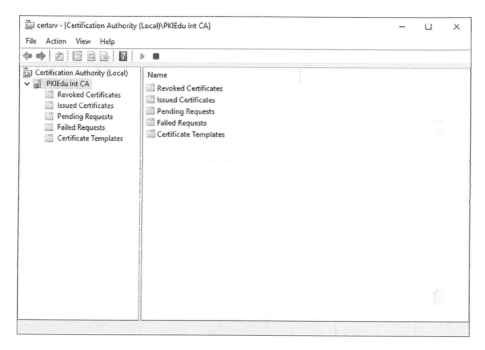

Figure 14-30. *Managing Subordinate CA*

Click *Issued Certificates*. You should see a list of all the certificates you have issued. Note that in my case, I issued a TLS Server Cert for intca. us.hughesnet.org (Request #4) and then issued another one (Request #5) because I wanted to make the private key exportable. We no longer need Certificate #4, so let's revoke it.

Right-click Request #4, and select *All Tasks, Revoke Certificate*.

You will see a Certificate Revocation dialog (Figure 14-31).

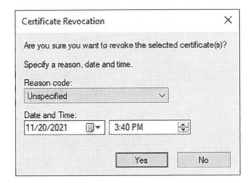

Figure 14-31. *Certificate Revocation dialog*

Select Reason code **Superseded**, shown in Figure 14-32.

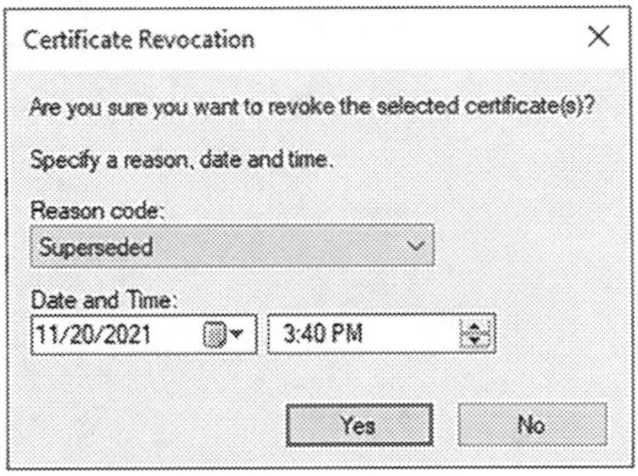

Figure 14-32. *Reason code "Superseded"*

Click *Yes*. See Figure 14-33.

Figure 14-33. *Issued Certificates*

Note that Request 4 is no longer listed under *Issued Certificates.*
Select *Revoked Certificates.* See Figure 14-34.

Figure 14-34. *Request #4 now appears on this list*

This is how you can revoke certificates.

Check CA Health in PKIView

Right-click *Start*, then select *Run*, and then enter *PKIView.msc*. Expand
your Root CA. You should see your Subordinate CA underneath it
(Figure 14-35).

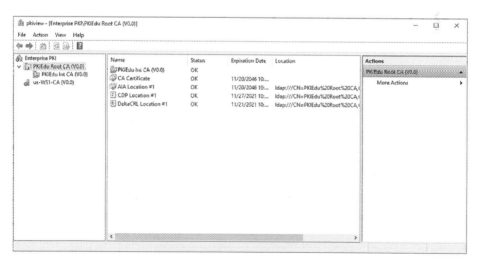

Figure 14-35. *Expanding your Root CA*

Right-click *CDP Location #1,* and select *View CRL.* Note that CDP stands for *Certificate Distribution Point.* That is where clients can find the most recent CRL for certificates issued by this CA.

You will view the first issued CRL for the Root CA (Figure 14-36).

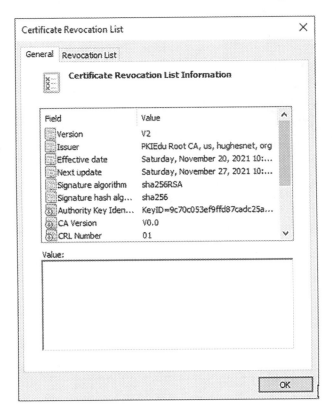

Figure 14-36. *Certificate Revocation List Information*

The *Issuer* is

```
CN = PKIEdu Root CA
DC = us
DC = hughesnet
DC = org
```

The *Effective Date* (when this CRL is effective) is

```
Saturday, November 20, 2021 10:33:47 AM
```

The *Next Update* (when the next CRL will be issued) is roughly one week later:

```
Saturday, November 27, 2021 10:53:47 PM
```

The CRL Number is

```
01
```

Now select the *Revocation List* tab (Figure 14-37).

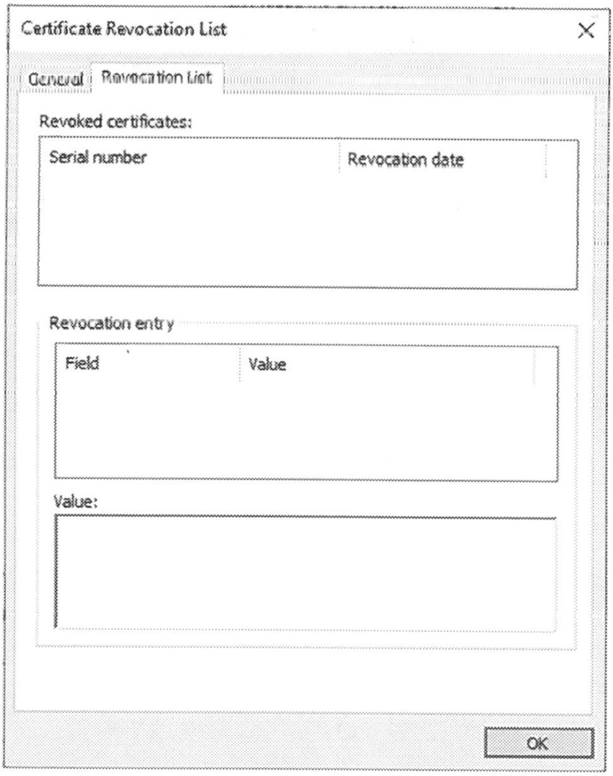

Figure 14-37. *Revocation List tab*

Note that there are currently no revoked certificates on this CRL. The only certificate that might be on the CRL for the Root CA is the Root Certificate, so it would be unusual to see one here. That means all relevant certs (in this case, only the Root Cert) has not been revoked.

Now check your Subordinate CA (in my case, PKIEdu Int CA).

Right-click *CDP Location #1*, and select *View CRL*. See Figure 14-38.

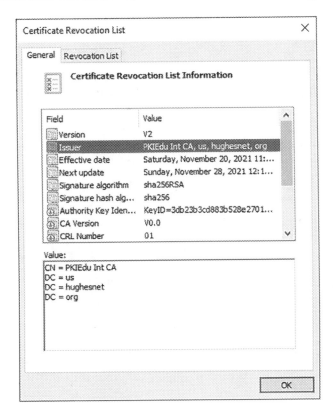

Figure 14-38. Issuer

The *Issuer* is

```
CN = PKIEdu Int CA
DC = us
DC = hughesnet
DC = org
```

The *Effective Date* (when this CRL is effective) is

    Saturday, November 20, 2021 11:58:00 AM

The *Next Update* (when the next CRL will be issued) is roughly one week later:

    Saturday, November 28, 2021 12:17:13 AM

The CRL Number is

    01

Now select the *Revocation List* tab. See Figure 14-39.

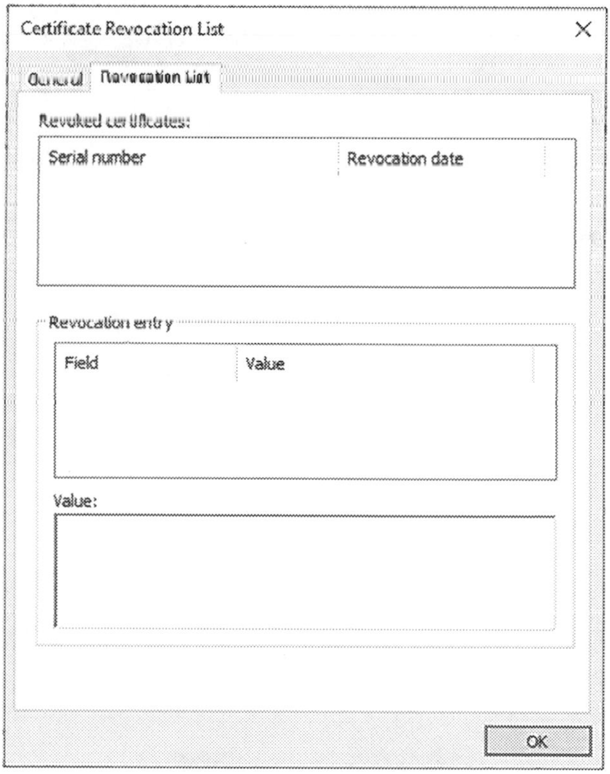

Figure 14-39. *Certificate Revocation List tab*

Note that there are no certificates listed.

But we just revoked a server cert we had issued! Why is it not listed? CRLs are only issued periodically (in this case, once a week). The cert we revoked will appear on the *next* CRL issued, which will be on Saturday, November 28, 2021, 12:17:13 AM. Until then, nobody will know that the cert has been revoked. This is not an error; it's just the way CRLs work.

You can adjust how frequently CRLs will be issued, if once a week is not sufficient. To do this, go to *certsrv*, right-click *Revoked Certificates*, and select *Properties* (see Figure 14-40).

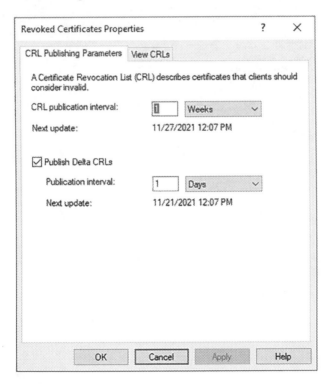

Figure 14-40. *Revoked Certificated Properties*

Set whatever intervals you want with this control.

Since OCSP just provides another way to access the issued CRLs, it will not show this cert as revoked until the next CRL is issued, either.

Force Publication of a New CRL

You *can* force Certificate Services to publish a new CRL.

In certsrv, right-click *Revoked Certificates,* and select *All Tasks*/Publish.

It will ask what CRLs to publish (see Figure 14-41).

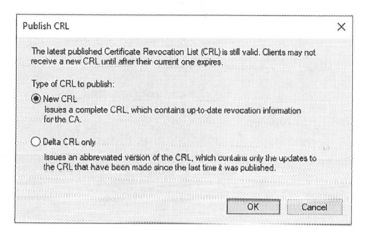

Figure 14-41. Select New CRL and click OK

Now go to PKIView. Right-click *CDP Location #1,* and click *Refresh.*

Then right-click *CDP Location #1,* and click *View CRL.* See Figure 14-42.

Figure 14-42. *View CRL*

Note that this is now *CRL Number 02*. Also, the *Effective Date* is the current time.

Select the *Revocation List* tab. There is now a revoked certificate listed. Click it. See Figure 14-43.

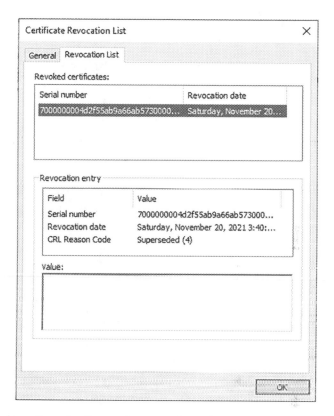

Figure 14-43. *Revoked certificate is listed now*

Note that there is now a revoked certificate listed. You can see the serial number of the revoked certificate, plus when it was revoked, and why ("superseded").

The only problem is that any users who retrieved the old CRL will still be relying on the *Next Update* value in that and not know how to retrieve this new one to update their CRL cache.

However, anyone that gets a new CRL will get the up-to-date information.

Install OCSP Responder

If we want our users to be able to use OCSP to check revocation status, we need to deploy an OCSP Responder (OCSP server) on our Subordinate CA.

Note   You could include this when you install *Certificate Services* for the first time.

In *Server Manager*, click *Manage* and then select *Add Roles and Features*.

You will see the *Select installation type* screen (Figure 14-44).

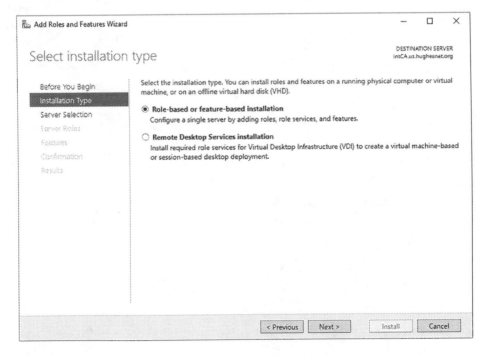

Figure 14-44. *Select role-based or feature-based installation.*
Click Next

You will see *Select destination server*. See Figure 14-45.

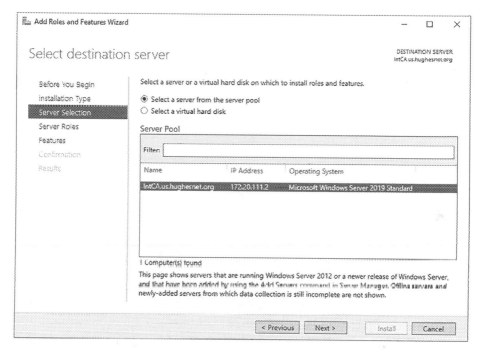

Figure 14-45. *Click Next*

You will see the *Select server roles* screen. Expand *Active Directory Certificate Services*. Add *Online Responder*.

When you do, it will ask for some additional features (Figure 14-46).

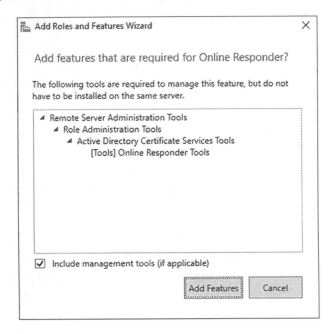

Figure 14-46. *Click Add Features*

Back on the *Select server roles,* click *Next.*

You will then see *Select features.* See Figure 14-47.

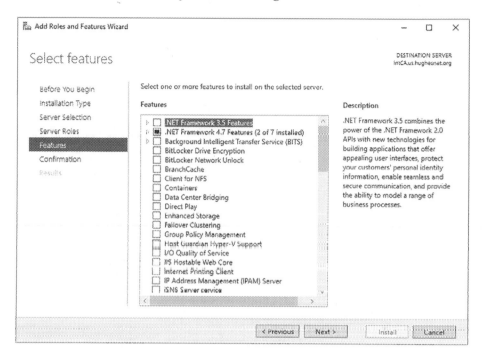

Figure 14-47. *Click Next*

You will then see *Confirm installation selections,* as shown in Figure 14-48.

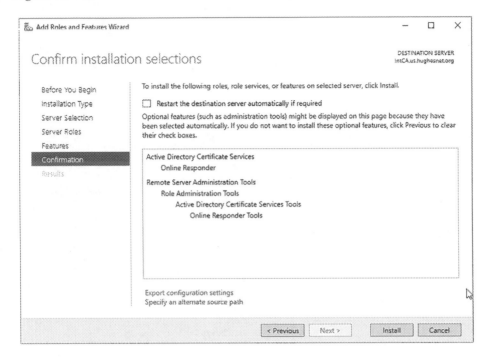

Figure 14-48. *Click Install*

It will then install the selected features (Figure 14-49).

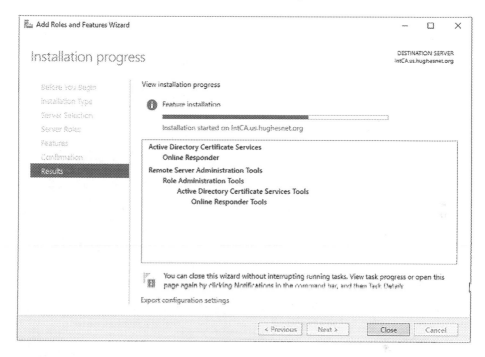

Figure 14-49. *Installation progress window*

When it is done, click *Close*.

There will be a yellow triangle at the top of Server Manager (Figure 14-50).

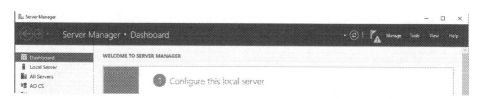

Figure 14-50. *Click the yellow triangle*

Click the link *Configure Active Directory Certificate Services on the Destination Server*.

You will see the *Credentials* screen (Figure 14-51).

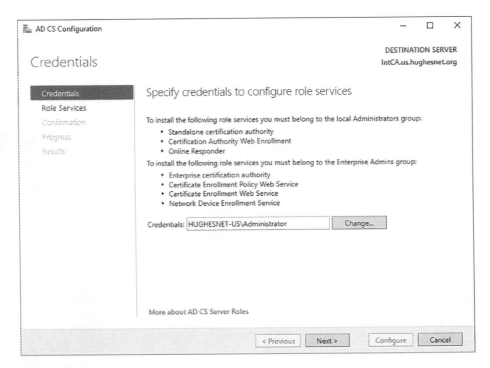

Figure 14-51. *Enter the domain administrator account name and click Next*

You will see the *Role Services* screen (Figure 14-52).

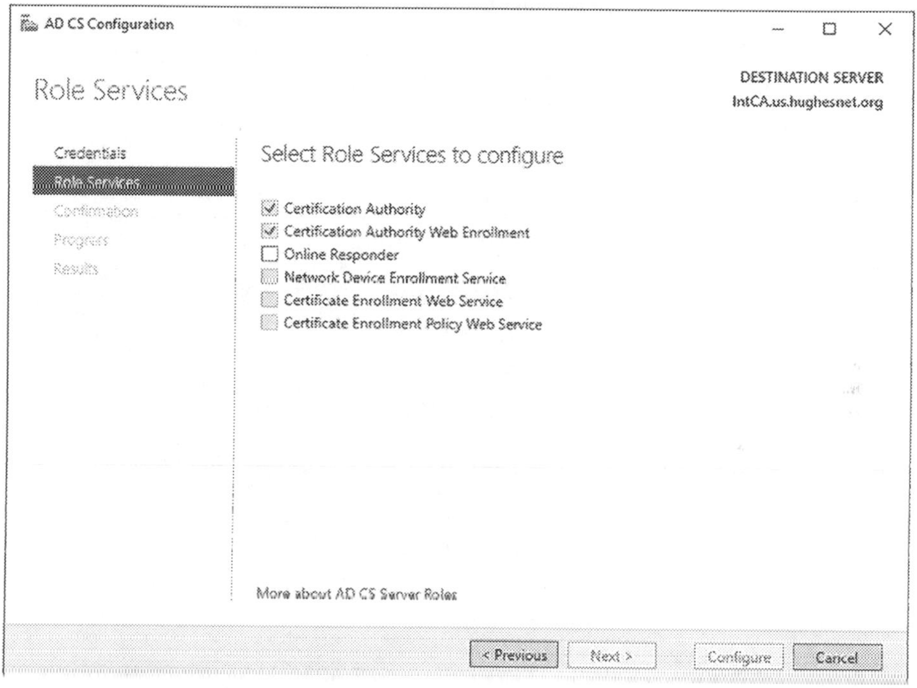

Figure 14-52. *Select Online Responder*

Click *Next*.

You will see the *Confirmation* screen (Figure 14-53).

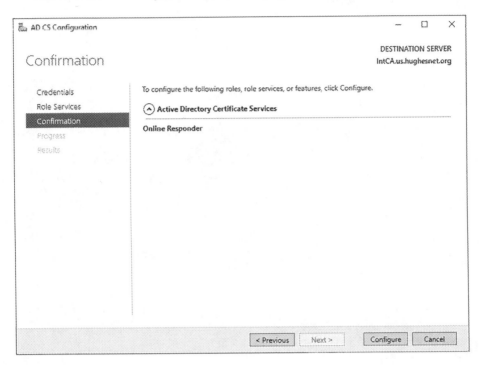

Figure 14-53. *Click Configure*

You will now see the *Results* screen (Figure 14-54).

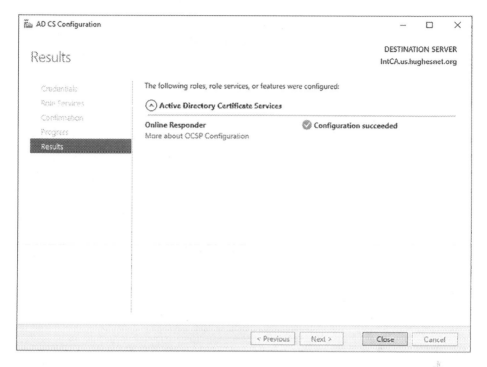

Figure 14-54. *Click Close*

You have now installed and configured an *Online Responder* on your Subordinate CA server for OCSP clients to obtain revocation information.

CHAPTER 15

Issue and Manage TLS Client Certificates

A TLS Client Certificate contains several important items:

- A *Subject Distinguished Name* (SubjectDN) that identifies a person or device. It contains a *Common Name* such as the person's full name, for example, *Lawrence E. Hughes*. It can include additional information that can include the person's organization name, their city, their state, and their country, for example, PKIEdu Inc. in Frisco, Texas, US. The complete distinguished name in this case would be *CN=Lawrence E. Hughes, O=PKIEdu Inc., L=Frisco, ST=Texas, C=US*.

- An *Issuer Distinguished Name* (IssuerDN) that identifies the Certification Authority that issued this certificate. An IssuerDN for a certificate issued by our CA might be: *CN=PKIEdu Root CA, DC=us, DC=hughesnet, DC=org*. This is used to find the parent certificate (whose SubjectDN is the same as this certificate's IssuerDN).

© Lawrence E. Hughes 2022
L. E. Hughes, *Pro Active Directory Certificate Services*,
https://doi.org/10.1007/978-1-4842-7486-6_15

A *trust chain* is formed in this manner up to a Trusted Root Certificate that is *self-signed*.

- Various *Usage* flags that determine what this certificate can be used for, for example, *Client Authentication*.

- A *ValidFrom* date that specifies when this certificate's validity period begins, for example, *Wednesday, September 9, 2020, 6:00:00 PM*. If the current date is *before* this date, the certificate will be rejected.

- A *ValidTo* date that specifies when this certificate's validity period ends, for example, *Friday, September 10, 2021, 5:59:59 PM*. If the current date is *after* this date, the certificate will be rejected.

- It may contain one or more *Subject Alternative Names*, like *Other Name: Principal Name=lhughes@ us.hughesnet.org*.

- A *public key* that is unique to this certificate and *bound* to the other identifying information by it. This can be an RSA key with 2048 (or more) bits, or an ECC key. It is half of a matched pair of keys. The other key is the corresponding *private key*, which is typically on the user's computer (but not in the certificate).

- Information on where to check the current revocation status of the certificate, either by *Certificate Revocation List* or *Online Certificate Revocation Protocol* (OCSP).

- A *digital signature* that was affixed by the Certification Authority at time of issue and covers all the other fields. If anyone changes this signature or any of the other items, the verification will fail, and the certificate will be rejected.

A TLS Client Certificate is used to authenticate a client node to the server node during a TLS handshake. This authentication takes place *after* the server-to-client authentication (which depends on the server having a TLS Server Certificate), but before the encrypted session begins. For TLS *Strong Client Authentication* (SCA), each user must obtain a unique client certificate that identifies *them* (not their node). In a *TLS Client Certificate*, the Subject Distinguished Name field identifies a particular *person* (or device) in the world, as opposed to some *server* node name. A *TLS Client Certificate* can be used from any node – it is not tied to a node name as a *TLS Server Certificate* is. Note that to be able to perform SCA, the client node needs to be able to present the *TLS Client Certificate* to the server (when requested by the server) and then respond to the crypto challenge from the server using its own private key. Only a node that has the appropriate private key can correctly respond to the crypto challenge.

You can export your key material (*TLS Client Certificate* and private key) in PKCS #12 format and import it on another node (e.g., use your work key material from home or from any other computer). It is possible to import your key material into a hardware token (USB or smart card). If the key material is created *inside* the token from the start, there is no way to back up the key material (the private key can never be exported from the hardware token). You can move the token (containing the key material) to another computer, but it can only be used from one computer at a time. Alternatively, you can obtain the key material in PKCS #12 form, back it up, and then import that into a hardware token (or any number of hardware tokens). This allows you to create a new hardware token from the PKCS #12 file in the event the original hardware token is lost.

If you are only going to use your key material for *authentication* and/ or *digital signatures*, there is no need to back up your key material, so it is acceptable to create the key pair and certificate inside a hardware token (a new one with a different key pair can easily be created and used if the current key material is lost). If you are going to use your key material for *encryption*, then you should back up the key material, so in that case, it is not recommended to create the key material and certificate inside a hardware token. If the private key is lost, all files encrypted by the corresponding digital certificate are unrecoverable.

We will create a template for *TLS Client Certificates* that has only the *Client Authentication* flag set. For a TLS Client Certificate, there is no need for any *Subject Alternative Name*.

Note with Client Certificates, you can include various fields in the *Subject Distinguished Name*, from the following choices:

CN	CommonName	User's full name (e.g., *Lawrence Hughes*)
E	EmailAddress	User's email address (e.g., *lhughes@hughesnet.org*)
O	Organization	User's organization (e.g., *PKIEdu Inc.*)
OU	Organization unit	User's department (e.g., *IT*)
L	Locality	User's city (e.g., *Frisco*)
ST	State	User's state or province (e.g., *Texas*)
C	Country	User's country (e.g., US)

There are numerous other fields possible in a Subject Distinguished Name, but each item included must be validated by the Registration Authority before the certificate is signed by the Certification Authority.

Create TLS Client Certificate

The next step is to create a certificate template for issuing certificates for TLS Strong Client Authentication. This is like a TLS Server Certificate, with the following changes:

- **Enhanced Usage flags** – Instead of *Server Authentication* flag, set *Client Authentication* flag.

- **Subject Distinguished Name** – Instead of CN=Fully Qualified Domain Name of server, it now specifies a person or device. This can have any of the fields listed earlier (CN, E, O, OU, L, ST, or C).

Set Up Template for TLS Client Certificate

On the VM running the Subordinate CA (in my case, *intca.us.hughesnet. org*), in Server Manager, click *Tools/Certification Authority*.

Expand *PKIEdu IntCA*. You should see the following (Figure 15-1).

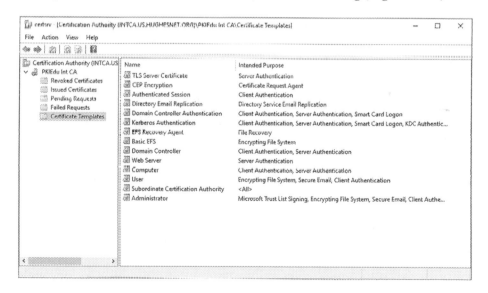

Figure 15-1. *Certificate templates list*

Right-click *Certificate Templates* and choose *Manage.* You should see the following (Figure 15-2).

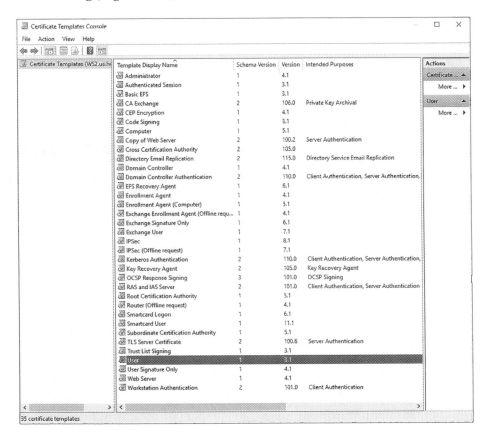

Figure 15-2. *Manage*

Right-click *User* (the appropriate starting point for a *TLS Client Certificate* template), and select *Duplicate Template.* You should see the following (Figure 15-3).

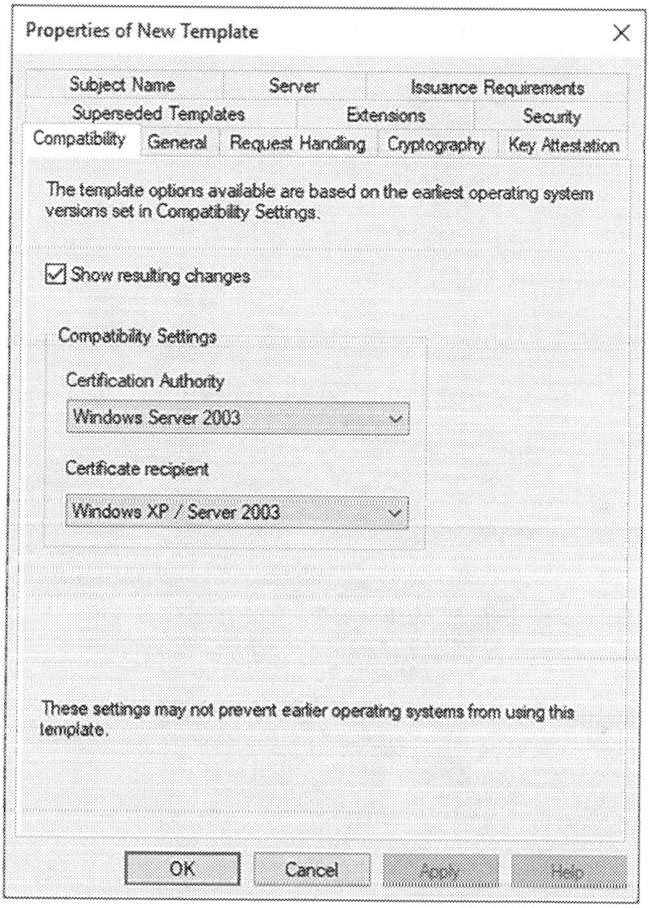

Figure 15-3. *Properties of New Template*

Click the *General* tab.

Set the Template Display Name to TLS Client Certificate. This will change the template name to *TLSClientCertificate*.

Set the Validity period to one year.

Select *Publish certificate in Active Directory*.

It should look like this (Figure 15-4).

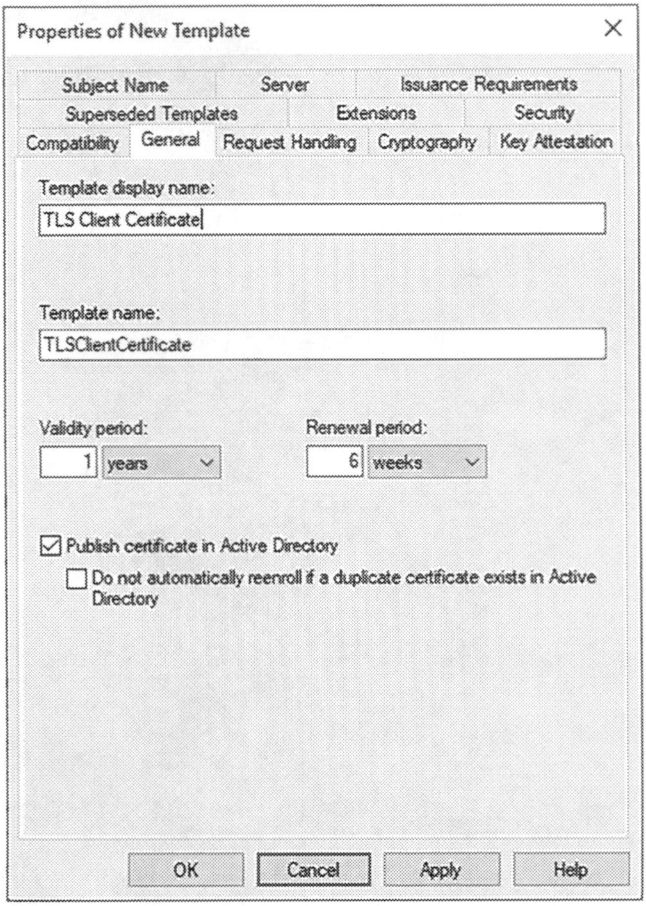

Figure 15-4. *Do not click OK yet*

Select the *Subject Name* tab. Select *Build from this Active Directory information.*

Select *Subject name format* as **Fully distinguished name**.

Under *Include this information in alternate subject name,* select only *User principal name.*

It should look like this (Figure 15-5).

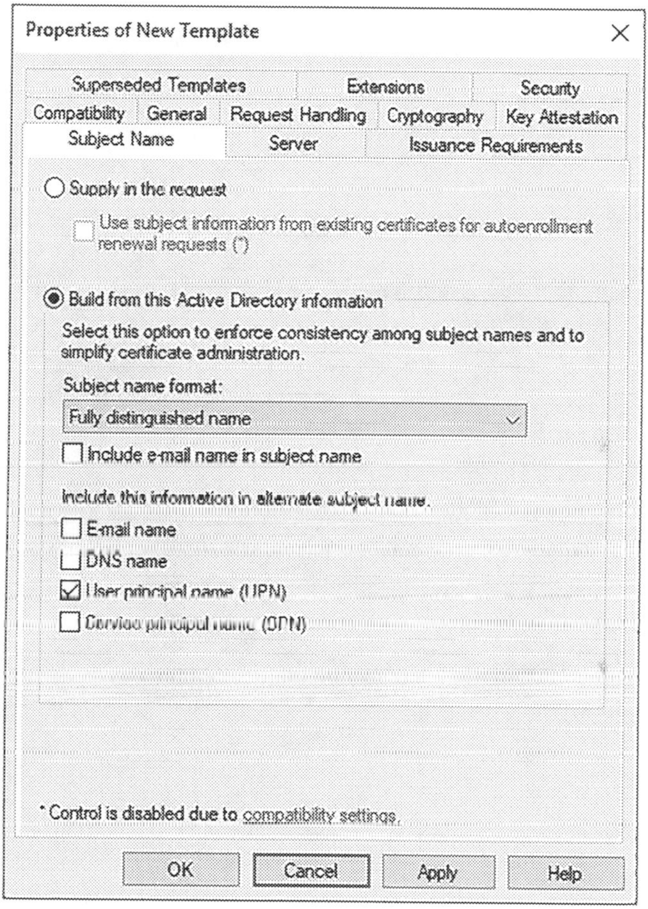

Figure 15-5. *Do not click OK yet*

Select the *Extensions* tab.

You will see that the *Application Policies* defaults to **Encrypting File System**, **Secure Email**, and **Client Authentication** (from the *User* template).

The first two are not needed for TLS SCA. We can remove them to make a *TLS Client Certificate*. See Figure 15-6.

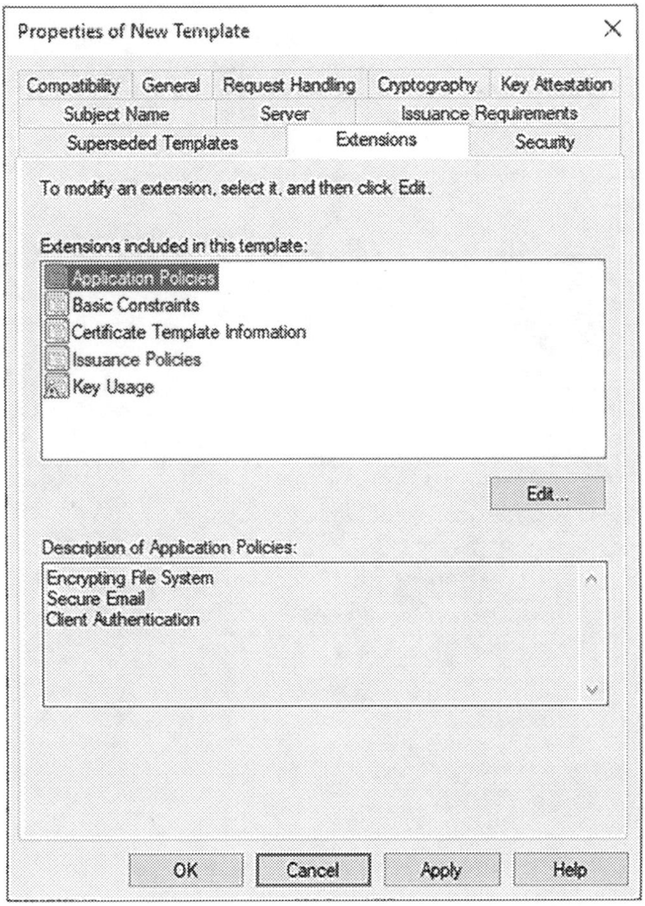

Figure 15-6. *Click Edit*

You should now see the Extension policies.

Highlight *Encrypting File System* and *Secure Email,* and click *Remove.*

You should now see the following (Figure 15-7).

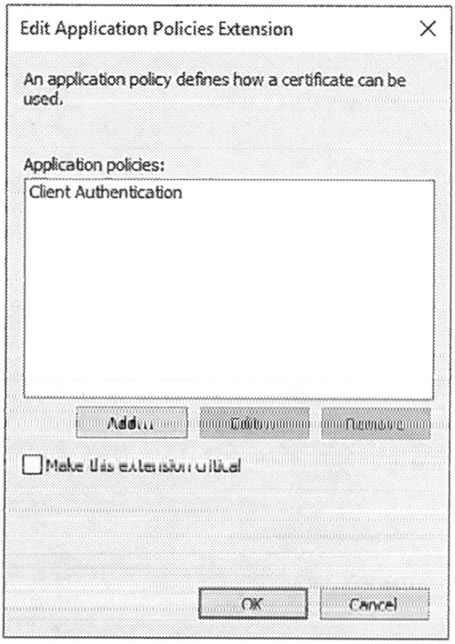

Figure 15-7. Click on OK

You should now see the final Certificate Properties. See Figure 15-8.

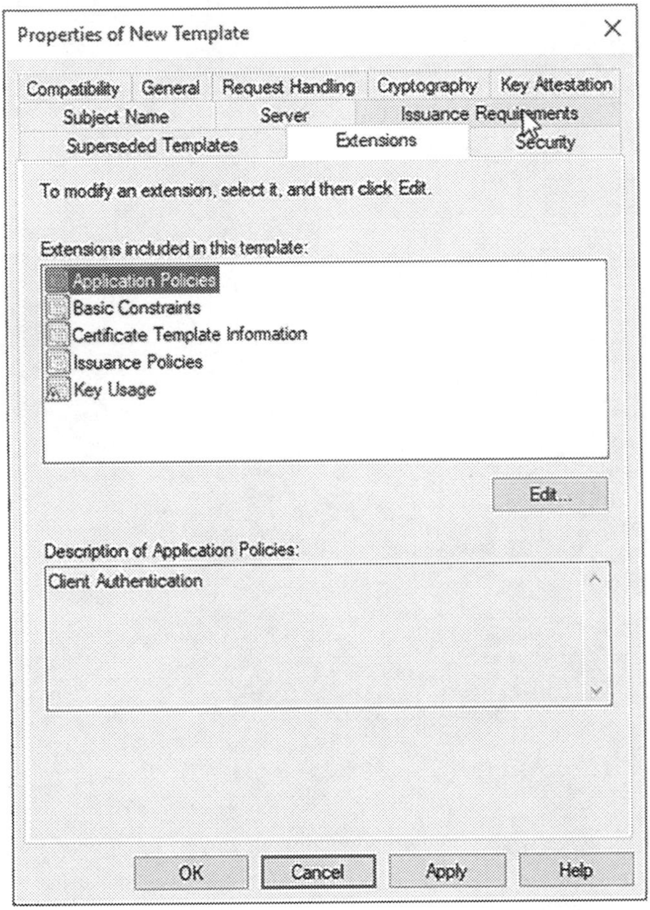

Figure 15-8. Click OK

There is now a new certificate template called *TLS Client Certificate*.
See Figure 15-9.

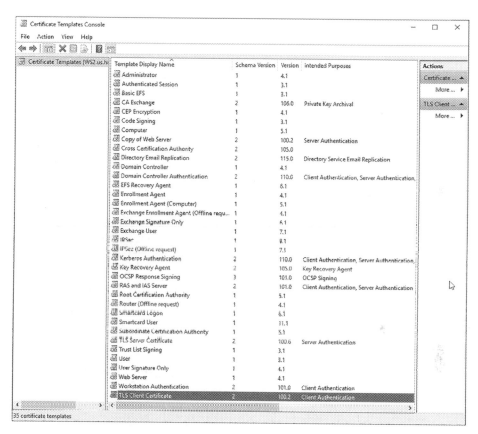

Figure 15-9. *TLS Client Certificate*

You can dismiss the *Certificate Templates Console* window (X in upper-right corner).

Prepare for Issuing TLS Client Certificates

In the Certification Authority app (certsrv), right-click *Certificate Templates*
and select *New/Certificate Template to issue.*

From the list of certificate templates, find *TLS Client Certificate*. See Figure 15-10.

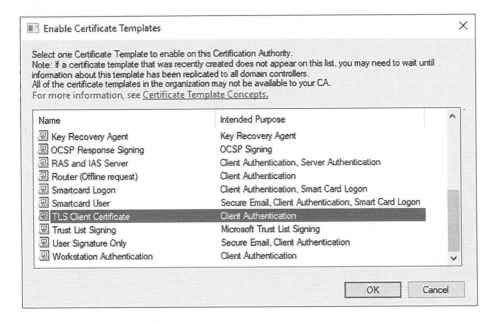

Figure 15-10. *List of certificate templates*

Select it by clicking it, and then click *OK*. This will enable your new template to be used for issuing certificates.

Now right-click *Certificate Templates* and select *Manage*.

Find *TLS Client Certificate* in the list of templates.

Right-click it and select *Properties*.

Select the *Security* tab. See Figure 15-11.

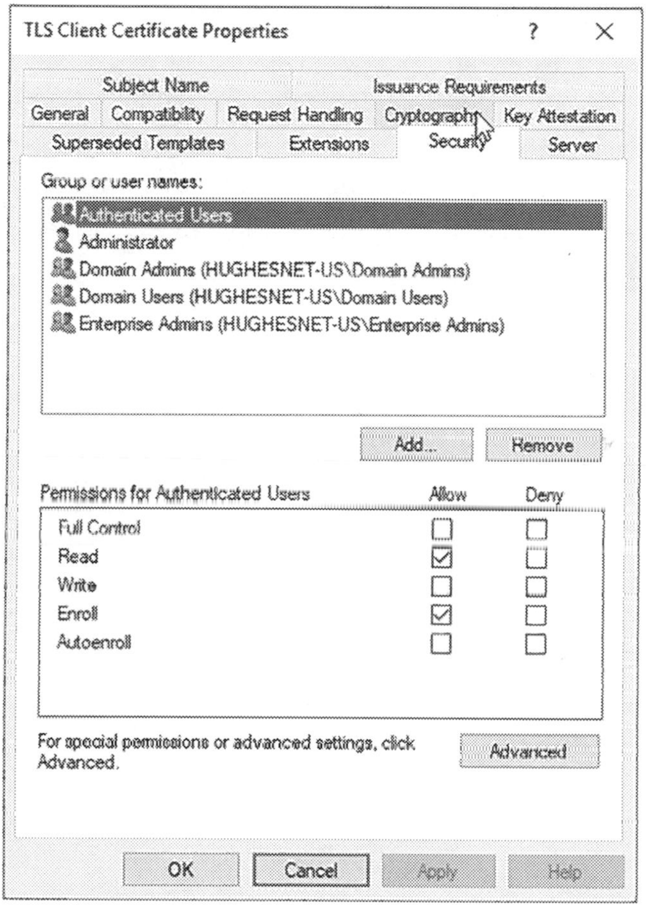

Figure 15-11. *Authenticated Users*

Select who you want to be able to enroll for *TLS Client Certificates* (e.g., *Authenticated Users*), and enable *Read* and *Enroll*.

Click *OK*.

Request and Obtain a TLS Client Certificate Using mmc.exe

The next step is to use mmc.exe (Microsoft Management Console) to request a *TLS Client Certificate* for Administrator (the currently logged in user). Be sure that you aren't using the one for local computer.

Start mmc.exe by selecting *Start/Run* and entering **mmc.exe**.

Click *File/Add/Remove Snap-in*.

Select *Certificates* and then click *Add*.

Select *My user account*.

Click *OK*.

Expand *Personal*. Expand *Certificates*. You should see the following (Figure 15-12).

Figure 15-12. *Expanded certificates list*

There may already be a certificate listed from previous labs.

Right-click the middle pane, and select *All Tasks/Request New Certificate*.

Ignore the *Before You Begin* page. Click *Next*.

You should now see the following (Figure 15-13).

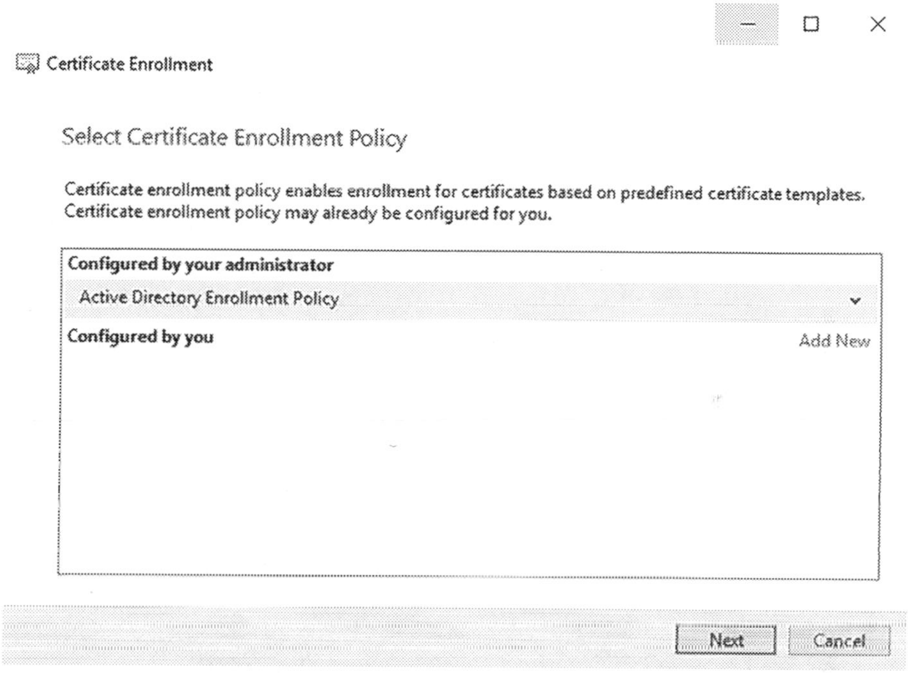

Figure 15-13. *Click Next*

You should now see the following (Figure 15-14).

Figure 15-14. *Select TLS Client Certificate. Click Enroll*

Note   If you want to make any changes to the request, click the *Details* link after TLS Client Certificate.

You should now see the following (Figure 15-15).

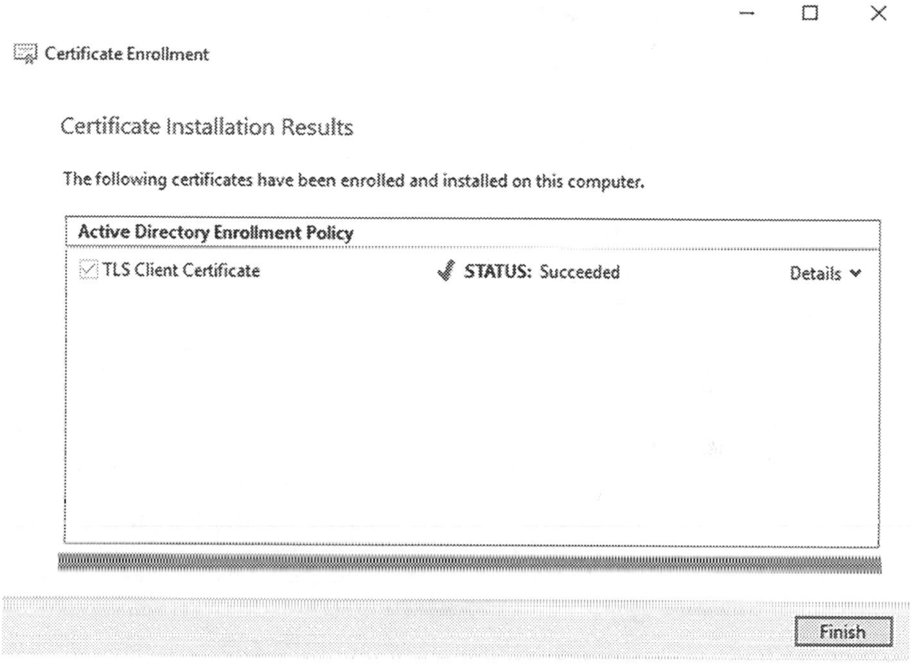

— □ ×

🖥 Certificate Enrollment

Certificate Installation Results

The following certificates have been enrolled and installed on this computer.

Active Directory Enrollment Policy		
☑ TLS Client Certificate	✔ STATUS: Succeeded	Details ⌄

Finish

Figure 15-15. *Certificate Installation Results*

Congratulations, you have just issued a TLS Client Cert for the current user (Administrator). Click *Finish*.

In mmc.exe, you should now see the new certificate (Figure 15-16).

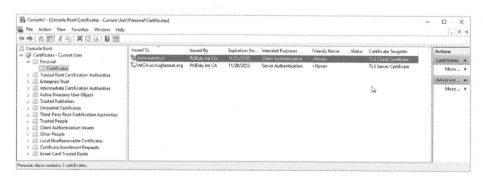

Figure 15-16. *New certificate list*

Double-click the new certificate to view its properties (Figure 15-17).

Figure 15-17. *General Certificate Information*

It was issued to Administrator.

It was issued (signed) by PKI Int CA.

The *ValidFrom* date is the day I did this.

The *ValidTo date* is one year from that.

You have a private key that corresponds to this certificate.

Now select the *Details* tab.

Under *Subject,* you should see

```
CN = Administrator
CN = Users
DC = us
DC = hughesnet
DC = org
```

Under *Issuer,* you should see

```
CN = PKIEdu Int CA
DC = us
DC = hughesnet
DC = org
```

Under *Enhanced Key Usage,* you should see

```
Client Authentication (1.3.6.1.5.5.7.3.2)
```

Under *CRL Distribution Point,* you should see

```
[1]CRL Distribution Point
    Distribution Point Name:
        Full Name:
                URL=ldap:///CN=PKIEdu Int CA,CN=IntCA,
                CN=CDP,CN=Public Key Services,CN=Services,
                CN=Configuration,DC=us,DC=hughesnet,
                DC=org?certificateRevocationList?base?
                objectClass=cRLDistributionPoint
                (ldap:///CN=PKIEdu%20Int%20CA,CN=IntCA,
                CN=CDP,CN=Public%20Key%20Services,
                CN=Services,CN=Configuration,DC=us,
                DC=hughesnet,DC=org?certificate
                RevocationList?base?objectClass=
                cRLDistributionPoint)
```

Under *Subject Alternative Name*, should you see Other Name:

Principal Name=Administrator@us.hughesnet.org

This is exactly what you need for a *TLS Client Certificate*.

Now select the *Certification Path* tab. You should see the following (Figure 15-18).

Figure 15-18. *Certification path*

Your new certificate chains up to the PKIEdu Int CA Intermediate Certificate.

That chains up to the PKI Root CA Root Certificate.

Congratulations! You have just issued a TLS Client Certificate for Administrator.

Test TLS Client Certificate for SCA with PKIEduRootCA

Testing a *TLS Client Certificate* is a bit more difficult than testing a *TLS Server Certificate*.

We will create a tiny PHP script that displays the SubjectDN (Subject Distinguished Name) from the selected *TLS Client Certificate*.

First, we need to install PHP using the Web Platform Installer.

This is found at `www.microsoft.com/web/downloads/platform.aspx`.

Once installed, run it, and choose the *Products* tab at the top. Search for "PHP." Find product PHP X.X.X (x64) (I found PHP 8.0.0), and click *Add*. Click *Install*. See Figure 15-19.

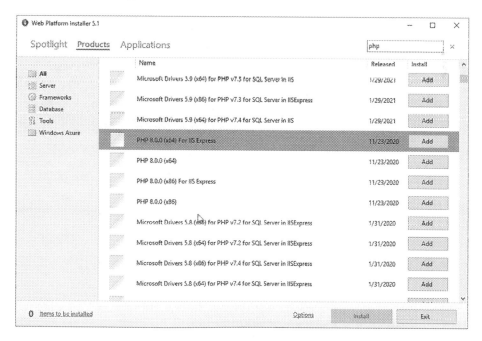

Figure 15-19. *Products tab*

When installation is complete, you should see the following (Figure 15-20).

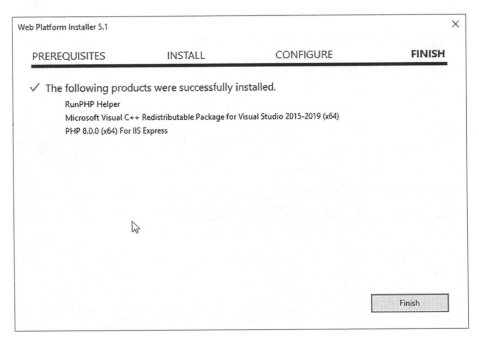

Figure 15-20. *Finish screen*

You also need to install ASP.Net and CGI.

Use *Server Manager/Add Roles and Features.* In *Server Roles*, under IIS, add ASP.NET 3.5 and CGI. See Figure 15-21.

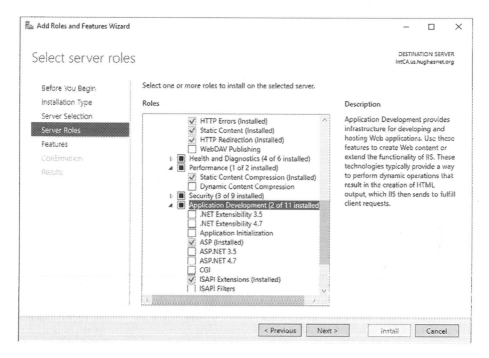

Figure 15-21. *Server Roles*

When you select ASP.NET 3.5, it will ask for additional features (see Figure 15-22).

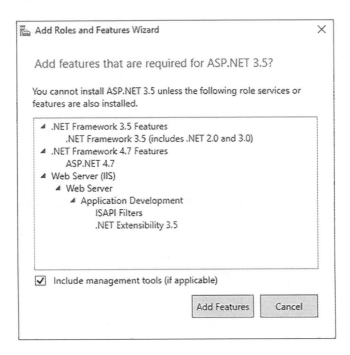

Figure 15-22. *Additional features*

Click *Add Features*. Complete the installation as usual. Restart your Subordinate CA server.

You can now run PHP scripts on your IIS Server.

Create the file login.php in directory C:\inetpub\wwwroot with the following contents:

```php
<?php
    echo 'Client Cert SubjectDN: ';
    echo $_SERVER['CERT_SUBJECT'];
    echo '<br>';
    echo 'Client Cert IssuerDN: ';
    echo $_SERVER['CERT_ISSUER'];
    echo '<br>';
?>
```

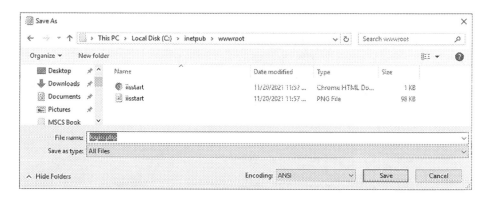

Figure 15-23. *Save as screen*

Be sure to use single quotes in the preceding script. If you use Notepad, be sure it doesn't append ".txt" to the file name.

Now we need to enable Strong Client Authentication (authentication using a client cert) in IIS

Start IIS Manager. Expand the server's name. Expand *Sites.* Click *Default Web Site.*

You should see the following (Figure 15-24).

Figure 15-24. *Default Web Site*

Double-click SSL Settings. Select *Require SSL*. Under *Client Certificates*, select *Accept*. It should look like this (Figure 15-25).

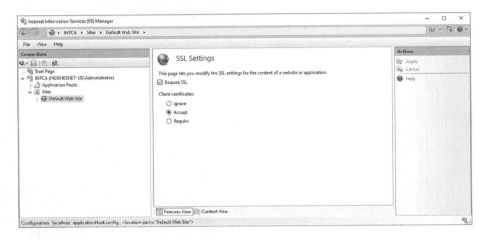

Figure 15-25. *SSL Settings*

This means the server will request a client certificate during the TLS handshake, but if one is not supplied, it will fall back to username/ password authentication. If you want to allow *only* SCA, select *Require*.

Click *Apply* in the top right.

Now under *Default Web Site*, double-click *Authentication*. See Figure 15-26.

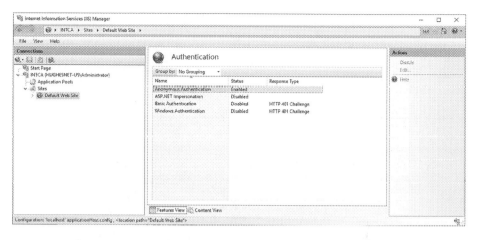

Figure 15-26. *Authentication screen*

Enable *Anonymous Authentication*. This will keep it from asking for a username/password login on the default website.

Now surf to `https://intca.us.hughesnet.org/login.php` (use your own node name).

It should ask you to select a TLS Client Certificate from your MS Certificate Store (Figure 15-27).

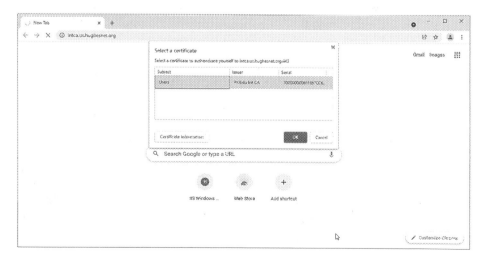

Figure 15-27. *Selecting a TLS Client Certificate*

View this certificate by clicking *Certificate Information*. The certificate listed is the one we just created. See Figure 15-28.

Figure 15-28. *Certificate Information*

To get it to accept the certificate, click *OK* in the *Select a certificate* dialog. You should see the following (Figure 15-29).

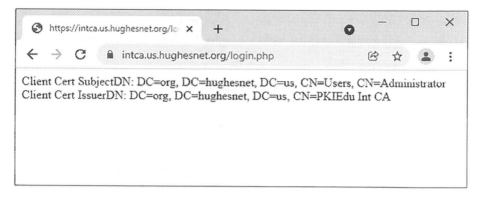

Figure 15-29. *Select a certificate dialog*

Your own PHP application can use this information to identify the user rather than ask them to provide a username and password.

If you don't select a certificate (click *Cancel* instead of *OK*), you will see the following (Figure 15-30).

Figure 15-30. *This indicates that no TLS Client Certificate was provided*

Note that in all browsers I have tried, once you select a *TLS Client Certificate*, the browser will latch onto that certificate until you kill all instances of that browser. This is very strange behavior, but none of the browser vendors are willing to change this or provide any other way to make the current instance of the browser turn loose of the *TLS Client*

Certificate. This makes it difficult to use *TLS Client Certificates* in web applications. It is much easier to use *TLS Client Certificates* and Strong Client Authentication if you create your own TLS-based client and server applications.

This is not an issue with TLS, SCA, or client certificates. It is a problem with *browsers*. You can use SCA with any protocol that supports TLS. The server has to enable SCA and be able to process the certificate supplied. The client needs to allow the user to select a client certificate in response to the request from the server.

TLS Strong Client Authentication allows *replacing* username/password authentication with far more secure cryptographic authentication. You should not do both Strong Client Authentication *and* username/password authentication (e.g., HTTP Basic Authentication). It's time to do away with passwords!

PeerTLS

I have been working with a version of TLS called *PeerTLS*. This is for end-to-end direct connections where both parties use a client cert (no TLS Server Cert is used). This provides true end-to-end encryption and mutual strong authentication. It works only with single links (no intermediary server). I have used this with chat, FTPS, and SMTP. The connection cannot cross a NAT gateway, so it works best over IPv6, where it works globally (no NAT, essentially unlimited global addresses). This is the logical conclusion of edge computing – true decentralization.

CHAPTER 16

Issue and Manage S/MIME Secure Email Certificates

S/MIME is an IETF open standard (currently specified in RFC 8551, "Secure/Multipurpose Internet Mail Extensions (S/MIME) Version 4.0 Message Specification," April 2019). It is based on S/MIME personal digital certificates created by a trusted Public Key Infrastructure (PKI). Each participant must obtain a unique S/MIME Certificate that identifies themselves. That cert must be trusted by all other parties that they will be communicating with. S/MIME allows adding a digital signature (for message integrity and detection of tampering) and/or a digital envelope (for privacy) to any Internet email message. These messages can be delivered in various ways, including over SMTP via existing email servers. The messages pass transparently through these servers. Secure messages are created on the sending node and opened on the receiving node. This provides true end-to-end privacy and sender-to-recipient authentication.

An *S/MIME Digital Certificate* is similar to a *TLS Client Certificate*. It is used for S/MIME secure email. There are two primary differences between a *TLS Client Certificate* and an *S/MIME Certificate*:

© Lawrence E. Hughes 2022
L. E. Hughes, *Pro Active Directory Certificate Services*,
https://doi.org/10.1007/978-1-4842-7486-6_16

- For a *TLS Client Certificate*, the X.509 *Enhanced Usage* field must have the *Client Authentication* flag set (as opposed to the *Server Authentication* flag in a TLS Server Certificate). In an S/MIME Certificate, the *Enhanced Usage* field must have the *Email Security* flag set.

- For an S/MIME Certificate, the X.509 *Subject Alternative Name* field must contain an RFC822 name which is the user's email address, for example, *RFC822Name = lhughes@hughesnet.org*. There is no need for any *Subject Alternative Name* field in a TLS Client Certificate, but the presence of one does not interfere with its use for TLS SCA.

It is possible to create a single certificate that will work for both TLS SCA and S/MIME by setting both *Enhanced Usage* flags and the *Subject Alternative Name*. I call that a "dual use" or "dual purpose" certificate.

Normally for S/MIME secure email, you would want for each user to obtain a "public hierarchy" S/MIME Certificate. A public hierarchy digital certificate is one that chains up to a Trusted Root Certificate that has been approved by WebTrust and is automatically installed in all leading operating systems. Such certificates are issued by a public Certification Authority, such as DigiCert, GlobalSign, Entrust, or Sectigo (formerly Comodo).

However, for use within a closed group (e.g., in-company secure email), you can use "private hierarchy" S/MIME Certificates (either issued by a public CA or an in-house CA, like *Microsoft Active Directory Certificate Services*). Private hierarchy digital certificates chain up to a Root Certificate that must somehow be installed in all relying nodes, since it is not installed automatically in all leading operating systems. Once that Root Cert is installed in a computer's Certificate Store, the private hierarchy certificate works just like a public hierarchy certificate on that computer. The Root

Certificate can be deployed in all nodes in an organization in various ways. With *Microsoft Active Directory Certificate Services*, the Root Certificate is deployed automatically to all nodes that are members of the Microsoft Domain involved.

Issuing S/MIME Digital Certificates with Microsoft AD CS

We will now configure *Microsoft Active Directory Certificate Services* to issue S/MIME Client Certificates that can be used to deploy S/MIME secure email. For S/MIME secure email, each user must obtain a unique S/MIME Certificate that identifies them. In an S/MIME Certificate, the *Subject Distinguished Name* field identifies a particular *person* in the world, as opposed to some *server* node name. An S/MIME Certificate can be used from any node – it is not tied to a node name as a server certificate is. Note that to use S/MIME secure email, each user must have access to their own private key on every node that they will be using to sign outgoing emails or receiving incoming encrypted emails. In addition, when *sending* an S/MIME encrypted email, the sender needs access to the current S/MIME Certificate for all recipients of that message. This can be accomplished via a shared address book (e.g., in *Active Directory*) that contains the S/MIME Certificate for all users. It helps if that shared address book is built automatically as S/MIME Certificates are issued by the CA.

Note that while only one TLS Server Certificate is needed regardless of how many people use that secure server, with S/MIME secure email, *every user* must be issued a unique S/MIME Certificate that identifies that user. There are several vendors that provide automated systems for providing large numbers of users with S/MIME Certificates, including building a shared address book in AD, and even optional private key escrow. Sixscape Communications provides such a system.

You can export your key material (S/MIME Certificate and private key) in PKCS #12 format and import it on another node (e.g., use your work key material from home or from any other computer). It is possible to import your key material into a hardware token (USB or smart card). If the key material is created *inside* the token from the start, there is no way to back up the key material (the private key can never be exported from the hardware token). You can move the token (containing the key material) to another computer, but it can only be used from one computer at a time. Alternatively, you can obtain the key material in PKCS #12 form, back it up, and then import the PKCS #12 file into a hardware token (or any number of hardware tokens). This allows you to restore your S/MIME Certificate and create a new hardware token from the PKCS #12 file in the event the original hardware token is lost.

If you are only going to use your key material for *digital signatures*, there is no need to back up your key material, so it is acceptable to create the key pair and certificate inside a hardware token (a new one with a different key pair can easily be created and used if the current key material is lost). If you are going to use your key material for *encryption*, then you should **back up the key material**. In that case, it is not recommended to create the key material and certificate directly inside a hardware token. If the private key is lost, all files encrypted by the corresponding digital certificate are unrecoverable.

We will create a new certificate template for S/MIME Certificates that has only the *Email Security* flag set and the user's RFC822 Name (email address) in the *Subject Alternative Name*.

Note with any client certificate type, you can include various fields in the *Subject Distinguished Name*, from the following choices.

CN	CommonName	User's full name (e.g., *Lawrence Hughes*)
E	EmailAddress	User's email address (e.g., *lhughes@ hughesnet.org*)
O	Organization	User's organization (e.g., *PKIEdu Inc.*)
OU	Organization unit	User's department (e.g., *IT*)
L	Locality	User's city (e.g., *Frisco*)
ST	State	User's state or province (e.g., *Texas*)
C	Country	User's country (e.g., US)

There are numerous other fields possible in a Subject Distinguished Name, but each item included must be validated by the Registration Authority before the certificate is issued by the Certification Authority. With public CAs, the more fields in your SubjectDN, the more the CA charges for the cert, because most of their cost is in verification of your identity. With AD CS, this verification is done by your PKI administrator.

The next step is to create a certificate template for issuing certificates for S/MIME secure email. This is like a TLS Client Certificate, with the following changes:

- **Enhanced Usage flags** – Instead of *Client Authentication* flag, set the *Email Security* flag.

- **Subject Alternative Name** – Must contain the user's email address as an *RFC822 Name*.

- **Subject Distinguished Name** – As with TLS Client Certificate, it specifies a person or device. This can have any of the fields listed earlier (CN, E, O, OU, L, ST, or C).

Create Template for S/MIME Certificate

On the VM running your subordinate CA (in my case, intca.us.hughes.org),
in *Server Manager*, click *Tools/Certification Authority*. This will start *certsrv*.

Expand *PKIEdu Int CA*. Expand *Certificate Templates*. You should see
the following (Figure 16-1).

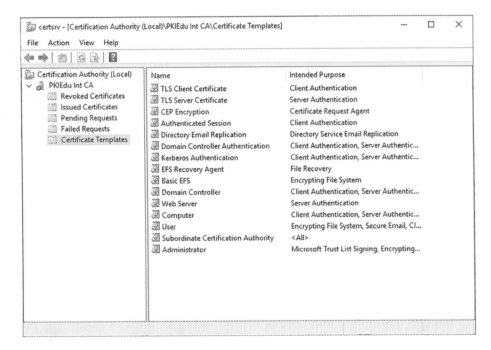

Figure 16-1. *Certificate Templates list*

Right-click *Certificate Templates* and choose *Manage*. You should see
the following (Figure 16-2)

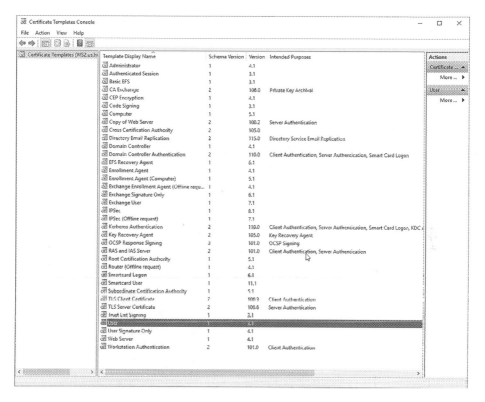

Figure 16-2. *Manage*

Right-click *User* and select *Duplicate Template*. You should see the following (Figure 16-3).

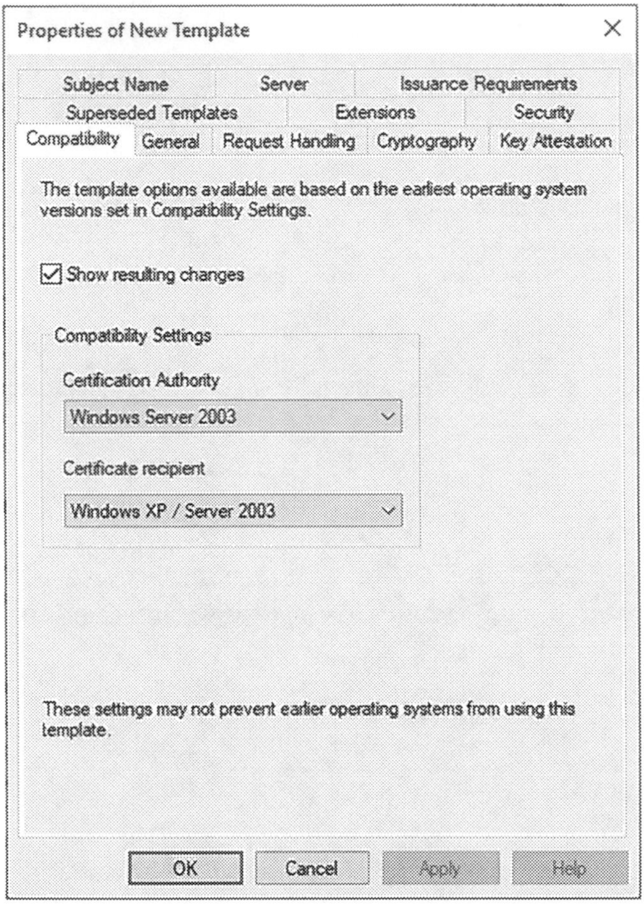

Figure 16-3. *Properties of New Templates*

Click the **General** tab.

Set the *Template display name to S/MIME Certificate*. This will change the *Template name to S/MIMECertificate*.

Set the Validity period to one year.

Select *Publish certificate in Active Directory*.

It should look like this (Figure 16-4).

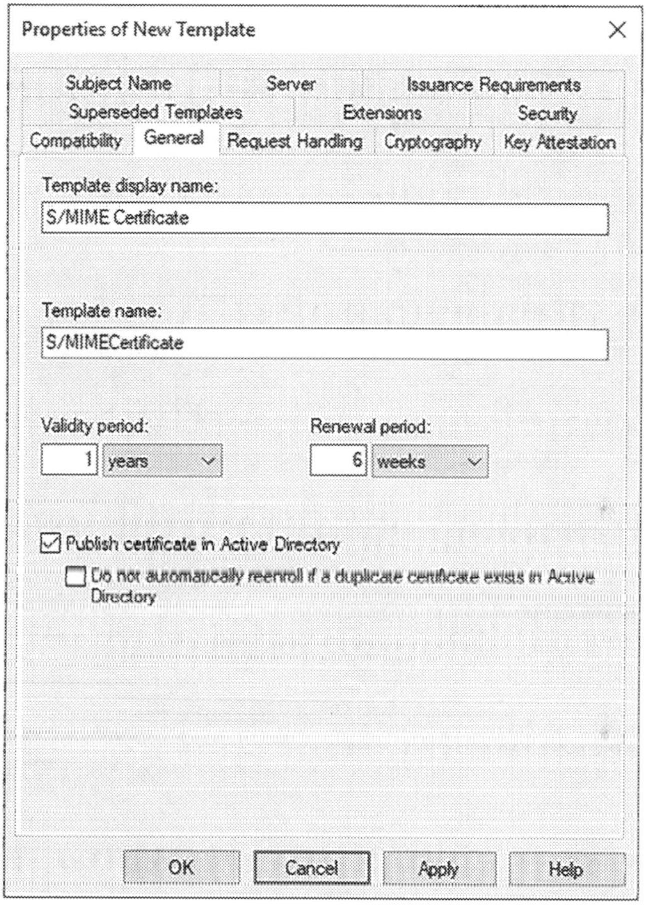

Figure 16-4. *Do not click OK yet*

Select the **Subject Name** tab.

Select *Build from this Active Directory information*.

Select *Subject name format* as **Fully distinguished name**.

Select *Include e-mail name in subject name*.

Under *Include this information in alternate subject name*, select *E-mail name and User principal name*.

It should look like this (Figure 16-5).

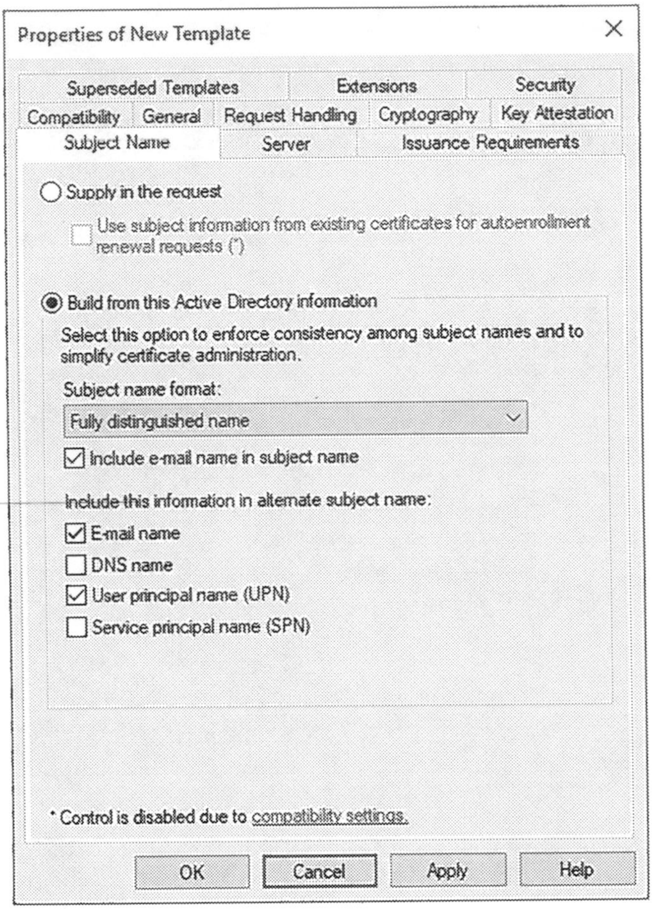

Figure 16-5. *Do not click OK yet*

Select the **Extensions** tab.

You will see that the *Application Policies* are currently set to **Encrypting File System**, **Secure Email**, and **Client Authentication**. See Figure 16-6.

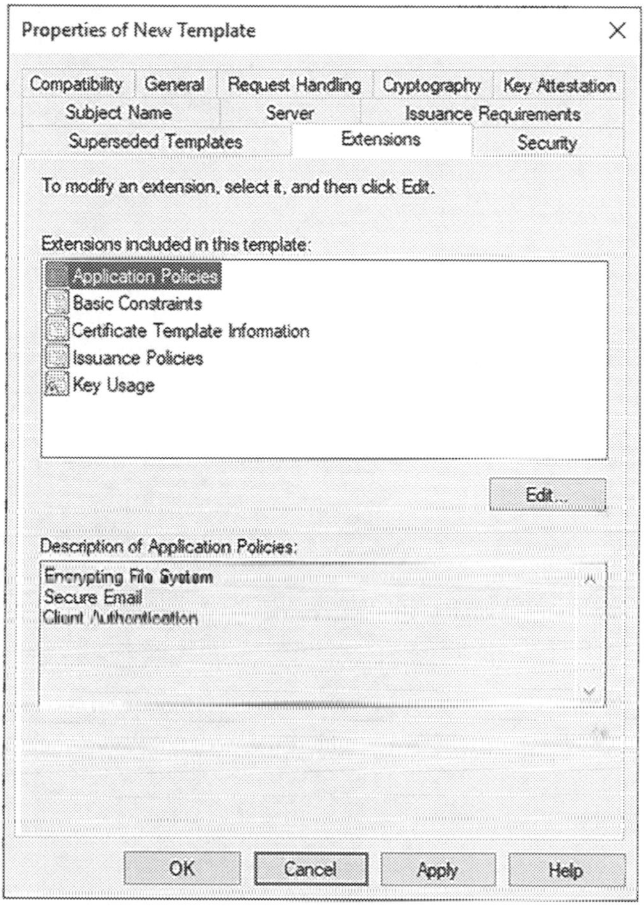

Figure 16-6. *Application Policies*

Only **Secure Email** is required. Click *Edit*.

You should now see the Extension policies. Highlight *Encrypting File System* and *Client Authentication* and click *Remove*. You should now see the following (Figure 16-7).

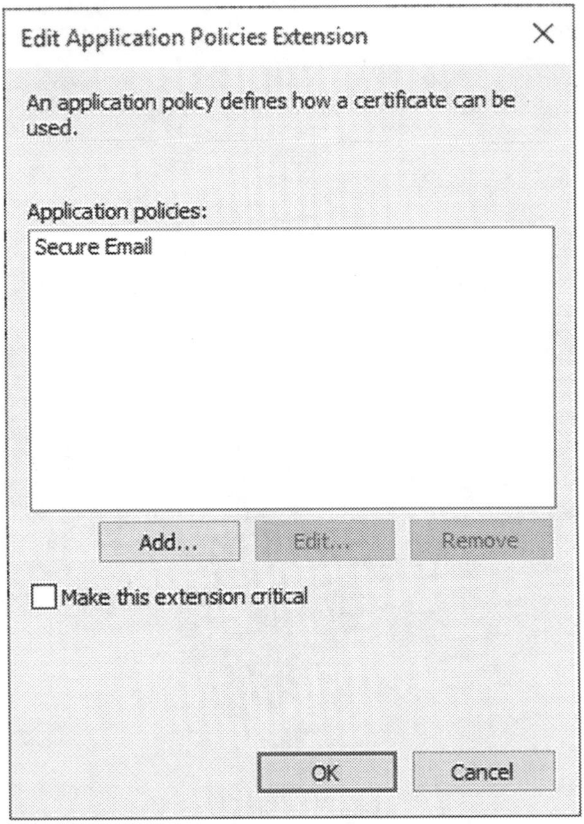

Figure 16-7. *Click OK*

You should now see the final New Template Properties. See
Figure 16-8.

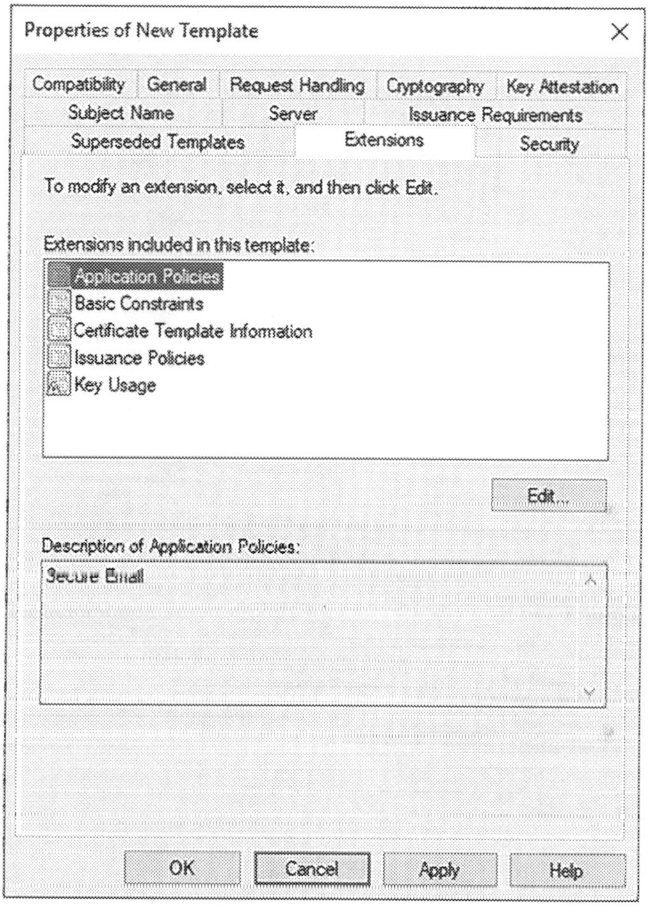

Figure 16-8. *Now you can click OK*

There is now a new template called *S/MIME Certificate,* as shown in Figure 16-9.

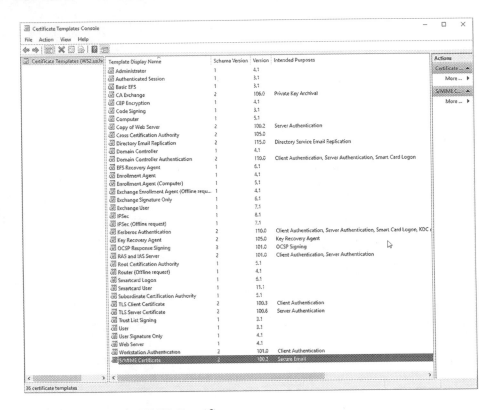

Figure 16-9. *S/MIME Certificate*

You can now dismiss the *Certificate Templates Console* (X in upper-right corner).

Prepare for Issuing S/MIME Certificates

In the Certification Authority app, right-click *Certificate Templates* and select *New/Certificate Template to issue.* From the list of certificate templates, find *S/MIME Certificate.* See Figure 16-10.

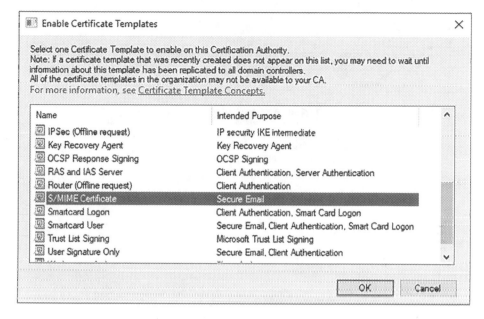

Figure 16-10. *Certification Authority app*

Select *S/MIME Certificate* by clicking it, and then click *OK*. This will enable your new S/MIME Certificate Template to issue certificates.

Now right-click *Certificate Templates* and select *Manage*.

Find *S/MIME Certificate* in the list of templates. Right-click it and select *Properties*.

Select the *Security* tab.

You should see the following (Figure 16-11).

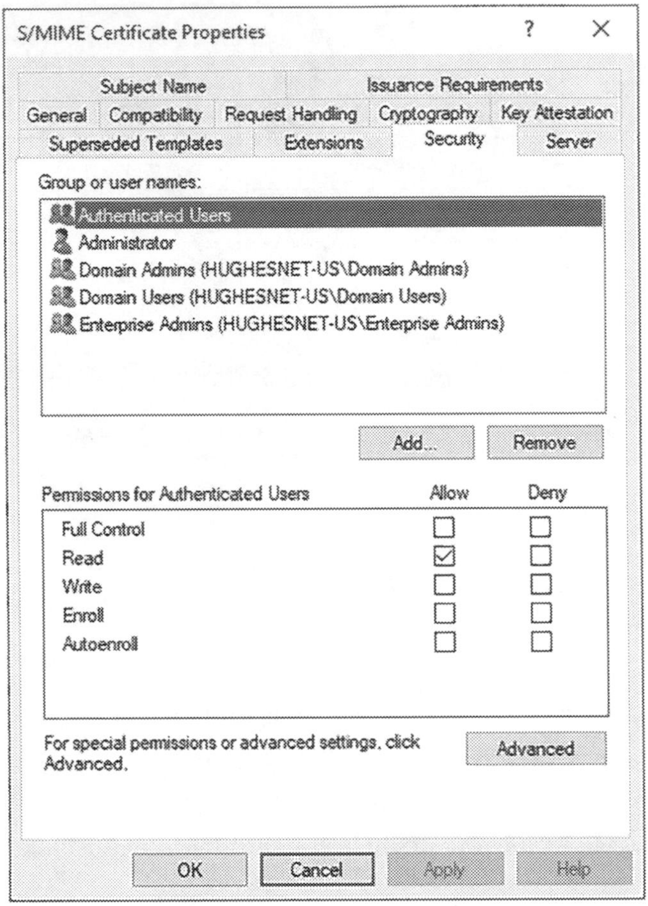

Figure 16-11. *S/MIME Certificate Properties*

Select who you want to be able to enroll S/MIME Certificates (e.g., *Authenticated Users*), and select *Read* and *Enroll*. Click *Apply*.

It will now look like this (Figure 16-12).

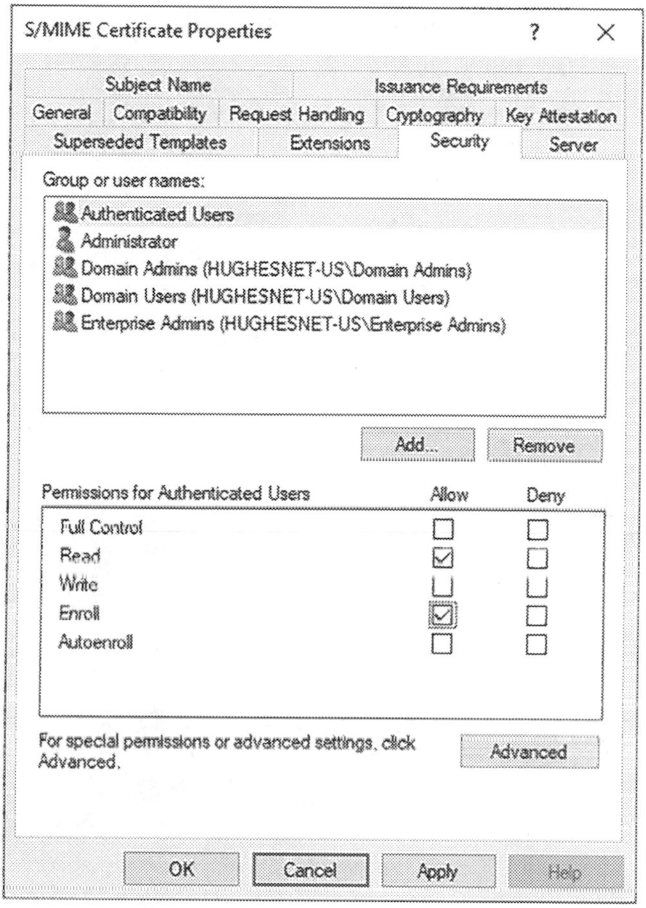

Figure 16-12. *Choose "Read" and "Enroll"*

Click *OK*.

Request and Obtain an S/MIME Certificate Using mmc.exe

The next step is to use mmc.exe to request an *S/MIME Certificate* for Administrator (the currently logged in user).

Start mmc.exe by selecting *Start/Run* and entering **mmc.exe**.

Click *File/Add/Remove Snap-in*. Select *Certificates* and then click *Add*. Select *My user account*. Click *Finish*. It should now look like the following (Figure 16-13).

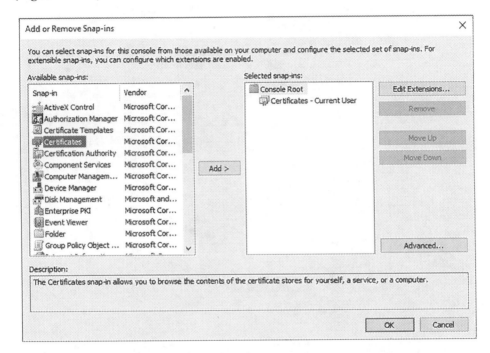

Figure 16-13. *Add or Remove Snap-ins*

Click *OK*. *Certificates*. Expand *Personal*. Expand *Certificates*. You should see the following (Figure 16-14).

Figure 16-14. *Expand Certificates*

Before requesting an S/MIME Cert for Administrator, make sure there is an email account for that user (e.g., administrator@hughesnet.org). I host the email for hughesnet.org at Rackspace, so I just added a new user there. Alternatively, you could create an S/MIME Cert for any existing email account.

Right-click the middle pane, and select *All Tasks/Request New Certificate.*

Ignore the *Before You Begin* page. Click *Next.* You should now see the following (Figure 16-15).

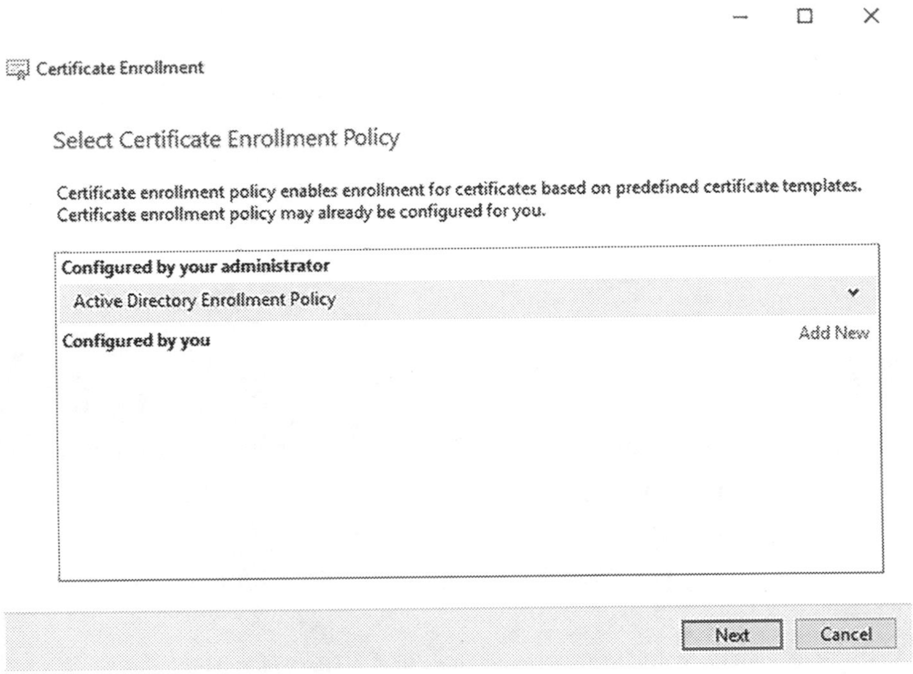

—   □   ×

🖳 Certificate Enrollment

Select Certificate Enrollment Policy

Certificate enrollment policy enables enrollment for certificates based on predefined certificate templates.
Certificate enrollment policy may already be configured for you.

Configured by your administrator	
Active Directory Enrollment Policy	⌄
Configured by you	Add New

Next   Cancel

Figure 16-15. *Click Next*

You should now see the following (Figure 16-16).

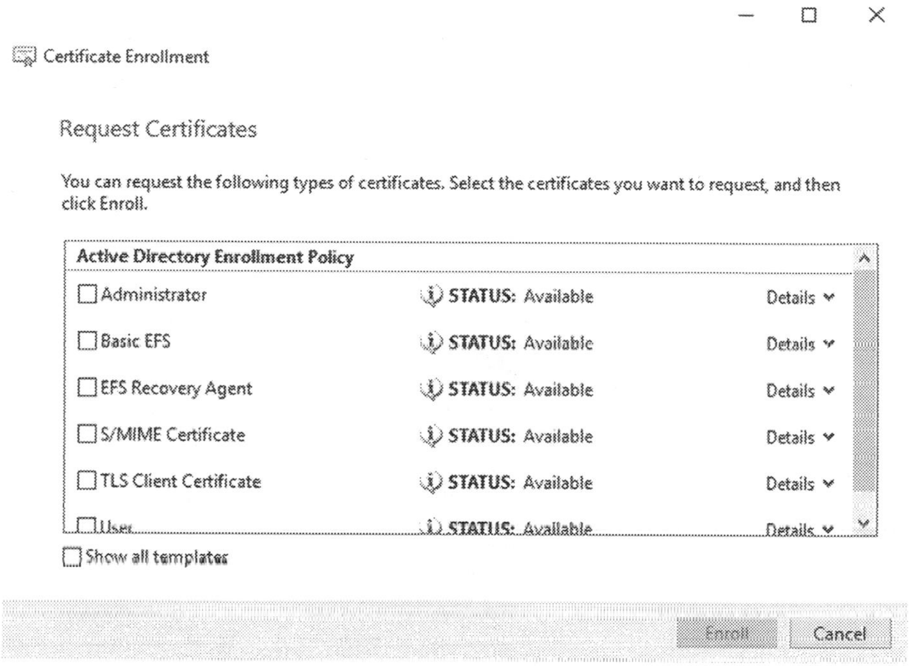

Figure 16-16. *Request Certificates*

Select *S/MIME Certificate*. Expand Details. See Figure 16-17.

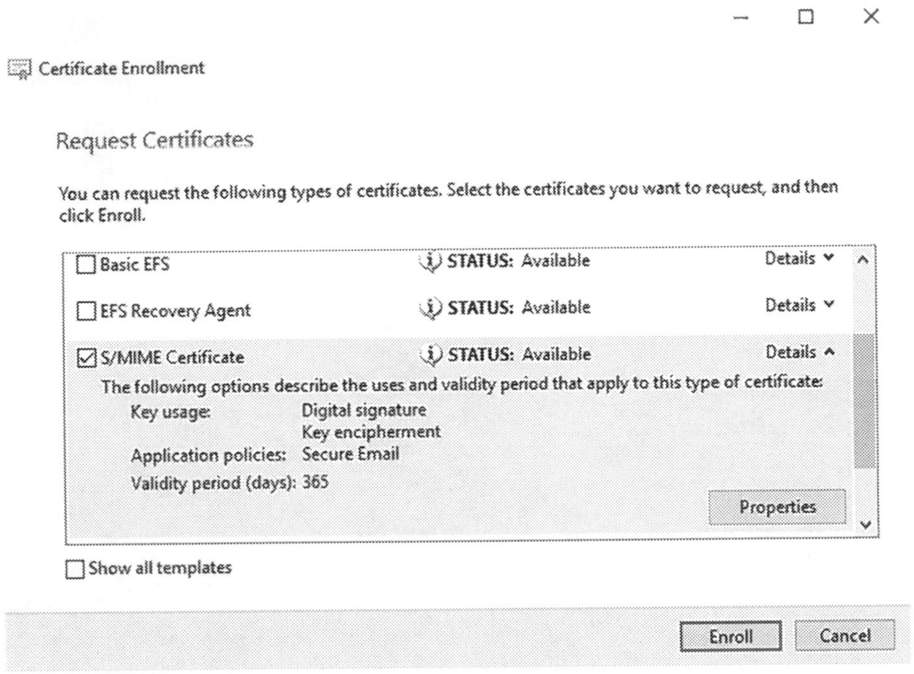

Figure 16-17. *Expand details*

Click *Properties.* Select the *Private Key* tab. Make sure the private key is exportable (Figure 16-18).

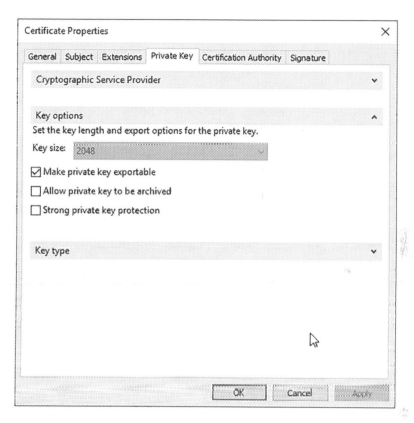

Figure 16-18. *Click OK*

Click *Enroll.*

You should now see the following (Figure 16-19).

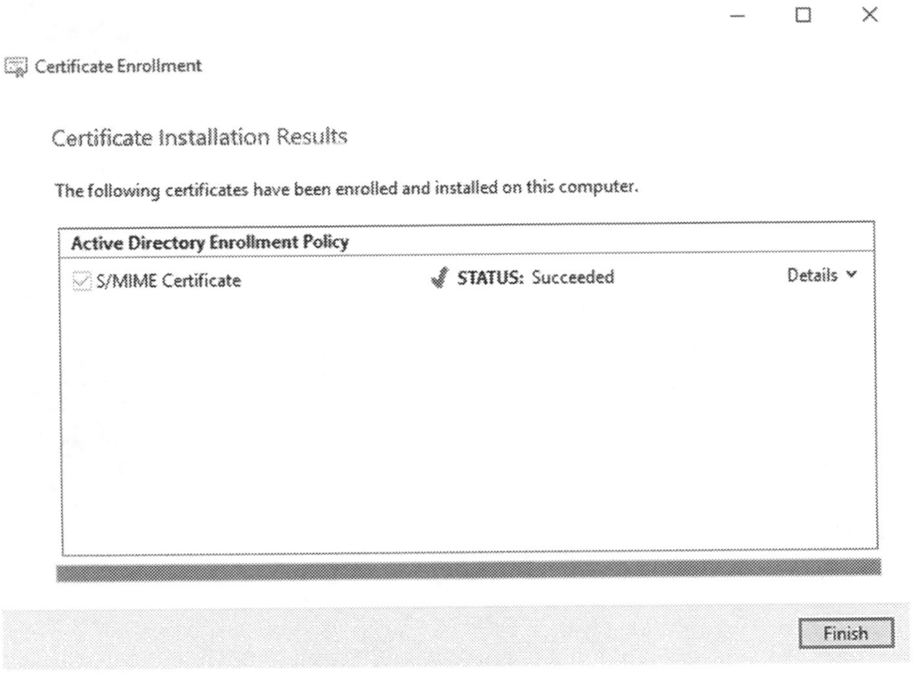

—   □   ×

🖳 Certificate Enrollment

Certificate Installation Results

The following certificates have been enrolled and installed on this computer.

Active Directory Enrollment Policy		
☑ S/MIME Certificate	✔ STATUS: Succeeded	Details ∨

Finish

Figure 16-19. *Certificate Installation Results*

Congratulations, you have just issued an S/MIME Certificate for the current user (Administrator). Click *Finish*.

In mmc.exe, you should now see the new certificate (Figure 16-20).

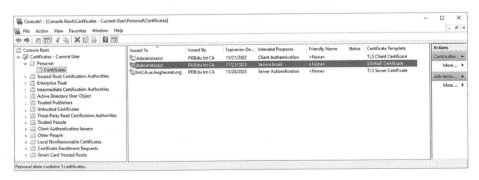

Figure 16-20. *New certificate*

Note that one of them is for Secure Email. Double-click that one to view its properties (Figure 16-21).

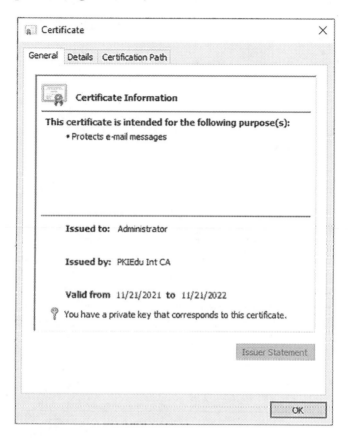

Figure 16-21. *Certificate Information*

It was issued to *Administrator*.

It was issued (signed) by *PKIEdu Int CA*.

The *ValidFrom* date is the date of issue (when I issued this cert).

The *ValidTo date* is one year from then.

You have a private key that corresponds to this certificate.

Now select the *Details* tab.

Under *Subject*, you should see

```
E = administrator@hughesnet.org
CN = Administrator
CN = Users
DC = us
DC = hughesnet
DC = org
```

Under *Issuer*, you should see

```
CN = PKIEdu Int CA
DC = us
DC = hughesnet
DC = org
```

Under *Enhanced Key Usage*, you should see

```
Secure Email (1.3.6.1.5.5.7.3.4)
```

Under *CRL Distribution Point*, you should see an LDAP URL pointing to your AD server.

Under *Subject Alternative Name*, should you see

```
Other Name:
      Principal Name=Administrator@us.hughesnet.org
RFC822 Name=administrator@hughesnet.org
```

This is exactly what you need for an S/MIME Certificate.

Now select the *Certification Path* tab. You should see the following (Figure 16-22).

Figure 16-22. *Certificate Path tab*

The new certificate chains up to the PKI Int CA Intermediate Cert. The PKI Int CA Intermediate Cert chains up to the PKIEdu Root CA Root Cert, which is trusted. This is a three-level hierarchy.

Congratulations! You have just issued an S/MIME Certificate for Administrator.

Test Your New S/MIME Certificate

To test this, you must have Outlook installed on any node in your domain, with an account for administrator@hughesnet.org (or whatever your domain is). In my case, this account is hosted at Rackspace, as an IMAP account. Verify you can send an email to yourself.

If you are not doing this on your Subordinate CA server, you can export the cert and copy it to the node where you have Outlook installed. Alternatively, you can request another S/MIME Cert on the node where Outlook is installed. One way or another, the S/MIME Cert must be on the node where you are running Outlook.

Now configure that account to use S/MIME. This is a bit complicated.

In Outlook, select the *File* menu. You will see something like this (Figure 16-23).

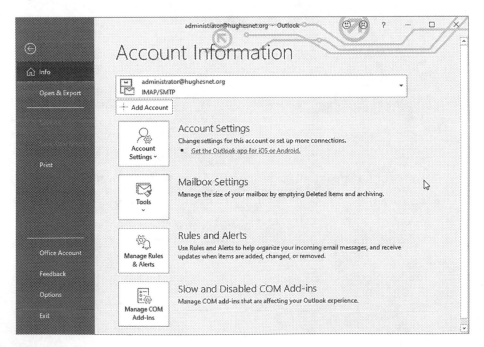

Figure 16-23. *Outlook "File" menu*

Click *Options* at lower left. You will see the following (Figure 16-24).

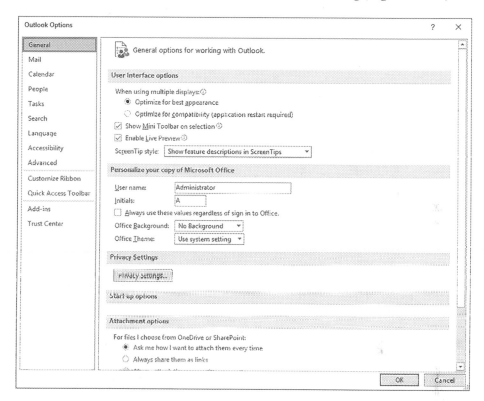

Figure 16-24. *Options*

Click *Trust Center* at lower left. In the right pane, click *Trust Center Settings*.

You will now see the following (Figure 16-25).

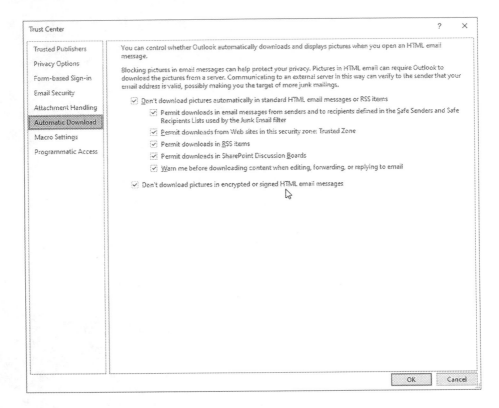

Figure 16-25. *Trust Center options*

In the left pane, click *Email Security*.

You will now see the following (Figure 16-26).

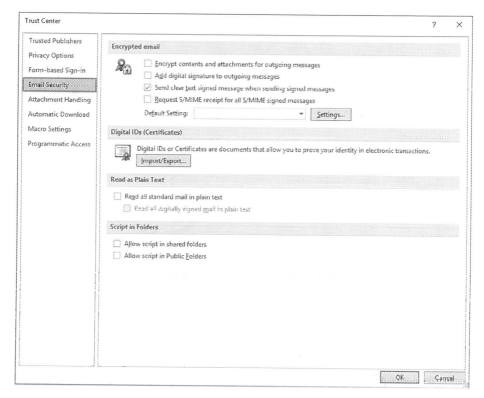

Figure 16-26. *Email Security*

Under *Encrypted email,* click the *Settings* button.

You will now see something like this (Figure 16-27).

Figure 16-27. *Encrypted email settings*

Change the *hash algorithm* to SHA256 (SHA1 was deprecated some time ago). Your S/MIME Cert for Administrator was selected (being the only one found).

Click *OK*. Dismiss the *Trust Center* dialog with *OK*. Dismiss the *Outlook Options* dialog with *OK*. See Figure 16-28.

Create a Digitally Signed Email

Create a new email (top left corner) to administrator@hughesnet.org (to your account).

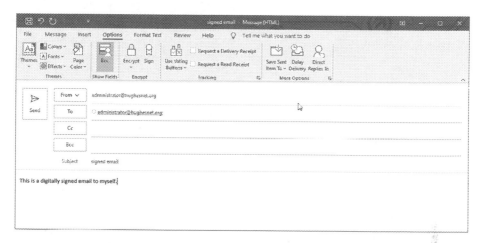

Figure 16-28. *Create a new email*

In the top menu, select *Options*. See Figure 16-29.

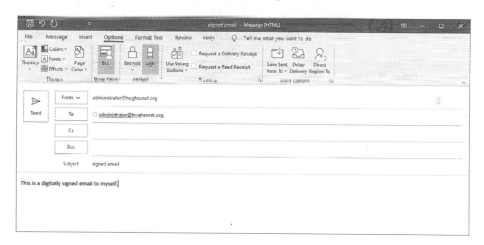

Figure 16-29. *Options*

Click the *Sign* option and send the message.

In a few seconds, the signed message will appear in your Inbox. See Figure 16-30.

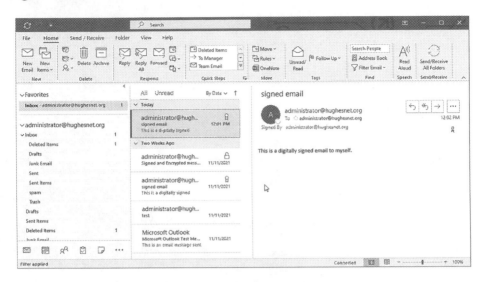

Figure 16-30. *Signed message*

Notice the red ribbon icon in the reading pane. Click it to see details (Figure 16-31).

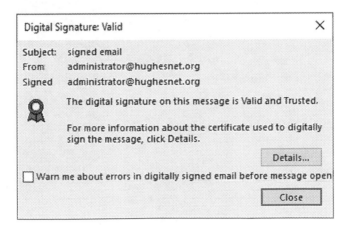

Figure 16-31. *Digital signature*

The signature is valid. The message is from administrator@hughesnet.org and was signed by administrator@hughesnet.org.

Click *Details*. See Figure 16-32.

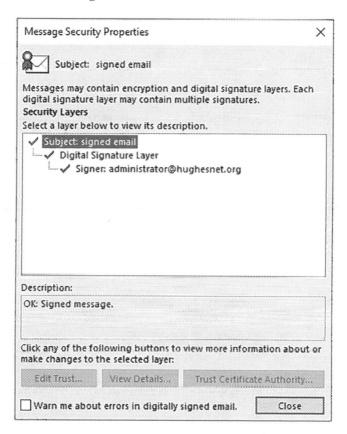

Figure 16-32. *Message Security Properties*

Click the *Signer* line (Figure 16-33).

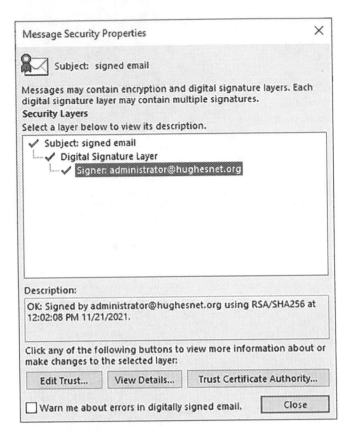

Figure 16-33. *Click "Signer" line*

This message was signed by administrator@hughesnet.org on 11/21/2021.

Click *View Details*. See Figure 16-34.

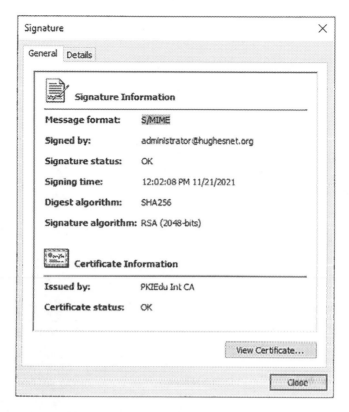

Figure 16-34. *Signature Information*

Click *View Certificate*. See Figure 16-35.

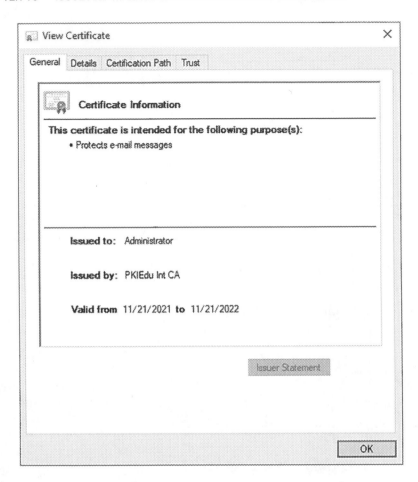

Figure 16-35. *This is the S/MIME Cert we just created*

Send a Digitally Enveloped Message

To do this, we need to capture our digital cert in a contact. In the reading pane, right-click the recipient, and select *Add to Outlook Contacts*. You will see the following (Figure 16-36).

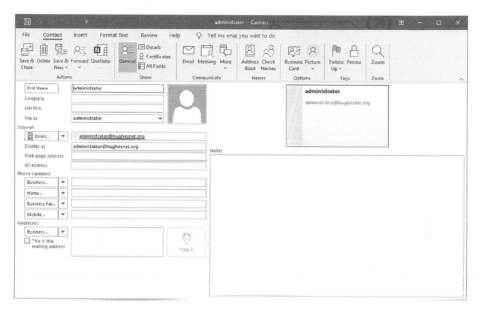

Figure 16-36. *Add to Outlook Contacts*

Click *Show/Certificates* (Figure 16-37).

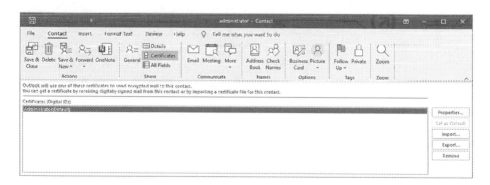

Figure 16-37. *Show/Certificates*

You can see that it captured the certificate from the signed message in our Outlook contacts.

Click *Save and Close.*

Now create another new email (Figure 16-38).

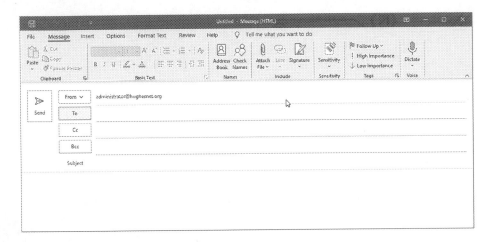

Figure 16-38. *Create new email*

Click the *To* button. See Figure 16-39.

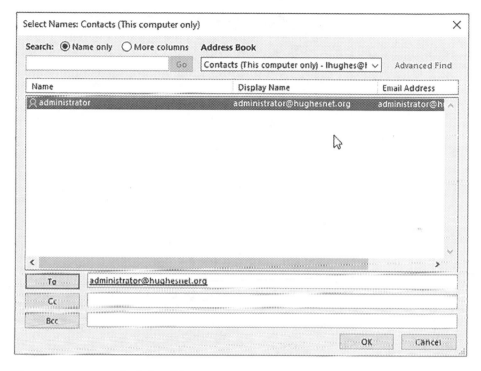

Figure 16-39. *Click "To" button*

The administrator contact we created is now there. Click the *To* button at the bottom to use it as the recipient.

Click *OK*.

Add a subject line and message (Figure 16-40).

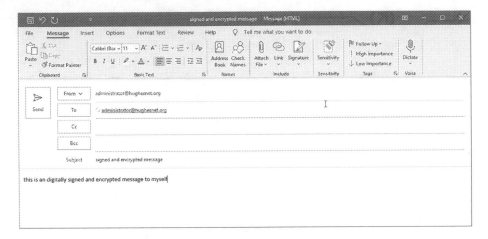

Figure 16-40. *Add subject line and message*

Click the *Options* item in the top menu. Select both *Encrypt* and *Sign*.
See Figure 16-41.

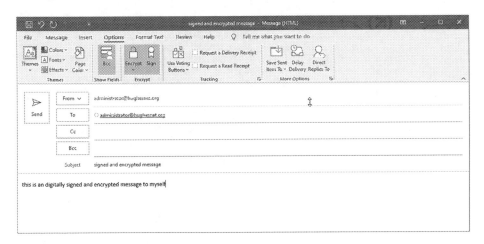

Figure 16-41. *Select "Encrypt" and "Sign"*

Send the message. If the send fails, it didn't find the recipient's
certificate.

Assuming everything went well, the new message will appear in your
Inbox (Figure 16-42).

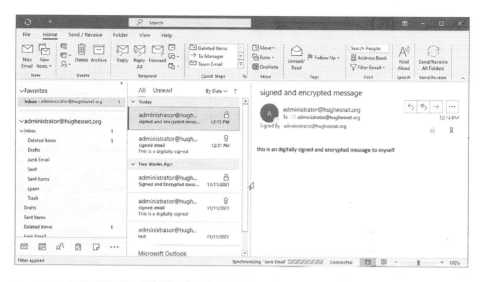

Figure 16-42. *Message shown in Inbox*

Note the new message in the reading pane has both the padlock (encrypted) and seal (signed).

Click the padlock icon (Figure 16-43).

Figure 16-43. *Padlock icon*

There are now both *Encryption* and *Signature* layers.

Click *Details*. See Figure 16-44.

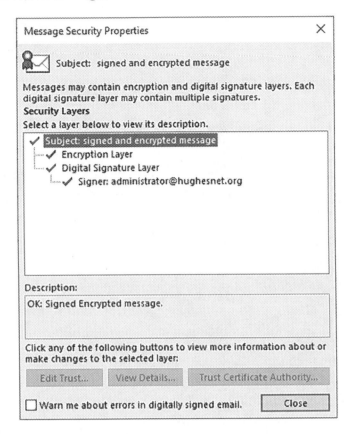

Figure 16-44. *Details*

Click the *Encryption Layer*. See Figure 16-45.

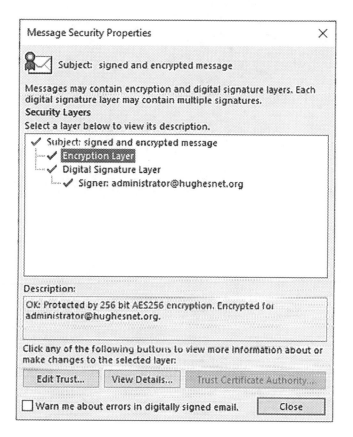

Figure 16-45. *Encryption Layer*

The message was encrypted using AES256, for administrator@ hughesnet.org.

Now click the *Signer* line (Figure 16-46).

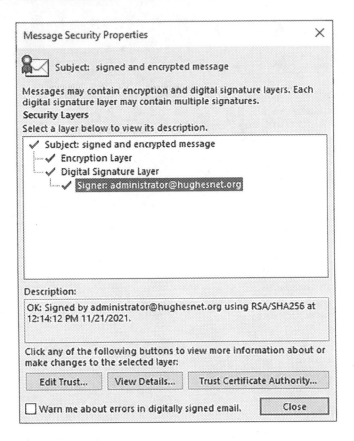

Figure 16-46. *Signer line*

The message was signed by the sender, using RSA/SHA256.

You can see the signer's certificate via *View Details* as before.

As you can see, we have created a valid S/MIME Certificate using *Active Directory Certificate* Services and sent both signed and encrypted emails using it.

CHAPTER 17

Issue and Manage Windows Logon Certificates

Most people who use Windows (even in corporate networks) authenticate with username/password. To be specific, here, the username is actually the *User Principal Name* (UPN), which can be entered as *HUGHESNET-US\lhughes* or *lhughes@us.hughesnet.org* in my network. The password is the one in the user's Active Directory account (when using domain login).

It is possible to create *Windows Logon Smart cards*, which is just a PKI smart card that contains a certificate with the SubjectDN containing the user's *User Principal Name* and the corresponding private key. The Windows computer has to be configured for *Smart card Login*. When the user wants to log in, they select *Smart card* and insert their smart card into a smart card reader on their computer.

A *Windows Logon digital certificate* is similar to a *TLS Client Certificate*. It is used for Windows Smart card Login. There are two primary differences between a *TLS Client Certificate* and a *Windows Logon Certificate*:

- For a *TLS Client Certificate*, the X.509 *Enhanced Usage* field must have the *Client Authentication* flag set (as opposed to the *Server Authentication* flag in a TLS

© Lawrence E. Hughes 2022
L. E. Hughes, *Pro Active Directory Certificate Services*,
https://doi.org/10.1007/978-1-4842-7486-6_17

Server Certificate). In a *Windows Logon* Certificate, the *Enhanced Usage* field must also have the *Client Authentication* flag set.

- For a Windows Logon Certificate, the X.509 *Subject Alternative Name* field must contain the user's UPN. There is no need for any *Subject Alternative Name* field in a *TLS Client Certificate*, but the presence of one does not interfere with its use for TLS client authentication.

There is no advantage of public hierarchy in a Windows Logon Certificate; private hierarchy is all that is needed. This is an ideal use for *Active Directory Certificate Services*.

Configure Active Directory Certificate Services to Issue Windows Logon Certificates

We will now configure *Microsoft Certificate Services* to issue *Windows Logon* Certificates that can be used for Windows Smart card Login. Each user must obtain a unique *Windows Logon* Certificate that identifies them with their UPN. In a *Windows Logon* Certificate, the *Subject Distinguished Name* field identifies a particular *user* in Active Directory. A *Windows Logon* Certificate can be used from any Windows workstation – it is not tied to particular node.

You can export your key material (*Windows Logon* Certificate and private key) in PKCS12 format and import it into one or more smart cards. If the key material is created *inside* the token from the start, there is no way to back up the key material (the private key can never be exported from the hardware token).

We will create a new certificate template for *Windows Logon* Certificates that has only the *Client Authentication* flag set and the user's UPN in the *Subject Alternative Name.*

Create Template for Windows Logon Certificate

On the VM running your Subordinate CA (in my case, intca.us.hughesnet.org), in *Server Manager*, click *Tools/Certification Authority.*

Expand *PKIEdu Int CA.* Click *Certificate Templates.* You should see the following (Figure 17-1).

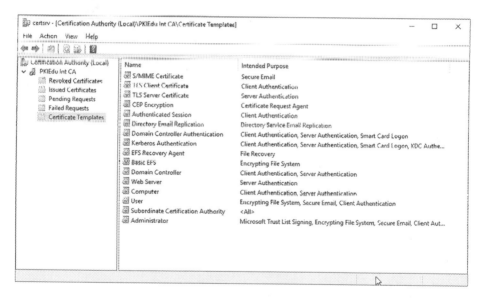

Figure 17-1. *Certificate Templates*

Right-click *Certificate Templates* and choose *Manage.* You should see the following (Figure 17-2).

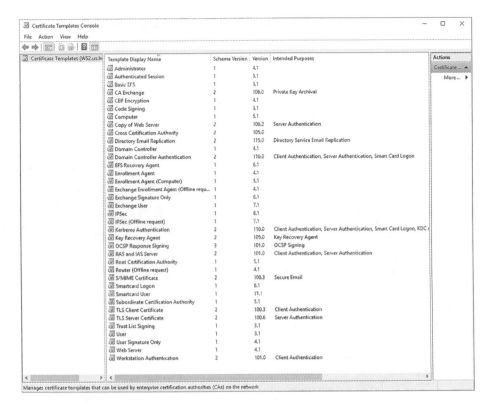

Figure 17-2. *Manage*

Right-click *Smart card Logon* and select *Duplicate Template*. You should see the following (Figure 17-3).

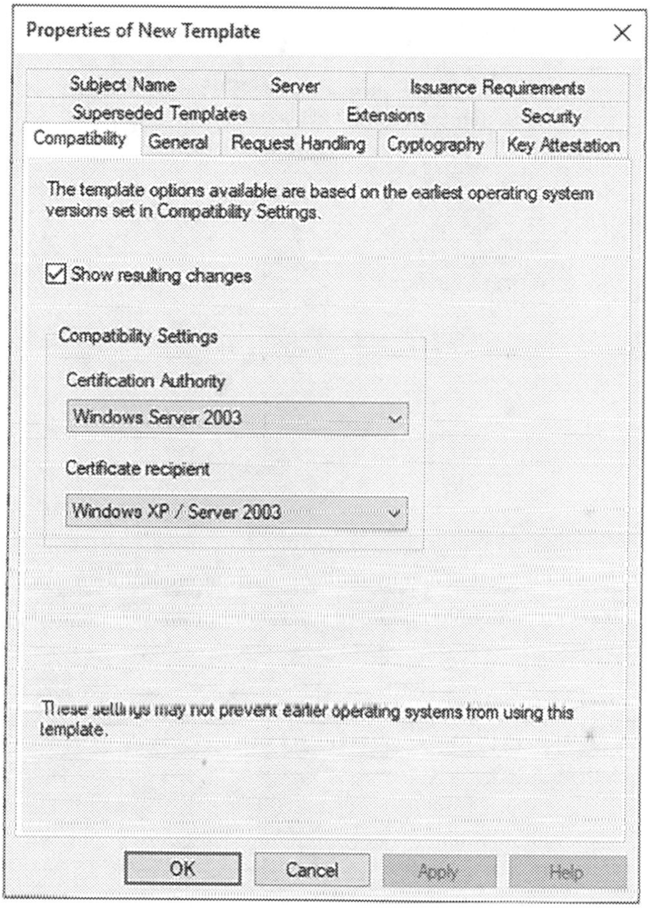

Figure 17-3. *Properties of New Template*

Click the **General** tab.

Set the *Template display name* to *Windows Logon*. This will change the *Template name* to *WindowsLogon*.

Set the Validity period to one year.

Select *Publish certificate in Active Directory*.

It should look like this (Figure 17-4).

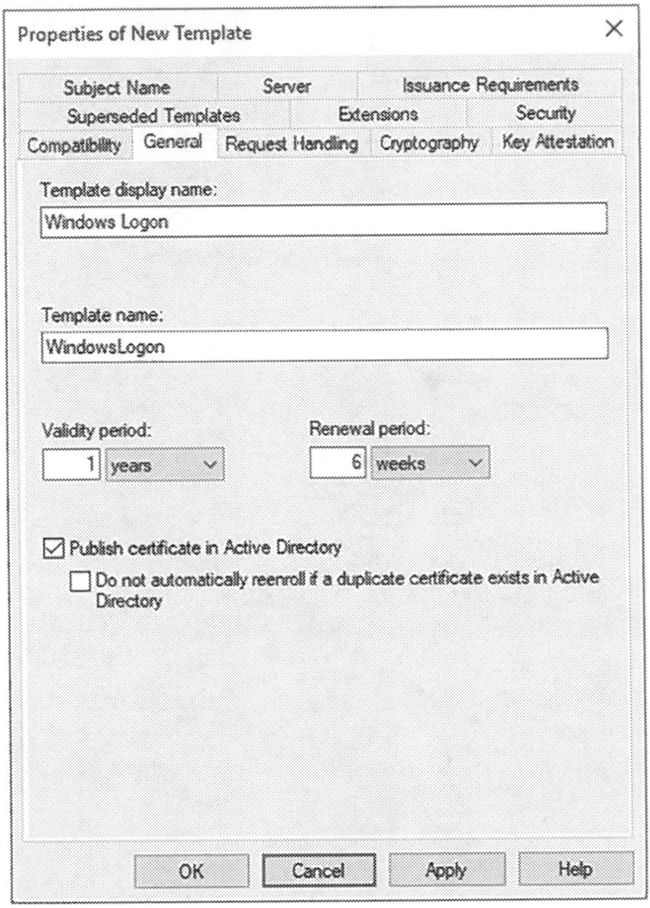

Figure 17-4. *"General" tab*

Do not click *OK* yet.

Select the **Subject Name** tab.

Select *Build from this Active Directory information.*

Select *Subject name format* as **Fully distinguished name**.

Under *Include this information in alternate subject name,* select *User principal name (UPN).*

It should look like this (Figure 17-5).

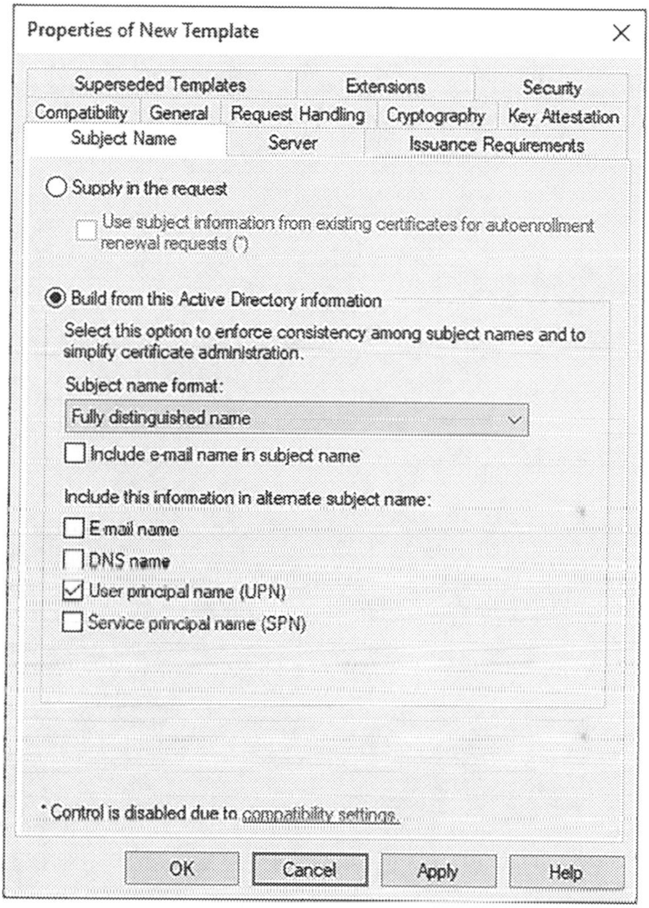

Figure 17-5. *Do not click OK yet*

Select the ***Extensions*** tab.

You will see that the *Application Policies* are currently set to **Client
Authentication** and **Smart card Login**.

Those are correct for Windows Logon Certificates. See Figure 17-6.

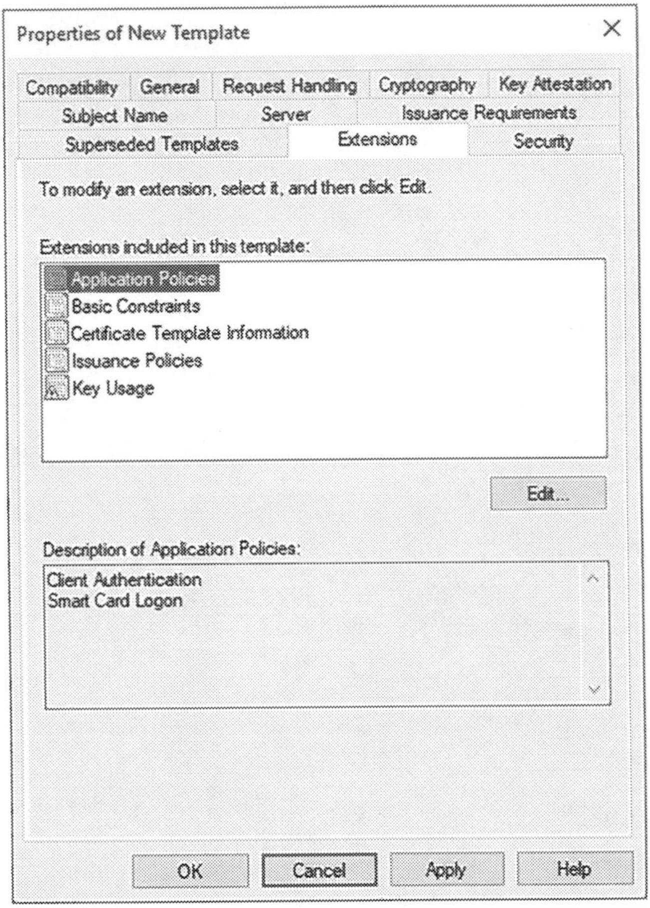

Figure 17-6. *Now you can click OK*

There is now a new template called *Windows Logon*. See Figure 17-7.

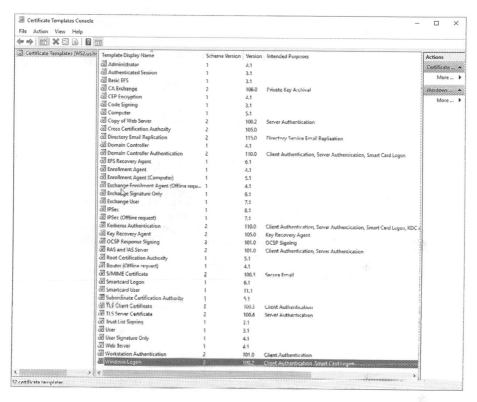

Figure 17-7. *Windows Logon Template*

Prepare for Issuing Windows Logon Certificates

In the Certification Authority app, right-click *Certificate Templates* and
select *New/Certificate Template to issue.* From the list of certificate
templates, find *Windows Logon.* See Figure 17-8.

413

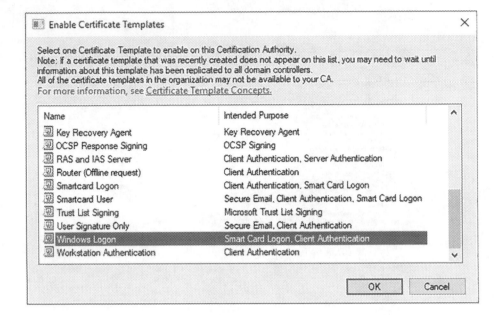

Figure 17-8. *Windows Logon*

Select it by clicking it, and then click *OK*. This will enable your new certificate template to be used for issuing new certificates.

Now right-click *Certificate Templates* and select *Manage*.

Find *Windows Login* in the list of templates. Right-click it and select *Properties*.

Select the *Security* tab (Figure 17-9).

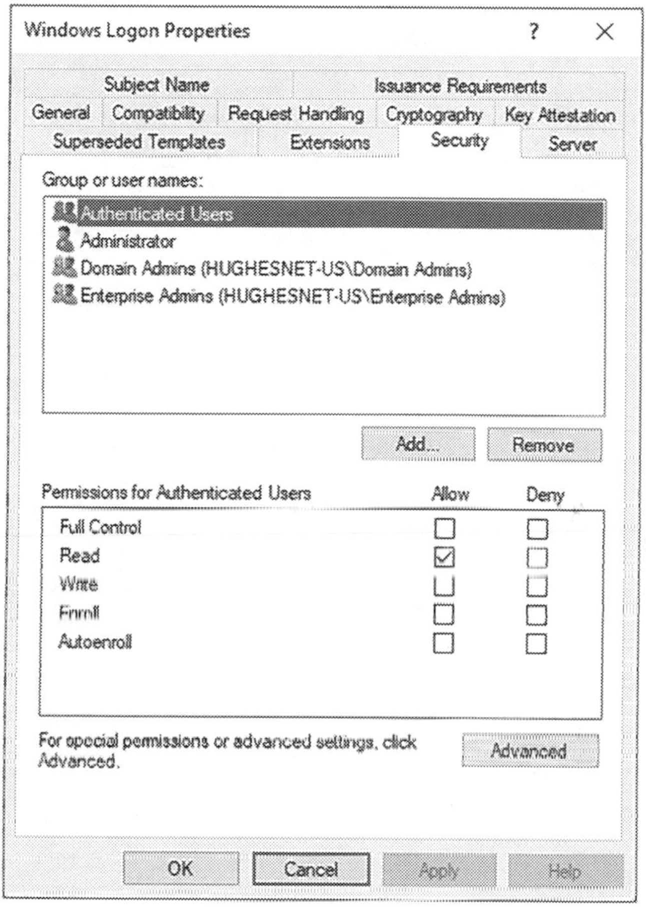

Figure 17-9. *Windows Logon Properties*

Select who you want to be able to enroll Windows Logon Certificates (e.g., *Authenticated Users*), and select *Read* and *Enroll*.

It will now look like this (Figure 17-10).

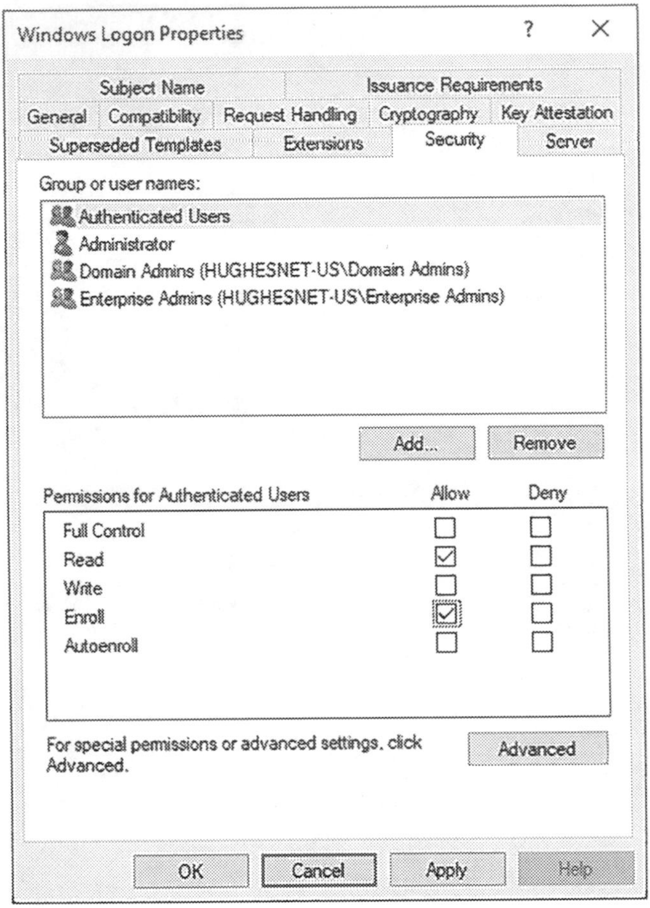

Figure 17-10. *Click OK*

Request and Obtain a Windows Logon Certificate Using mmc.exe

The next step is to use mmc.exe to request *a Windows Logon Certificate* for Administrator (the currently logged in user).

Start mmc.exe by selecting *Start/Run* and entering **mmc.exe**.

Click *File/Add/Remove Snap-in*. Select *Certificates* and then click *Add*. Select *My user account*. Click *OK*. Expand *Certificates – Current User*. Expand *Personal*. Expand *Certificates*. You should see something like the following (Figure 17-11).

Figure 17-11. *Expand "Certificates"*

Right-click the middle pane, and select *All Tasks/Request New Certificate*.

Ignore the *Before You Begin* page. Click *Next*.

You should now see the following (Figure 17-12).

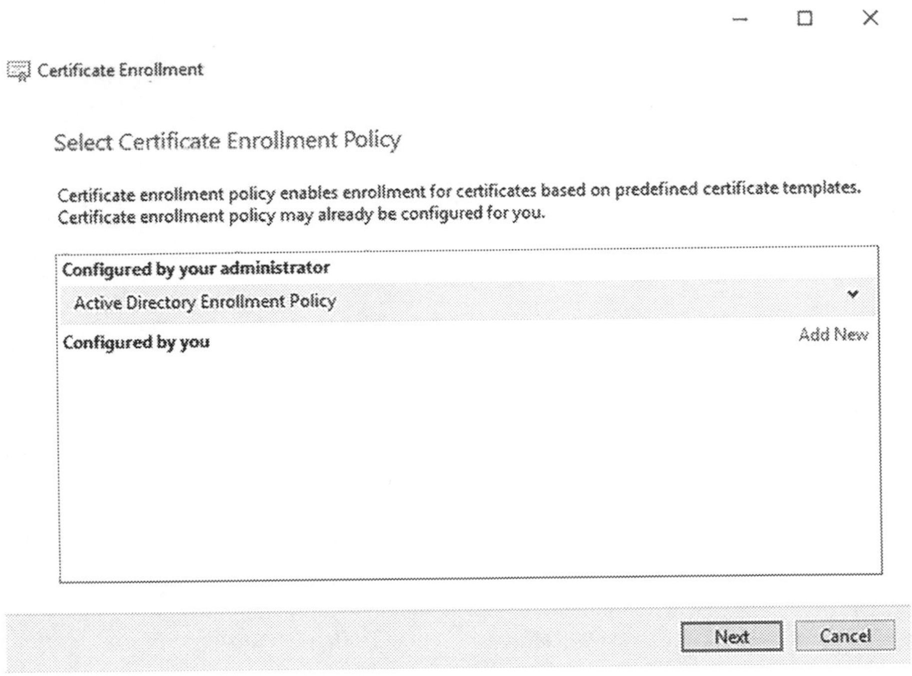

— ☐ ✕

🖳 Certificate Enrollment

Select Certificate Enrollment Policy

Certificate enrollment policy enables enrollment for certificates based on predefined certificate templates.
Certificate enrollment policy may already be configured for you.

Configured by your administrator	
Active Directory Enrollment Policy	⌄
Configured by you	Add New

Next   Cancel

Figure 17-12. *Certificate Enrollment*

Click *Next*.

You should now see the following (Figure 17-13).

Figure 17-13. Request Certificates window

Select *Windows Logon*. Click *Enroll*.

You should now see the following (Figure 17-14).

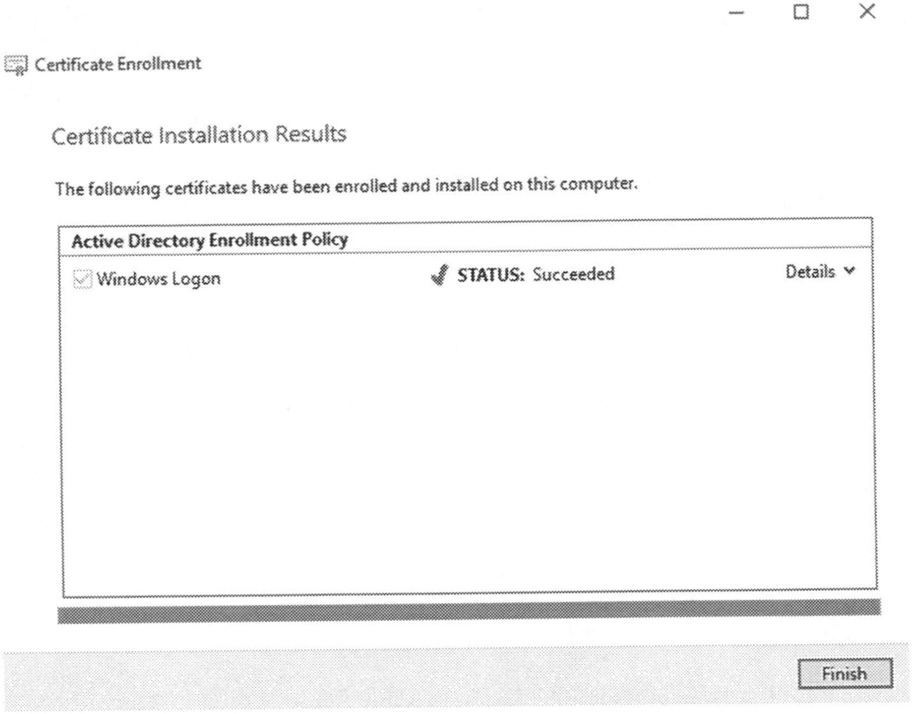

— ☐ ✕

🖳 Certificate Enrollment

Certificate Installation Results

The following certificates have been enrolled and installed on this computer.

Active Directory Enrollment Policy		
☑ Windows Logon	✔ **STATUS:** Succeeded	Details ⌄

Finish

Figure 17-14. *Certificate Installation Results*

Congratulations, you have just issued a Windows Logon Certificate for the current user (Administrator). Click *Finish*.

In mmc.exe, you should now see the new certificate (Figure 17-15).

Figure 17-15. *New certificate screen*

Double-click the new certificate to view its properties (Figure 17-16).

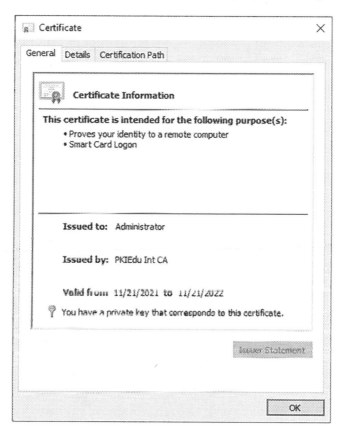

Figure 17-16.   *Certificate properties*

The *ValidFrom* date is when I issued this certificate.

The *ValidTo date* is one year from then.

I have a private key that corresponds to this certificate.

Now select the *Details* tab.

Under *Subject,* you should see

```
CN = Administrator
CN = Users
DC = us
```

```
DC = hughesnet
DC = org
```

Under *Issuer*, you should see

```
CN = PKIEdu Int CA
DC = us
DC = hughesnet
DC = org
```

Under *Enhanced Key Usage*, you should see

```
Smart Card Logon (1.3.6.1.4.1.311.20.2.2)
Client Authentication (1.3.6.1.5.5.7.3.2)
```

Under *CRL Distribution Point*, you should see an LDAP URL pointing to your AD server.

Under *Subject Alternative Name*, should you see

```
Other Name:
        Principal Name=Administrator@us.hughesnet.org
```

This is exactly what you need for a Windows Logon Certificate.

Now select the *Certification Path* tab. You should see the following (Figure 17-17).

Figure 17-17. *Certificate Path tab*

The new certificate chains up to the PKIEdu Int CA Intermediate Cert. That cert chains up to the PKIEdu Root CA Root Certificate, which is trusted.

Congratulations! You have just issued a Windows Logon Certificate for Administrator.

Logging into Windows with a Windows Logon Certificate

To do this, you need a PKI type smart card (e.g., ACS ACOS5 EVO), a compatible smart card reader, and the ability to import your Windows Logon Certificate into it. All smart card vendors supply Windows apps to initialize blank cards and manage the contents (certificates and private keys) in those smart cards.

Microsoft Certificate Services installs your certificate in the *Personal* folder of your Certificate Store. In my case, the ACS Certificate Manager cannot import from the Certificate Store, but only from a PKCS12 file. By default, you cannot export the private key of your Windows Logon Certificate, so you have to request that the cert be exportable when you enroll for it.

On my workstation (LEHPC), which is a member of my HUGHESNET-US domain, I used mmc.exe to request a Windows Logon Certificate for my lhughes domain account. I right-clicked the Personal/Certificates list of certificates and chose *Request New Certificate*. See Figure 17-18.

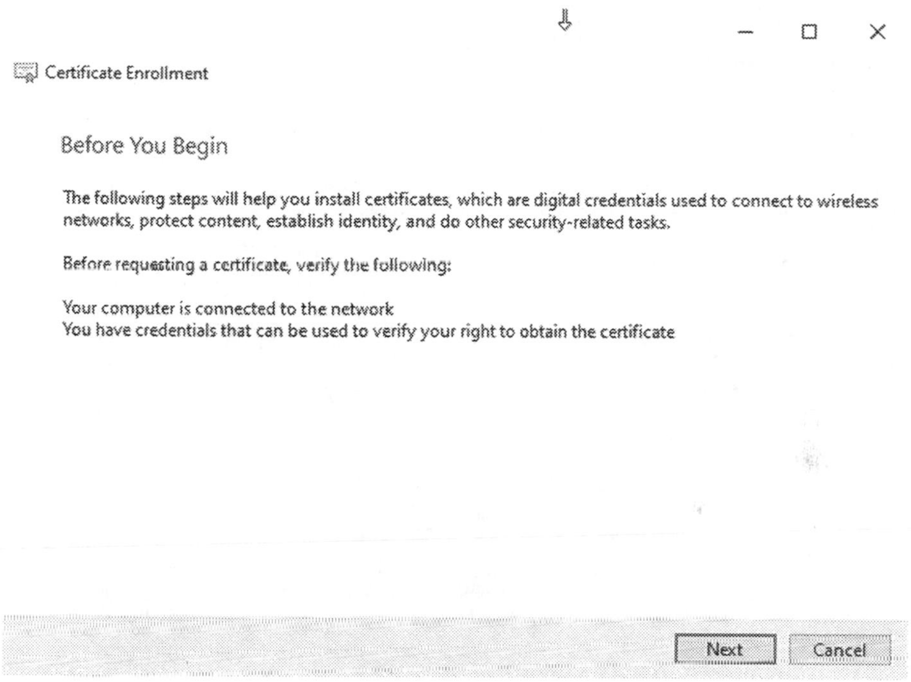

Figure 17-18. *"Before You Begin" screen*

Click *Next*. See Figure 17-19.

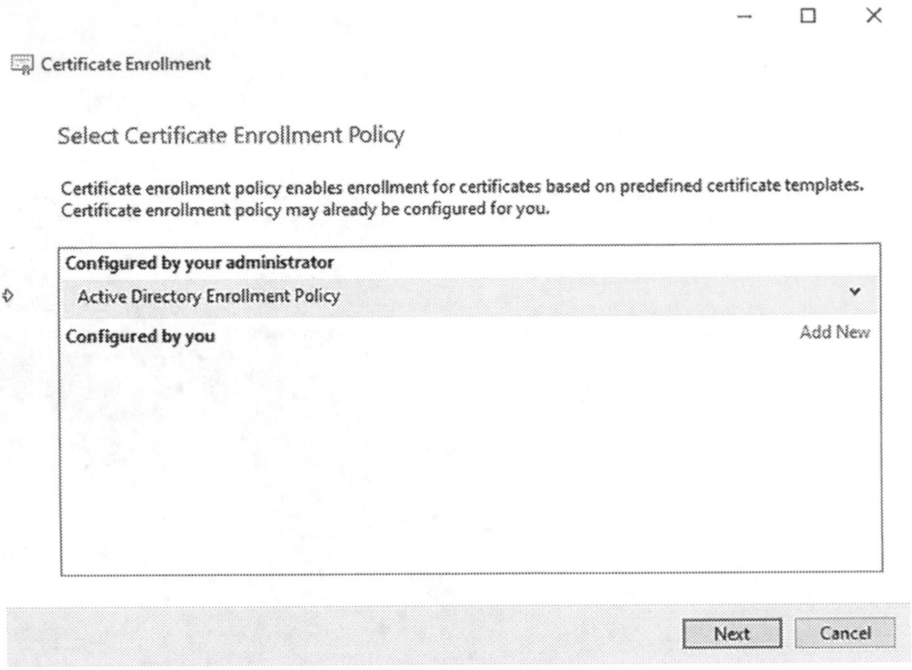

—   □   ×

⬛ Certificate Enrollment

Select Certificate Enrollment Policy

Certificate enrollment policy enables enrollment for certificates based on predefined certificate templates.
Certificate enrollment policy may already be configured for you.

Configured by your administrator	
Active Directory Enrollment Policy	⌄
Configured by you	Add New

Next   Cancel

Figure 17-19. *Certificate Enrollment Policy*

I am going to use a domain Certificate Services enrollment policy, so I
click *Next*. See Figure 17-20.

— ☐ ✕

🖳 Certificate Enrollment

Request Certificates

You can request the following types of certificates. Select the certificates you want to request, and then click Enroll.

☐ Basic EFS	ⓘ **STATUS:** Available	Details ⌄
☐ EFS Recovery Agent	ⓘ **STATUS:** Available	Details ⌄
☐ S/MIME Certfiicate	ⓘ **STATUS:** Available	Details ⌄
☐ TLS Client Certificate	ⓘ **STATUS:** Available	Details ⌄
☐ User	ⓘ **STATUS:** Available	Details ⌄
☑ Windows Login	ⓘ **STATUS:** Available	Details ⌄

☐ Show all templates

Enroll   Cancel

Figure 17-20. *Certificates list*

I select the Windows Login template and expand *Details* (on the right), as shown in Figure 17-21.

Figure 17-21. *Selecting certificates*

To allow the certificate to be exportable, I click *Properties*.

In the Properties dialog, I go to the *Private Key* tab and then the *Key options* field. I check *Make private key exportable*. See Figure 17-22.

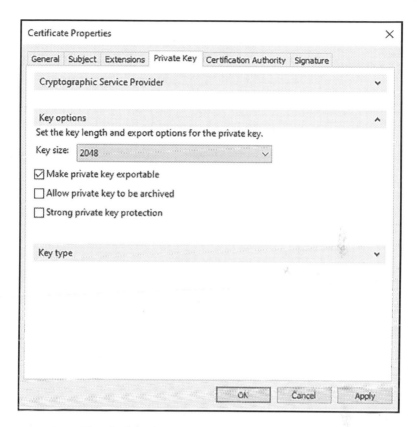

Figure 17-22. *Check "Make private key exportable"*

I then click *OK*. In the *Certificate Enrollment* dialog, I click *Enroll*. The enrollment is successful (Figure 17-23).

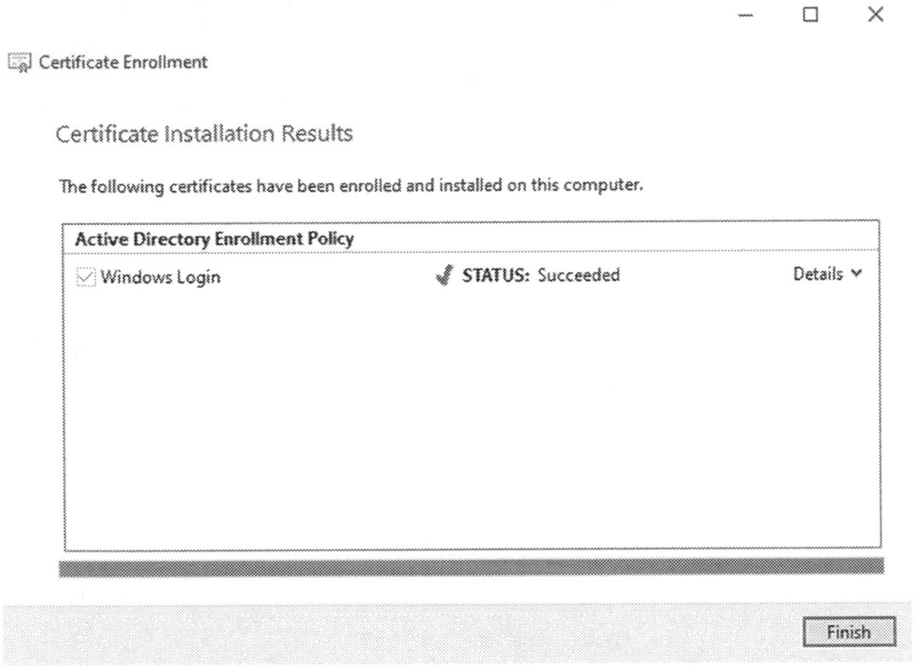

—   □   ✕

🖼 Certificate Enrollment

Certificate Installation Results

The following certificates have been enrolled and installed on this computer.

Active Directory Enrollment Policy		
☑ Windows Login	✓ STATUS: Succeeded	Details ⌄

Finish

Figure 17-23. *Click Finish*

In mmc.exe, the new certificate appears (Figure 17-24).

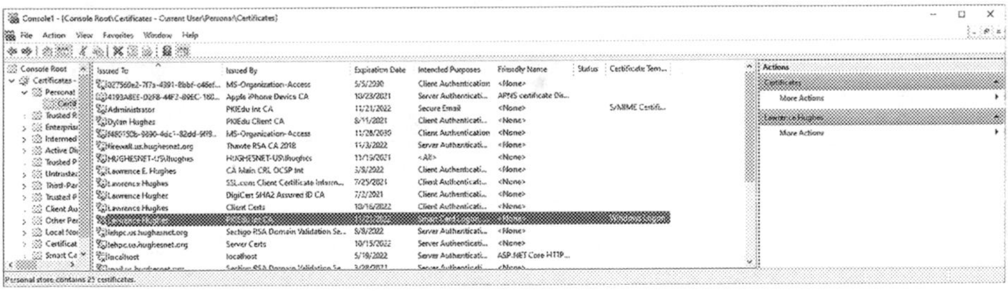

Figure 17-24. *Shows new certificate*

I double-click the new certificate to view it. See Figure 17-25.

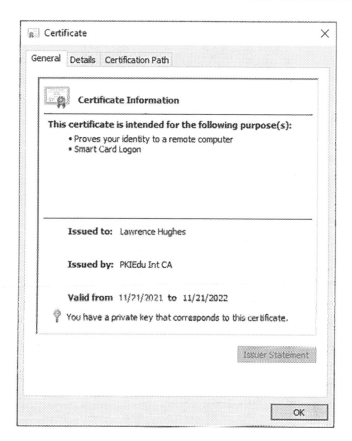

Figure 17-25. *New certification information*

Note that the purposes include *Smart card Logon*.

The cert was issued to *Lawrence Hughes*.

It was issued (signed) by *PKIEdu Int CA*.

The *ValidFrom* date is the day I issued the cert.

The *ValidTo* date is one year later.

On the Details tab, I can see more detailed information on this certificate:

The *Subject DN* contains

```
CN = Lawrence Hughes
CN = Users
```

```
DC = us
DC = hughesnet
DC = org
```

The *Issuer DN* contains

```
CN = PKIEdu Int CA
DC = us
DC = hughesnet
DC = org
```

The *Enhanced Key Usage* contains

```
Smart Card Logon (1.3.6.1.4.1.311.20.2.2)
Client Authentication (1.3.6.1.5.5.7.3.2)
```

The *Subject Alternative name* contains

```
Other Name:
        Principal Name=lhughes@us.hughesnet.org
```

Select *Certification Path* tab, as shown in Figure 17-26.

Figure 17-26. *Certification Path tab*

This certificate chains up to the PKIEdu Int CA Intermediate Certificate. That cert chains up to the PKIEdu Root CA Root Certificate, which is trusted.

This is exactly what I need for a Windows Logon Certificate for me. I export the certificate in PKCS12 format:

- Right-click my certificate in mmc.exe, and select *All Tasks*, *Export*.

- I select *Yes, export the private key*.

- I accept default settings on Export File Format (PFX).

433

- I enter a passphrase to protect my PKCS12 (and confirm it).

- I choose a folder to export my certificate into (in my case, C:\Certs).

- I specify the file name as *Lawrence Hughes Windows Logon Certificate.*

I now insert a blank ACS ACOS5 EVO smart card in my USB smart card reader and use the *ACS Initialization Manager* App to initialize it.

I now use the *ACS Certificate Manager* app and enter the smart card PIN to allow me to import my Windows Logon Certificate into the smart card (Figure 17-27).

Figure 17-27. *ACS Certificate Manager app*

I click the green plus sign to add a new certificate. I select the PKCS12 file and enter the passphrase it is protected with. See Figure 17-28.

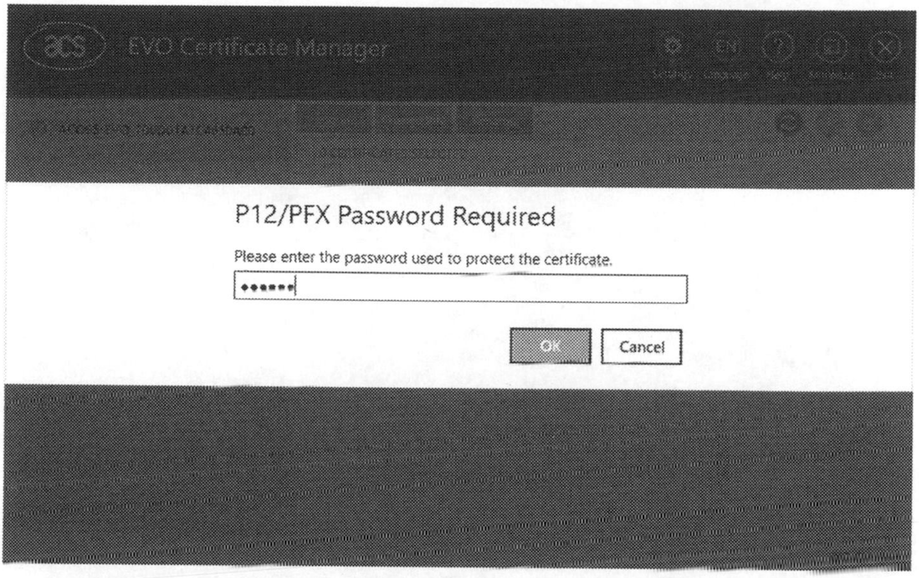

Figure 17-28.   Password screen

My Windows Logon Certificate is now in my smart card. See
Figure 17-29.

Figure 17-29. *Windows Logon Certificate now listed*

Now I log out of my Windows workstation and log back in. This time, I select Smart card (if it is not already selected) and insert my smart card into the reader. I enter the smart card PIN. In a few seconds, I am logged in as *lhughes@us.hughesnet.org*, without having to enter my UPN or any password.

Note   If you installed your CA in VMs running on your computer, when you log out, the CA is no longer running, so login will not work. You can move your VMs to another computer or do this exercise on a different computer.

If I lose my smart card, I can create another one from the PKCS12 container or even issue a new Windows Logon Certificate and load *that* into a new smart card.

APPENDIX

Relevant Standards

There are several standards relevant to the digital certificates and PKI covered in this book. Some of these were from RSA, the creators of the first successful public key cryptosystem (the RSA algorithm). These are referred to as the Public Key Cryptography Standards (PKCS). Some of these are from the Internet Engineering Task Force (IETF), the technical group responsible for the standards underlying the Internet. These are called Requests for Comments (RFCs). Others are from US government agencies, such as the National Institute for Standards and Technology (NIST) and the Federal Information Processing Standards (FIPS).

PKCS – Public Key Cryptography Standards

Unlike the other standards listed here, these were created by a single company (RSA). Some had updated versions released by RSA. Some of the PKCS standards are still being used today, although they have since been adopted by the IETF, subjected to consensus review, and cleaned up or extended based on more recent technology. The IETF does not allow any standard based on patented or proprietary technology to be issued as an RFC, so PKCS #1 could not be incorporated in an RFC until after its patent expired in 2000. Most people in the field still refer to these standards by the PKCS numbers (e.g., a "PKCS #12 container"). In the following, we will reference the current RFC numbers that now specify these standards.

© Lawrence E. Hughes 2022
L. E. Hughes, *Pro Active Directory Certificate Services*,
https://doi.org/10.1007/978-1-4842-7486-6

PKCS #1 – RSA Cryptography Standard

This specified the "RSA algorithm." The final version from RSA was v2.2. It is now specified in RFC 8017, "PKCS #1: RSA Cryptography Specifications Version 2.2," November 2016. Although the Diffie-Hellman Key Agreement algorithm preceded it, the RSA cryptosystem was the first one to support general encryption and decryption using asymmetric key cryptography. It is still in widespread use although it is now reaching the end of its useful life (due to constantly increasing CPU performance and the inevitable release of viable quantum computing).

The RSA algorithm is based on one of the classic "hard problems" in mathematics, which is factoring the product of two large primes. Instead of each participant being issued a single "secret" key (symmetric key cryptography), with asymmetric key cryptography, each participant is issued a related pair of keys, one public and one private. The public key is published in some way so that anyone can use it. It is normally protected by inclusion in a public key digital certificate, along with information identifying the person or device that the key belongs to, information identifying the issuer of the certificate, validity dates, usage flags, and other information. The private key is kept secret by the key owner.

PKCS #2 – RSA Encryption of Message Digests (Withdrawn)

This standard was withdrawn by RSA and its subject incorporated into PKCS #1. It was never incorporated into an IETF RFC.

PKCS #3 – Diffie-Hellman Key Agreement

Although this was not invented by RSA personnel, it was included in the PKCS series. It is now specified in RFC 2631, "Diffie-Hellman Key Agreement Method," June 1999 (with no mention of PKCS #3). Nobody refers to this algorithm as "PKCS #3".

This is actually the first widely used algorithm based on asymmetric key cryptography, invented by Whitfield Diffie and Martin Hellman and published in 1976. It was never patented.

It is based on another classic "hard problem" in mathematics, known as "discrete logarithms." It cannot be used for general-purpose encryption and decryption (although the later ElGamal algorithm, also based on discrete logarithms, is capable of that). Recent implementations of TLS often use Diffie-Hellman Key Agreement to securely exchange a symmetric session key.

It allows two nodes to exchange numeric values over an insecure channel, resulting in a securely shared symmetric key. A hacker can intercept all of the exchanged messages and still not be able to reconstruct the shared symmetric key (at least it is very difficult and time-consuming to do so).

PKCS #4 – RSA Key Syntax (Withdrawn)

This PKCS standard specified a syntax for representing RSA keys and was incorporated into a later version of PKCS #1 in 2010. No RFC incorporated this standard.

PKCS #5 – Password-Based Encryption Standard

This is an algorithm for creating a symmetric key from an alphanumeric passphrase in a secure, repeatable manner. It is now specified in RFC 8018, "PKCS #5: Password-Based Cryptography Specification v2.1," January 2017.

Symmetric keys are long (128 to 256 bits) and difficult for humans to remember or specify. This algorithm allows them to use an alphanumeric passphrase (which is not the same as a password) instead of the binary key. A passphrase is far easier for a human to use or enter than a binary key. It can create a unique binary key from a given passphrase in a repeatable manner – anyone can use it to create the correct symmetric key given the correct passphrase. Like a message digest, given the symmetric key, it is very difficult to derive the passphrase from it. The most important requirement for a good passphrase is length (number of characters). Ideally, passphrases should be at least 14 characters long.

As an example, a PKCS #12 container allows you to specify a passphrase to create or open one. It uses PKCS #5 to securely create a symmetric key (typically 3DES) from the passphrase. The generated symmetric key is actually used to encrypt or decrypt the contents of the container.

A related algorithm is PBKDF2, referenced in RFC 8018. This adds the concept of "Salt," a value used in the generation of the symmetric key from the passphrase that makes it more difficult to recover the passphrase (or password) from the hashed value using "rainbow tables" of precomputed hashes. PBKDF2 is often used to protect passwords on a server that uses username/password authentication.

PKCS #6 – Extended-Certificate Syntax Standard (Obsoleted by X.509 v3)

This specified the syntax for X.509 v1 certificates. We now use X.509 v3 certificates, so this standard is no longer in use. The current RFC that covers the syntax of X.509 v3 certificates (and X.509 v2 CRLs) is RFC 5280, "Internet X.509 Public Key Infrastructure Certificate and Certificate Revocation List (CRL) Profile," May 2008.

PKCS #7 Cryptographic Message Syntax Standard

This specifies how to sign and/or encrypt messages using a digital certificate issued by a PKI. This was used in the creation of S/MIME which is the IETF standard for end-to-end encryption and sender authentication (originally used for Internet email). It was incorporated into an IETF standards track RFC, RFC 5652, "Cryptographic Message Syntax (CMS)," September 2009.

The standard file type for PKCS #7 objects is ".p7".

Cryptographic Message Syntax (CMS) was originally used in Privacy Enhanced Mail (PEM) in four standards track RFCs:

- RFC 1421, "Privacy Enhancement for Internet Electronic Mail: Part I: Message Encryption and Authentication Procedures," February 1993.

- RFC 1422, "Privacy Enhancement for Internet Electronic Mail: Part II: Certificate-Based Key Management," February 1993

- RFC 1423, "Privacy Enhancement for Internet Electronic Mail: Part III: Algorithms, Modes and Identifiers," February 1993

- RFC 1424, "Privacy Enhancement for Internet Electronic Mail: Part IV: Key Certification and Related Services," February 1993

We still use PEM format files for exported cryptographic keys and other objects.

PEM was not widely adopted, and replaced by S/MIME, now at version 4.0. Almost all Internet email clients support S/MIME (at least v3.1).

S/MIME is currently specified in RFC 8551, "Secure/Multipurpose Internet Mail Extensions (S/MIME) Version 4.0 Message Specification," April 2019. This is an extension to Multipurpose Internet Mail Extensions (MIME) by adding MIME messages parts for digital signatures, digital envelopes, and digital certificates. It is still based on CMS and ultimately PKCS #7. S/MIME is designed for native applications, not webmail. It is transparent to intermediate servers (S/MIME-protected messages just look like normal email messages to servers). All encryption and signing is done in the sending client application, and all decryption and signature verification is done in the receiving client application. The web model is not compatible with this requirement (all processing is done on a centralized web server).

The user's private key is used by the sending client application to create digital signatures and decrypt incoming encrypted messages. The receiving client application requires the sender's public key (in a certificate) to verify digital signatures (usually included as part of the signed message). The sending client application requires the public keys (in certificates) for all recipients at time of message creation. This can be obtained by asking the recipient to send a signed message or from a centralized address book that supports digital certificates.

PKCS #8 – Private-Key Information Syntax Standard

This standard specifies a syntax for representing asymmetric private keys in a secure manner. It is now specified as part of RFC 5958, "Asymmetric Key Packages," August 2010.

Asymmetric Key Packages use DER (Distinguished Encoding Rules), which is a binary format. It is specified in ITU-T X.690. DER syntax is a way of representing ASN.1 objects, such as asymmetric keys. These can also be encoded in PEM format, which uses alphanumeric Base64 encoding with well-known headers and trailers.

The standard file type for PKCS #8 files is ".p8".

PKCS #9 – Selected Attribute Types

This defines selected attribute types for use in PKCS #6 extended certificates, PKCS #7 digitally signed messages, PKCS #8 private-key information, and PKCS #10 certificate-signing requests.

This was incorporated in the IETF RFCs as an informational document in RFC 2985, "PKCS #9: Selected Object Classes and Attribute Types Version 2.0," November 2000.

Most people (unless they are creating a cryptographic API) do not need to use PKCS #9.

PKCS #10: Certification Request Standard

The syntax of a message is sent to a Certification Authority to request the creation of a digital certificate. Now specified in RFC 2986, "PKCS #10: Certification Request Syntax Specification v1.7," November 2000. It is commonly referred to as a PKCS #10 request or a Certificate-Signing Request (CSR).

A CSR contains several things needed by a Certification Authority to issue a digital certificate, including

- The subject's public key, including algorithm and key length

- The Subject Distinguished Name (SubjectDN), which identifies the subject (applicant), for example, *CN=Lawrence Hughes, E=lhughes@pkiedu.com, O=PKIEdu Inc., OU=IT, L=Frisco, ST=Texas, C=US*

- Requested Key Usage flags

- Requested Enhanced Key Usage flags

Note that the CSR never includes the subject's private key. Normally, only the generated certificate is returned to the applicant (e.g., by email or web download). The generated certificate must be reassociated with the private key created by the user to make usable key material (certificate + private key). It is possible for the CA to create the key pair, in which case the certificate and the private key are returned in a PKCS #12 container. The submitted CSR is digitally signed using the subject's private key. This signature is validated using the subject's submitted public key.

The Certification Authority adds several things to the preceding information to create the issued certificate, including

- Issuer Distinguished Name that identifies the certificate issuer (CA)

- Certificate serial number

- Validity dates (ValidFrom and ValidTo)

- CRL Distribution Point (where you can find the CRL for this certificate)

- OCSP URL (where you can find the OCSP server for this certificate)

- Approved Key Usage flags

- Approved Enhanced Key Usage flags

- A digital signature that covers all fields of the certificate except for the signature itself, using a private key corresponding to the issuing certificate

Note that the Registration Authority or Certification Authority can modify the SubjectDN if needed (e.g., only include items that have been authenticated) as well as the Requested Key Usage and Enhanced Key Usage flags.

PKCS #11 – Cryptographic Token Interface (Cryptoki)

An API for communicating with a hardware cryptographic token, such as a USB PKI token or PKI Smart card. This allows you to initialize a token, load certificates and private keys into the token, view the current contents of the token, delete certificates and private keys from the token, etc.

Windows uses PKCS 11 to integrate hardware tokens into the Certificate Store (so they appear to be in the local Certificate Store but really are in the token).

Note that each cryptographic token includes a PKCS11 .DLL to allow a generic PKCS 11 API to communicate with that type of token. When you install the token driver, it usually installs this .DLL into your Windows subdirectory. The .DLL must be installed before you can work with that kind of token.

Many cryptographic APIs include PKCS #11 interfaces for working with hardware tokens.

RSA turned control over PKCS 11 to the OASIS PKCS 11 Technical Committee.

PKCS #12 – Personal Information Exchange Syntax Standard

This standard specifies a container that can securely hold certificates and private keys. It is currently specified in RFC 7292, "PKCS #12: Personal Information Exchange Syntax v1.1," July 2014.

When you create the container, you provide a passphrase (an alphanumeric string) that is converted into a 3DES key by PKCS #5. The private key is encrypted using this key. To open the container, you must supply the original passphrase used to create it. Because the private key is encrypted, it is safe to store PKCS12 files in a database or file system or send via unsecured channels such as email, FTP, etc.

For example, if the CA creates the key pair, they can provide the certificate and private key to the user in a PKCS12 container, but they must securely provide the passphrase needed to open it to the customer as well (via a different channel).

One clever use of PKCS12 containers is for private key escrow (where the organization can recover the private key of any user for law enforcement reasons or if the key owner leaves the organization without surrendering their private key). You create a PKCS12 container with their certificate and private key, using a randomly generated passphrase, and then encrypt the passphrase with a special "escrow" digital certificate. The corresponding private key can be kept securely with access limited to corporate executives with secure auditing. To recover the user's key, you decrypt the passphrase using the escrow private key and then open the container with the recovered passphrase.

The recommended file type for a PKCS12 container is ".p12", but on Windows, ".pfx" is commonly used. Microsoft refers to PKCS12 containers as "Personal Information Exchange" files.

Internet Request for Comments (RFCs)

There are currently over 8,000 RFCs, including the ones listed earlier that are the current specifications for the old PKCS standards from RSA.

There are quite a few standards created by the PKIX working group (for PKI using X.509 certificates). A long list of PKI-related RFCs can be found at www.oasis-pki.org/resources/techstandards/.

RFC 4211 – "Internet X.509 Public Key Infrastructure Certificate Request Message Format (CRMF)," September 2005. This RFC specifies the format for messages used to request a certificate (CSR).

RFC 3647 – "Internet X.509 Public Key Infrastructure Certificate Policies and Certification Practices Framework," November 2003. This RFC provides guidance on how to draft a Certification Practices Statement (CPS) that explains how your CA operates. Every issued certificate should include the URL of that CA's CPS. This CPS becomes legally a part of the certificate by this inclusion.

RFC 5272 – "Certificate Management over CMS (CMC)," June 2008. This RFC specifies how to do certificate management via CMS messages, typically over email.

RFC 5280 – "Internet X.509 Public Key Infrastructure Certificate and Certificate Revocation List (CRL) Profile," May 2008. This is the main specification for the X.509 v3 certificate as well as the Certificate Revocation List (CRL) v2.

The X.509 certificate was originally specified in ISO X.509, which was part of the OSI X.500 Directory Services (which ran on OSI networks). It included specifications for Distinguished Names and other concepts. The current version is v3. RFC 5280 is one of several "profiles" that specify the use of X.509 certificates in particular environments (in this case, the Internet).

A Certificate Revocation List (CRL) is a sorted list of serial numbers of revoked certificates from a given certificate hierarchy (and the reason those certificates were revoked). It is a "blacklist" that identifies only revoked certificates. If the serial number of the certificate in question is *not* on the list, then it has not been revoked. Each CRL is digitally signed by the CA to provide authentication of the issuing CA and detect tampering with the list.

Each certificate that supports revocation checking via CRL includes the URL of the CRL server at the CA (as the CRL Distribution Point). CRLs may be published via HTTP, HTTPS, LDAP, or LDAPS. CRLs are updated periodically (e.g., once a day, once a week, etc.). Each CRL indicates when the next CRL for this certificate hierarchy will be published.

RFC 6960 – "X.509 Internet Public Key Infrastructure Online Certificate Status Protocol – OCSP," June 2013. This is the main specification for the Online Certificate Status Protocol (OCSP) used by many CAs as an alternative to Certificate Revocation Lists (CRLs).

Each certificate that has an OCSP server includes the URL for that server in the certificate (in an AIA field). Unlike CRLs, you connect to the correct OCSP server and request the current revocation status of a single certificate by serial number. The response is digitally signed and can include one of three values for status: *good*, *revoked*, and *unknown*.

RFC 8446 – "The Transport Layer Security (TLS) Protocol Version 1.3," August 2018. This specifies the Transport Layer Security (TLS) protocol that can protect any text-based protocol with a request/response design. It is used with HTTP, SMTP, IMAP, LDAP, etc. It requires a TLS Server Certificate on the server to enable TLS and provide server-to-client authentication. It optionally can use a TLS Client Certificate on the client to provide strong client-to-server authentication. It also supports secure exchange of a symmetric session key to enable encryption of the entire session after the handshake. This can be done with asymmetric key encryption and decryption or via the Diffie-Hellman Key Agreement algorithm. Some applications are still using TLS v1.2, but versions 1.1 and earlier (including SSL 2.0 and 3.0) have been deprecated.

Federal Information Processing Standards (FIPS)

There is another set of standards created and managed by the US government for several technical things, including cryptography. Some of the most common ones relevant to cryptography and PKI are

FIPS 140-3 – Security Requirements for Cryptographic Modules

This standard specifies how a hardware cryptographic token (USB or smart card) must secure the contents and resist compromise by a hacker. The -3 version replaced the -2 version of FIPS-140 on March 22, 2019. There are several "levels" that you can certify such a device to. Level 1 is not very secure, and you can actually create a "virtual" token in software that meets this standard. Levels 2 and 3 are commonly used for hardware tokens (software tokens do not qualify for these levels). Level 4 includes extensive anti-tampering (such as self-destruction of the device when it detects certain attacks). Most requirements for cryptographic tokens (e.g., in banking) specify FIPS-140-3 level 2 or level 3.

FIPS-197 – Advanced Encryption Standard (AES). There are several RFCs related to *using* AES in various situations, but the actual standard for AES is FIPS-197. AES is the official successor to DES (Data Encryption Standard). AES uses 128-, 192-, or 256-bit keys. The block size is 128 bits.

Index

A

ACS Certificate Manager app, 434
Active Directory Domain, 219
Advanced Encryption
      Standard (AES), 4, 11, 449
Asymmetric key algorithms, 3, 9,
      27, 31, 124
Asymmetric key encryption
   algorithms, 29
   Alice, 26
   conceptual model, 30, 31
   Diffie-Hellman Key
      Exchange, 23
   ECC, 27
   public and private keys, 24
   secure session key
      exchange, 27
   server authentication, 24
   vs. symmetric key, 28
   TLS, 25
Asymmetric key management, 105
Authority information
      access (AIA), 67, 150, 297
Automated certificate management
      environment (ACME), 125

B

Alice, 8, 9
Bob, 8, 9

C

Caesar Cipher, 3, 23
Carrier Grade NAT (CGN), 172
Certificate authority, 25, 125, 215,
      252, 258
Certificate distribution
      point (CDP), 308
Certificate enrollment policy, 426
Certificate hierarchy, 97, 98,
      149, 150
Certificate management over
      CMS (CMC), 121, 447
Certificate management
      protocol (CMP), 107, 120
Certificate renewal, 95, 96, 122, 126
Certificate revocation, 96, 104
Certificate revocation list (CRL), 47,
      94, 97–102, 147, 308
   force publication, 313–315
   Root CA, 308

Certificate-signing request (CSR), 50, 75, 443
  certificate information, 89
  certificate view, 88
  check view, 82
  creation, 77, 83
  creation and management, 132–139
  encrypted private key, 79
  fields, 85, 90
  IDCentral, 84
  passphrase, 86, 87
  PCKS12 file to IRP server, 87
  PEM format, 80
  PKCS12 stored locally, 91
  protection level, private key, 86
  reassociate cert, 139–145
  status view, 86
  symmetric key, creation, 79
  viewer, 81
  visual, 84
Certificate Store, 81, 86, 114
Certificate trustworthiness, 48, 49
Certification authority (CA), 39, 124, 147, 149
Certification request standard, 443, 445
Cipher block chaining (CBC), 13
Cipher feedback (CFB), 13
Ciphertext, 4–6, 33
Cisco network, 122
Client authentication, 126, 127, 130, 335

Client-to-server authentication, 25, 164, 170, 448
Counter-XOR (CTR), 13
Crypto challenge demo, 32, 33
Cryptographic algorithm performance, 31
Cryptographic message syntax (CMS), 121, 441, 442
Cryptographic token interface (Cryptoki), 445
Cryptography, 3, 35, 40, 75

D

Data encryption standard (DES), 10, 449
Deploy Root CA
  AD services role to Windows Server 2019
  add features, 224
  CA Name, 239
  CA type, 235
  certificate services, 226
  certification authority selection, 232
  certification authority web enrollment, 227
  confirmation window, 241
  credentials, configuring role services, 231
  cryptography, CA window, 237
  database window, 240

feature-based
  installation, 221
HSM, 237
installation selections
  screen, 228
post-deployment
  configuration, 231
private key creation, 236
role services selection, 228
server roles screen, 223
setup type window, 234
tools list, 227
desktop experience on
  VirtualBox, 219
member server, 221
static IP addresses, 220
Deploy Subordinate CA
AD certificate services role
  AD CS window, 251
  add basic
    authentication, 256
  before you begin
    window, 245
  CA Name window, 266
  CA Type window, 263
  credentials screen, 259
  cryptography options, 265
  Database window, 268
  destination server
    window, 247
  feature-based
    installation, 246
  features window, 250

HSM, 265
installation selections
  screen, 257
private Key window, 264
request certificate, 266
role services selection, 252
server roles window, 248
setup type window, 262
tools list, 249
web enrollment, 260
web server role, 255
desktop experience on
  VirtualBox, 243
static IP addresses, 244
Diffie-Hellman key agreement, 169,
  438, 439, 448
Diffie-Hellman Key Exchange,
  23, 25, 29
Digital certificate, 51, 106
Digital envelope
  creation, 40
  definition, 40
  opening, 42
  recipient certificates, 41
  symmetric key cryptography, 40
Digitally enveloped
  message, 396–404
Digitally signed email, 390–396
Digitally signed message, 41,
  106, 184
Digital Signature Algorithm (DSA),
  28–30
  binary object, 35

Digital Signature
Algorithm (DSA) (*cont.*)
creation, 37
non-repudiation, 36
message integrity, 35
signer authentication, 36
uses, 39
validating, 37, 38
Domain controllers (DCs), 218, 219, 285
Dual key pairs, 117, 130, 134
Dynamic IP address, 172

E

Electronic code book (ECB), 12, 13
Elliptic Curve Cryptography (ECC), 27, 29, 131
Email security suite, 110
Encrypt certificates, 125
Encrypted email settings, 390
Encrypted message (EM), 41, 186, 187
Encrypted message digest (EMD), 36
Encryption modes, 12, 13, 169
End-entity certs, 97, 98, 218
Enhanced usage flags, 331, 360, 363
Enrollment over secure transport (EST), 107, 123, 124
Explicit TLS, 126, 158

F, G

Federal information processing standards (FIPS), 437, 449
Fully distinguished name, 334, 367

H

Hardware security module (HSM), 148, 219, 237
Hash function, 19, 36, 38

I, J

IDCentral, 82–84, 86
Identity registration protocol (IRP), 107, 125–127
Implicit TLS, 158, 159
Intermediate Cert, 97, 218
Internet information server (IIS), server cert installation, 299–304
Internet request for comments (RFCs), 447, 448
IPv4 address exhaustion, 172
IPv4 internet, 157, 171
IPv4 public addresses, 172
Issuer Distinguished Name (IssuerDN), 39, 70, 152, 153, 276, 327, 444

K

Key backup and recovery, 116
Key encipherment,46, 117

Key escrow, 117, 361, 446
Key management, symmetric key
    encryption, 9

L

LDAP management tool, 108
Link-oriented protocol, 180

M

Member server, 216, 218, 221
Message digest algorithm, 19–22
Message integrity, 22, 36
Message security properties, 393
Microsoft Active Directory
    Certificate Services (AD
    CS), 215, 218, 360
Multipurpose internet mail
    extensions (MIME), 177,
    359, 442

N

NAT traversal, 173
Network address translation
    (NAT), 157
Non-repudiation, 36

O

OCSP responder
    installation, 316–325
Online certificate status protocol
    (OCSP), 94, 102, 103, 148

P, Q

Password-based encryption
    standard, 440
PeerTLS, 173–175, 358
Personal address book (PAB),
    41, 42, 106
Personal information exchange
    syntax standard, 446
PKIView, CA Health, 272,
    273, 307–312
Private branch
    exchange (PBX), 171
Private certificate hierarchies, 183
Private IPv4 address, 171
Private key digital certificate, 26
Private-key information syntax
    standard, 443
Private key management
    definition, 110
    digital certificate, 113
    key material portable, 116
    manage hardware tokens, 115
    password creation, 112
    protection level, 111
    security level, 111
    USB hardware tokens, 114
Public hierarchy, 71, 110, 150
Public hierarchy digital
    certificate, 360
Public IPv4 addresses, 173
Public Key Cryptography
    Standards (PKCS)
    certification request standard,
    443, 445

Public Key Cryptography
  Standards (PKCS) (*cont.*)
  cryptographic message syntax
    standard, 441, 442
  Cryptoki, 445
  Diffie-Hellman key
    agreement, 439
  extended-certificate syntax
    standard, 441
  password-based encryption
    standard, 440
  Personal Information Exchange
    Syntax, 446
  private-key information
    syntax, 443
  RSA Cryptography
    Standard, 438
  RSA encryption of message
    digests, 438
  RSA key syntax, 439
  selected attribute types, 443
Public key infrastructure (PKI), 46,
    48, 120, 121, 147
  certificate hierarchy, 149, 150
  components, 147, 148
  registration authority, 147
  trust chain, 151–153
Public key management
  active directory users, 109
  attributes, 108
  automated systems,
    organizations, 110
  CMP, 107
  digital certificate, 106

directory, 107
LDAP management tool, 108
PAB, 106
post certificates, 109
publish certificate, 107
Public-private key encryption, *see*
    Asymmetric key encryption

R

Random string, 24, 32, 33
Reassociate certificate, 84
Recipient-to-sender
    authentication, 178
Regional internet
    registries (RIRs), 172
Registration authority (RA), 48, 147
Renewal with replacement, 95, 96
Renewal with rollover, 95
Root CA, set up templates,
    277–284
Root Cert, 97, 98, 128, 149, 360
RSA algorithm, 23, 437, 438

S

Secure hash algorithm (SHA), 20
Secure sockets layer (SSL), 46, 157
Server authentication, 276, 283
Signed message, 392
  digitally, 184
  properties, 185
  warning, 186
Signer authentication, 22, 36

Simple certificate enrollment protocol (SCEP), 107, 122, 123

Sixscape, 51, 145, 361

SixWallet
algorithm column, 131
certificate status, 153
certificate to display cert, 129
Cert Type column, 130
Common Name column, 131
CSR page, 132
CSRs tab, 130
key size column, 131
main window, 128
private key column, 131
Token column, 130

S/MIME certificate, 47, 54, 55, 124, 360

S/MIME Digital Certificate, 359

S/MIME secure email certificates
Certification Authority app, 373
digitally enveloped message, 396–404
digitally signed email, 390–396
issuing with Microsoft AD CS, 361–363
mmc.exe to request, 375–385
properties, 374
template creation, 364–372
testing, 386–390

S/MIME (Secure MIME)
applications, 211
certificate installation, Microsoft Outlook

certificate information, 211
certificate store, 190
encryption layer item, 209
enhanced key usage, 193
file menu header, 195
hash algorithm, 199
list of certificates, 197
message signed and encrypted, 207
send signed message, 200
signer item highlighted, 202
subject alternative name, 194
subject selection, 205
subject view, 192
trust center settings, 196
view certificate, 191, 204
view details, 203, 210

digital certificates, 181–183

end-to-end security protocol, 180

implementations, 178–180

MIME extensions, 178

SMTP authentication, 180

Stand-alone CA, 215, 216, 231

Static IP addresses, 172, 220, 244

Strong client authentication (SCA), 51, 127, 130, 329

Subject alternative name field, 181

Subject distinguished name, 50, 75, 331, 362

Subject Distinguished Name (SubjectDN), 275, 327

Subordinate CA
    management, 305–307
Symmetric key algorithms, 5, 11, 12
Symmetric key ciphers, 12
Symmetric key cryptographic
    algorithms, 7, 10, 11, 13–17
Symmetric Key Encryption
  bulk encryption, 27
  key lengths, 27
  key management, 9
Symmetric key management, 105
Symmetric session key (SSK), 40

T

Three-level hierarchy, 217–219, 385
TLS client certificate
  authenticated users, 341
  certificate installation
    results, 345
  certificate templates list, 340
  certification path, 348
  creation, 330
  digital signature, 328
  general certificate
    information, 346
  IssuerDN, 327
  PeerTLS, 358
  request using mmc.exe, 342–349
  SubjectDN, 327
  template creation, 330
  templates set up, 331–339
  testing, SCA with
    PKIEduRootCA, 349–358

TLS server certificates, 51, 53, 54
  CA health in PKIView, 307–312
  installation in IIS, 299–304
  issuing, 284–287
  items, 275, 276
  request and issue, mmc.
    exe, 287–298
  subordinate CA
    management, 305–307
TLS Server Digital Certificate, 51,
    405, 406
Transmission control
    protocol (TCP), 161
Transport layer security (TLS), 46
  client certificates, 155
  client/server network link,
    170, 171
  client-to-server
    authentication, 168
  cryptosuites, 169
  HTTP, 156
  implicit *vs.* explicit, 158–160
  network protocol, 161–165
  revisions, 157
  secure protocols, 163
  securing FTP, 166, 167
  server certificate, 155, 156, 158
  strong client authentication,
    167, 169
Transport Layer Security (TLS), 24,
    46, 155, 157, 448
Trust chain, 151–153
Trusted root cert, 150, 183, 276

Trusted root certificate
    authorities, 56
Two-factor authentication, 167
Two-level hierarchy, 216, 217

U, V

Uniform resource
    identifiers (URIs), 123
User datagram protocol (UDP), 161
User principal name (UPN),
    405, 410

W

Web server role (IIS), 255
Windows certificate store, 55, 57
Windows Logon certificates
    Active Directory Certificate
        Services, 406
    certificate templates list, 413
    definition, 406
    enrollment, 418
    installation results, 420

    logging into Windows, 424–436
    mmc.exe to request, 416–423
    properties, 415, 421
    template creation, 407–413
Windows Logon digital
    certificate, 405
Windows Logon Smart cards, 405

X, Y, Z

X.509 digital certificate
    certificate policies, 63
    certificate
        trustworthiness, 48, 49
    information, 58
    intermediate certificate, 71
    issuer distinguished name, 60
    S/MIME certificates, 72
    subject distinguished
        name, 50, 59
    TLS client certificates and S/
        MIME certificates, 54, 55
    TLS Server (SSL) certificates,
        51, 53, 54

Printed in the United States
by Baker & Taylor Publisher Services